THE
HISTORY OF
SOUTH AFRICA

THE
HISTORY OF
SOUTH AFRICA

Roger B. Beck

The Greenwood Histories of the Modern Nations
Frank W. Thackeray and John E. Findling, Series Editors

Greenwood Press
Westport, Connecticut • London

Library of Congress Cataloging-in-Publication Data

Beck, Roger B.
    The history of South Africa / Roger B. Beck.
        p.   cm.—(The Greenwood histories of the modern nations, ISSN 1096–2905)
    Includes bibliographical references and index.
    ISBN 0–313–30730–X (alk. paper)
        1. South Africa—History.   I. Title.   II. Series.
    DT1787 B43   2000
    968—dc21   99–058880

British Library Cataloguing in Publication Data is available.

Library of Congress Catalog Card Number: 99–058880
ISBN: 0–313–30730–X
ISSN: 1096–2905

First published in 2000

Greenwood Press, 88 Post Road West, Westport, CT 06881
An imprint of Greenwood Publishing Group, Inc.
www.greenwood.com

Printed in the United States of America

The paper used in this book complies with the
Permanent Paper Standard issued by the National
Information Standards Organization (Z39.48–1984).

10 9 8 7 6 5 4 3 2 1

To Ann

Contents

Series Foreword

The Greenwood Histories of the Modern Nations series is intended to provide students and interested laypeople with up-to-date, concise, and analytical histories of many of the nations of the contemporary world. Not since the 1960s has there been a systematic attempt to publish a series of national histories, and, as series editors, we believe that this series will prove to be a valuable contribution to our understanding of other countries in our increasingly interdependent world.

Over thirty years ago, at the end of the 1960s, the Cold War was an accepted reality of global politics, the process of decolonization was still in progress, the idea of a unified Europe with a single currency was unheard of, the United States was mired in a war in Vietnam, and the economic boom of Asia was still years in the future. Richard Nixon was president of the United States, Mao Tse-tung (not yet Mao Zedong) ruled China, Leonid Brezhnev guided the Soviet Union, and Harold Wilson was prime minister of the United Kingdom. Authoritarian dictators still ruled most of Latin America, the Middle East was reeling in the wake of the Six-Day War, and Shah Reza Pahlavi was at the height of his power in Iran. Clearly, the past thirty years have been witness to a great deal of historical change, and it is to this change that this series is primarily addressed.

With the help of a distinguished advisory board, we have selected nations whose political, economic, and social affairs mark them as among the most important in the waning years of the twentieth century, and for each nation we have found an author who is recognized as a specialist in the history of that nation. These authors have worked most cooperatively with us and with Greenwood Press to produce volumes that reflect current research on their nation and that are interesting and informative to their prospective readers.

The importance of a series such as this cannot be underestimated. As a superpower whose influence is felt all over the world, the United States can claim a "special" relationship with almost every other nation. Yet many Americans know very little about the histories of the nations with which the United States relates. How did they get to be the way they are? What kind of political systems have evolved there? What kind of influence do they have in their own region? What are the dominant political, religious, and cultural forces that move their leaders? These and many other questions are answered in the volumes of this series.

The authors who have contributed to this series have written comprehensive histories of their nations, dating back to prehistoric time in some cases. Each of them, however, has devoted a significant portion of the book to events of the past thirty years, because the modern era has contributed the most to contemporary issues that have an impact on U.S. policy. Authors have made an effort to be as up-to-date as possible so that readers can benefit from the most recent scholarship and a narrative that includes very recent events.

In addition to the historical narrative, each volume in this series contains an introductory overview of the country's geography, political institutions, economic structure, and cultural attributes. This is designed to give readers a picture of the nation as it exists in the contemporary world. Each volume also contains additional chapters that add interesting and useful detail to the historical narrative. One chapter is a thorough chronology of important historical events, making it easy for readers to follow the flow of a particular nation's history. Another chapter features biographical sketches of the nation's most important figures in order to humanize some of the individuals who have contributed to the historical development of their nation. Each volume also contains a comprehensive bibliography, so that those readers whose interest has been sparked may find out more about the nation and its history. Finally, there is a carefully prepared topic and person index.

Readers of these volumes will find them fascinating to read and useful in understanding the contemporary world and the nations that comprise it. As series editors, it is our hope that this series will contribute to a heightened sense of global understanding as we enter a new century.

Frank W. Thackeray and John E. Findling
Indiana University Southeast

— global understanding

— Dutch arrived in 1652

Preface

[handwritten annotations: indiginous People SW `South Africa (nomad)` — Batu speaking / former name]

Anyone who writes or speaks about South Africa has to preface their work with a discussion of South African terminology and orthography. The problem began when the Dutch arrived in 1652 and called the Khoikhoi people Hottentots. For much of South Africa's history Whites used the word *kaffir* (Arabic for "infidel") for Africans, and that practice continued into the late twentieth century. These two terms are now regarded as extremely offensive, racist, and insulting; their use is even considered criminal. Starting in 1948 the apartheid government used language in such a manipulative and racist way that many other terms today offend certain ethnic groups. Even the term "African" has provoked debate. Whites generally apply it only to the Bantu-speaking peoples who migrated into South Africa over the last two thousand years and not to the Khoisan peoples who are indigenous to southern Africa and also Africans. White usage also frequently changed over time, so that different terms were used for the same people, such as "natives," "Bantu," "Blacks," and "Africans." To avoid confusion I have retained the terminology of the period; for example, the 1913 Natives Land Act, but the 1951 Bantu Authorities Act. The Dutch word *boer* for the earliest White settlers was often used by the English as a term of derision, and many *boers* today prefer the term "Afrikaners." I have used "Afrikaner" throughout, although in 1988 some ultra-right Afrikaners formed a "Boerestaat Party" (Boer Nation Party) with the intention of creating a Boer homeland. The so-called mixed-race people, the "Coloured," are themselves experiencing a severe identity crisis at present. Some identify themselves as Black, some as White, and many are now building pride in their Coloured heritage.

African orthography raises too many problems for a book of this length—one primarily intended for students and lay people—to treat thoroughly. Thus, I have not employed all the different prefixes for the various African languages and peoples. I refer to the Sotho (rather than Basotho) people, who speak the Sotho (rather than Sesotho) language. The Sotho live in Lesotho, which is the official name for that country. Finally, I have tried to be consistent in my descriptions of South Africa's people. "Black" refers to South Africans other than Caucasians. "African" refers to the peoples who make up the four main branches of Bantu-speaking peoples; the Nguni, Sotho, Venda, and Tsonga. "Whites" are those of European ancestry. "Coloured" refers to Malay or mixed-race peoples, including descendants of Khoisan and White unions. The terms "Khoikhoi," "San," "Griqua," and "Khoisan" are used as they occurred during phases of South Africa's history, while recognizing that these groups also were Africans. I invite the reader to peruse nearly any book about South Africa for other introductory explanations about South African terminology.

I wish to thank the editors of Greenwood's *Histories of the Modern Nations* series, Frank W. Thackeray and John E. Findling, for giving me the opportunity to write this history of South Africa. I deeply appreciate all the help and support they, and the executive editor, Barbara A. Rader, have given throughout the project. My thanks go also to Dr. Tshome Abebe, Provost for Academic Affairs at Eastern Illinois University, for a travel grant that enabled me to visit South Africa in the summer of 1999 and carry the book through to June 1999 and Nelson Mandela's retirement. The attractive maps in this volume were prepared by an Eastern Illinois University graduate, Ron Finger, with the help of Professor Vince Gutowski of the school's geography department. I am most grateful to Christopher Saunders at the University of Cape Town who read through the entire manuscript and offered me many valuable suggestions and recommendations for improving the text and also much appreciated encouragement.

All of you who have written books will understand when I say that my wife, Ann, deserves sainthood.

Timeline of Historical Events

BEFORE THE COMMON ERA (B.C.E.)

ca. 2.5–3 million years	Early Stone Age
ca. 1–3 million years	*Australopithecus africanus* in southern Africa
ca. 90,000–1 million years	*Homo erectus* in southern Africa
ca. 30,000–100,000 years	Middle Stone Age; *Homo sapiens* in southern Africa
ca. 27,000	Earliest dated rock art
ca. 20,000	Late Stone Age
ca. 15,000	San hunter-gatherers in southern Africa
ca. 2200	Khoikhoi San in northern Botswana domesticate livestock, move south

COMMON ERA (C.E.)

ca. third century	Early Iron Age; iron-using mixed-farmers settle south of the Limpopo River
sixth–seventh century	Lydenburg Heads; early Iron Age sites in Transkei
1300–1500	Sotho-Tswana–speakers in highveld interior; Nguni-speakers along southeastern coast and in the Drakensberg Mountains
1488	Portuguese navigator Bartolomeu Dias rounds the Cape
1497	Vasco da Gama rounds the Cape on way to East Africa and India
1652	Dutch East India Company founds refreshment station at Cape of Good Hope under Commander Jan van Riebeeck
1657	First freeburghers farm along the Liesbeek River
1658	First two shiploads of slaves from Angola and West Africa arrive at the Cape
1659	First Dutch-Khoikhoi War
1673–1677	Second Dutch-Khoikhoi War
1688	Huguenots arrive from France
ca. 1690s	*Trekboers* begin expansion east and north into the interior
1702	First contact between Whites and Bantu-speakers in eastern Cape
1713	Khoikhoi are decimated by smallpox
1717	Council of Policy supports slavery as main source of colonial labor
ca. 1775	Phalo's death; Xhosa are divided between Phalo's sons Gcaleka and Rharhabe
1779–1780	First (White-Xhosa) Frontier War
1793	Second Frontier War
1795	First British occupation of the Cape begins
1799–1803	Third Frontier War; Khoisan rebellion in Cape eastern districts; arrival of London Missionary Society missionaries

1803–1806	Dutch Batavian rule at Cape
1806	Second British occupation begins
1808	British slave trade is abolished
1809	Caledon Code places labor and residency on Khoikhoi
1811–1812	Fourth Frontier War; Black Circuit courts enable Blacks to testify against masters
1814	Lord Charles Somerset becomes governor
1815	Slagtersnek Rebellion
1816–1828	*Mfecane*; Shaka creates Zulu kingdom
1818	Ndlambe defeats Ngqika at Battle of Amalinde
1818–1819	Fifth Frontier war
1820	5,000 British settlers arrive in Cape colony
1823	Griqua and Tlhaping defeat Kololo at Battle of Dithakong
ca. 1824	The Sotho leader Moshoeshoe moves to Thaba Bosiu
1828	Ordinance 50 abolishes discriminatory practices against Khoikhoi and other free Blacks; Cape repeals pass laws; death of Zulu King Shaka
1829	Establishment of the Kat River Settlement, where Khoikhoi could own land
1834–1835	Slaves are emancipated; Sixth Frontier War
1835	The British murder Xhosa paramount chief Hintsa; Great Trek begins; Mfengu (refugees) move into Cape colony
1837	*Voortrekkers* defeat Mzilikazi's Ndebele
1837	The Ndebele leave Transvaal across the Limpopo River
1838	Zulu ruler Dingane massacres Piet Retief's party; Republic of Natalia is founded; Battle of Blood River; Andries Potgieter founds Potchefstroom
1840	Mpande overthrows Dingane
1841	Cape Masters and Servants Act
1843	Britain annexes Natal

1846–1847	Seventh Frontier War (War of the Ax)
1850–1852	Eighth Frontier War
1852–1854	Britain recognizes Transvaal and Orange Free State as independent Afrikaner republics
1853	Cape is granted representative government
1856–1857	The Xhosa Great Cattle Killing
1858	Lesotho defeats Orange Free State
1865–1867	Orange Free State defeats Lesotho
1867	Diamonds are discovered in Griqualand West
1868	Britain annexes Basutoland (Lesotho)
1870	Moshoeshoe dies
1876	The Pedi defeat South African Republic
1877	Britain annexes the Transvaal
1879	British win Anglo-Zulu War after major defeat at Isandlwana; British army defeats Sekhukhune, the Pedi ruler, and conquers the Pedi
1880	Transkeian rebellion; "Gun War" in Basutoland; Griqualand West is annexed to Cape colony
1880–1881	Transvaal (or First) War of Independence; Transvaal is granted limited self-rule after defeating the British at Majuba Hill
1884	Britain assumes direct rule over Basutoland
1885	Britain annexes Bechuanaland
1886	Gold is discovered on Witwatersrand; Johannesburg is founded
1887	Britain annexes Zululand and deports King Dinuzulu
1890	Cecil Rhodes is elected Cape prime minister
1893	Mohandas K. Gandhi arrives in South Africa
1894	Natal Indian Congress is founded
1895	British Bechuanaland is added to Cape; Jameson Raid into Transvaal
1896–1897	Rinderpest epidemic kills vast herds of cattle in southern Africa

1897	Enoch Sontonga writes "Nkosi sikelel 'iAfrika," Christian hymn and liberation movement anthem
1898	White conquest of all independent African populations in southern Africa is completed when Transvaal commandos conquer Venda
1899–1902	The South African War
1901–1902	Thousands of Boers and Africans die in British concentration camps
1902	Rhodes dies; (31 May) Treaty of Vereeniging ends South African War, with British victory
1904–1907	63,397 Chinese workers are imported to work in gold mines
1906	Bambatha Rebellion in Natal
1907	Transvaal and Orange River Colony are granted parliamentary government; White miners' strike on Rand
1910	(31 May) Union of South Africa is established; Louis Botha is first prime minister, Jan Smuts is deputy
1912	South African Native National Congress is formed with John Dube as first president, later renamed African National Congress (ANC)
1913	Natives Land Act limits African land ownership to designated reserves (7% of all South African land)
1913–1914	White miners strike
1914	National Party (NP) is founded; Gandhi returns to India
1914–1919	South Africa allies with Britain in World War I
1914	Afrikaner Rebellion
1916	South African Native College (Fort Hare) is opened; Beaumont (Natives Land) Commission Report
1918	Afrikaner Broederbond is founded to promote Afrikaner Nationalism
1919	Botha dies, Smuts becomes prime minister; Industrial and Commercial Workers' Union (ICU) is formed; South Africa receives League of Nations mandate over South West Africa

1920	African mine workers strike
1921	Bulhoek Massacre; Communist Party of South Africa is formed
1922	Rand Revolt
1923	Natives (Urban Areas) Act creates African locations in urban areas
1924	NP and Labour pact wins election; J.B.M. Hertzog becomes prime minister
1925	Afrikaans replaces Dutch as official language
1926	Mines and Works Amendment Act establishes color bar in employment
1927	Nationality and Flag Act; mass ICU protests; Immorality Act prohibits sexual relations between Whites and others
1930	White women receive franchise to vote; Natives (Urban Areas) Amendment Act
1931	Statute of Westminster
1932	Depression; Carnegie Commission Report on Poor Whites; Native Economic Commission Report; South Africa abandons gold standard
1933	Hertzog-Smuts coalition wins general election; Smuts becomes deputy prime minister
1934	NP and South African Party form United Party; D.F. Malan forms Purified National Party
1936	Africans are removed from Cape voters' roll; Natives' Trust and Land Act that set aside less than 14 percent of South African land for African reserves
1938	Great Trek centenary (*Eeufees*) is celebrated
1939	Smuts becomes prime minister; pro-Nazi Ossewabrandwag is formed
1939–1945	South Africa participates on Allied side in World War II
1940	Hertzog and Malan form Herenigde Nasionale Party
1941	African Mine Workers' Union is formed
1943	ANC Youth League is formed with Anton Lembede elected president

1945	World War II ends
1946	Police suppress strike by 70,000 to 100,000 African mine workers; Natives' Representative Council adjourns in protest
1948	Fagan Commission Report on native laws; National Party wins general election and begins to implement apartheid
1949	Prohibition of Mixed Marriages Act; ANC adopts Program of Action; Nelson Mandela, Walter Sisulu, and Oliver Tambo join ANC National Executive
1950	Suppression of Communism Act; Immorality Act is amended; Population Registration Act; Group Areas Act
1951	Bantu Authorities Act
1952	Nationwide Defiance Campaign; abolition of Passes Act
1953	South African Communist Party is formed; Reservation of Separate Amenities Act; Bantu Education Act; Public Safety Act; Criminal Law Amendment Act
1954	Federation of South African Women is formed; J.G. Strijdom becomes prime minister
1955	South African Congress of Trade Unions is formed; Congress of the People adopts Freedom Charter that called for a multiracial democratic South Africa
1956	Treason Trial of 156 members of Congress Alliance; Coloureds are removed from Cape common voters' roll
1958–1966	Hendrik F. Verwoerd is prime minister
1959	Robert Sobukwe forms Pan Africanist Congress (PAC); Progressive Party is founded; Promotion of Bantu Self-Government Act; Extension of University Education Act segregates higher education
1960	White representation of Africans in Parliament is abolished; British prime minister Macmillan delivers "wind of change" speech to South African Parliament; Sharpeville massacre; Unlawful Organizations Act; ANC and PAC are banned; assassination attempt on Verwoerd fails; White referendum on South Africa becoming a republic

1961	Treason Trial detainees are acquitted; Albert Luthuli receives Nobel Peace Prize; South Africa becomes a republic, leaves Commonwealth; ANC adopts armed struggle; Umkhonto we Sizwe is formed, and sabotage campaign begins
1962	Mandela is arrested
1963	General Law Amendment Act (detention for ninety days and more); Umkhonto High Command is arrested; Rivonia Trial begins; Transkei receives self-government
1964	The Armaments Corporation of South Africa (ARMSCOR) is established; Mandela and others are sentenced to life imprisonment at Rivonia Trial
1966	General Law Amendment Act; Verwoerd is stabbed to death in House of Assembly; B.J. Vorster becomes prime minister; South Africa's Namibia mandate is revoked by UN General Assembly
1966–1968	Lesotho, Botswana, and Swaziland become independent
1967	Terrorism Act; Luthuli dies
1968	Prohibition of Political Interference Act prohibits multiracial political parties; White representatives for Coloureds in Parliament are abolished
1969	Bureau of State Security (BOSS) is created, Steve Biko forms South African Students' Organization; Albert Hertzog forms Herstigte Nasionale Party
1970	Bantu Homelands Citizenship Act
1971	International Court of Justice rules South Africa's occupation of Namibia illegal
1973	61,000 Black workers strike in Natal; Afrikaner Weerstandsbeweging is formed
1974	Salazar/Caetano dictatorship is overthrown in Portugal
1975	South African Defence Force troops invade Angola and nearly reach Luanda; Inkatha movement is revived by Mangosuthu Buthelezi
1975–1976	Mozambique and Angola become independent
1976	South African forces withdraw from Angola; police fire on Soweto schoolchildren protesting mandatory Afrikaans learning in schools

1976–1977	Soweto riots spread throughout country
1976–1981	Transkei, Bophuthatswana, Venda, and the Ciskei are granted "independence"
1977	Steve Biko is murdered in police detention; seventeen Black Consciousness organizations and three newspapers are banned; United Nations imposes compulsory arms embargo against South Africa
1978	South Africa accepts independence plan for Namibia; Information ("Muldergate") scandal; Pan Africanist Congress leader Robert Sobukwe dies
1978–1984, 1984–1989	P.W. Botha is prime minister, then state president
1979	Federation of South African Trade Unions is formed; Black trade unions gain official recognition and are allowed to register and strike
1980	Gold price goes over $800 per ounce; Umkhonto bombs South African Coal, Oil, and Gas Corporation (SASOL) facilities; Multiracial President's Council replaces Senate; Zimbabwe becomes independent
1981–1988	South African Defence Forces (SADF) carry out raids and acts of sabotage against Lesotho, Zimbabwe, Zambia, Lesotho, also invade Angola; Umkhonto attacks main South African military base at Voortrekkerhoogte
1982	Andries Treurnicht and other right-wing members of Parliament form Conservative Party; Umkhonto attacks Koeberg nuclear plant
1983	United Democratic Front (UDF) is formed; White voters approve new constitution
1984–1986	Township revolts begin in Sharpeville, spread to East Rand, Soweto, and other parts of the nation
1984	South African troops withdraw from Angola; Nkomati Accord between Mozambique and South Africa; Botha becomes state president and the first tricameral parliament for Coloureds, Whites, and Indians is opened; Archbishop Desmond Tutu is awarded the Nobel Peace Prize
1985	Police fire on marchers near Uitenhage; Botha delivers "Rubicon Address"; White delegation meets ANC in Zambia

1986   Eminent Persons Group mission; nationwide state of
            emergency; Mixed Marriages Act, section 16 of
            Immorality Act, and Prohibition of Political
            Interference Act are repealed; pass laws and influx
            control are abolished; U.S. Congress overrides
            President Reagan's veto and passes the
            Comprehensive Anti-Apartheid Act

1987   Sixty-one Afrikaners meet ANC representatives in
            Dakar, Senegal; ANC activist Govan Mbeki is released

1989   F.W. de Klerk replaces Botha as National Party
            leader, then becomes acting state president; Walter
            Sisulu and seven other long-term political prisoners
            are released; Namibian elections

1990   (2 February) de Klerk legalizes ANC, PAC, SACP, and
            other opposition parties, announces Mandela's
            unconditional release; (11 February) Mandela is freed;
            Namibian independence; (April) Ciskei and Venda
            governments are overthrown; Separate Amenities Act is
            repealed; ANC suspends armed struggle

1991   1913 and 1936 Land Acts, Group Areas Act,
            Population Registration Act are repealed; the further
            Abolition of Racially Based Measures Act provides
            for removal of racial distinctions in other laws;
            Mandela is elected ANC president; National Peace
            Accord is signed by the government, ANC, the IFP,
            and others; South Africa signs nuclear
            nonproliferation treaty; nineteen parties attend
            Convention for a Democratic South Africa
            (CODESA), seventeen sign Declaration of Intent

1992   Whites-only referendum supports reform process;
            Boipatong Massacre of forty-five people brings ANC
            rolling mass action campaign of strikes, sit-ins,
            marches; ANC coup in Ciskei fails; South Africa
            attends Olympics after thirty-two years of being
            banned; four million workers support COSATU-
            sponsored stayaway; Record of Understanding is
            reached between ANC and government agreeing to
            democratically elected interim government of
            national unity; formation of Concerned South
            Africans Group (COSAG); ANC agrees to power-
            sharing after ANC activist Joe Slovo proposes
            "sunset" clauses that allow for power sharing in
            new government of national unity

1993	European Economic Community lifts sanctions; CODESA negotiations resume with twenty-six parties attending; de Klerk announces dismantling of South Africa's six nuclear weapons; Chris Hani is assassinated; Inkatha Freedom Party and Conservative Party form Freedom Alliance; armed AWB members invade World Trade Centre; report of Motsuenyane Commission into alleged human rights abuses against ANC detainees; UN lifts most sanctions; agreement is reached on interim constitution providing for a nonracial, multiparty democracy, three tiers of government and Bill of Rights in a unitary South Africa with nine provinces; Parliament approves interim constitution, marking end of apartheid
1994	Presidents Lucas Mangope (Bophuthatswana) and Brigadier Gqozo (Ciskei) are ousted; South Africa hands over Walvis Bay to Namibia; Shell House massacre (IFP members attack ANC's Johannesburg headquarters, killing fifty); (26–29 April) ANC victory in first democratic election; (27 April) interim constitution takes effect; Government of National Unity is formed; Transkei, Ciskei, Bophuthatswana, and Venda are reincorporated into South Africa; (10 May) Mandela is inaugurated as first democratically elected president; South Africa rejoins the British Commonwealth of Nations after thirty-three years, UNESCO after forty years, reclaims seat in UN General Assembly, also joins the Organization of African Unity and the Non-Aligned Movement; Constitutional Assembly begins drawing up South Africa's final constitution; UN lifts arms embargo; Reconstruction and Development Program is launched
1995	Masakhaine ("Let us build together") campaign is initiated to end rent and bond boycotts, Joe Slovo dies; death penalty is ruled unconstitutional; President Mandela appoints Truth and Reconciliation Commission (TRC) with Archbishop Desmond Tutu as chair

1996   Bafana Bafana, the national soccer team, wins Africa Cup of Nations, qualifies for World Cup; (April) TRC begins hearing victims' accounts of human rights abuses; National Party leaves Government of National Unity; Mandela becomes chair of Southern African Development Community; (10 December) Mandela signs Constitution at Sharpeville; Bishop Stanley Mogoba is elected president of Pan Africanist Congress

1997   (4 February) Constitution takes effect; National Council of Provinces is inaugurated; South Africa bans use of anti-personnel land mines; South Africa intervenes in Zairean crisis; Winnie Madikizela-Mandela is re-elected ANC Women's League president; (September) de Klerk resigns as NP leader and retires from active politics; deadline for amnesty for apartheid crimes expires; Roelof Meyer and Bantu Holomisa form United Democratic movement; Thabo Mbeki succeeds Mandela as ANC president; Jacob Zuma becomes ANC deputy president

1998   South Africa opens official diplomatic relations with the People's Republic of China; U.S. president Bill Clinton makes state visit to South Africa; South Africa becomes chair of Non-Aligned Movement; South Africa sends troops into Lesotho to quell uprising against government; (October) Truth and Reconciliation Commission files report; amnesty hearings continue

1999   (March) Mandela delivers farewell speech to Parliament; (June 2) ANC wins 66.36 percent of vote in nationwide elections under new constitution; (June 16) Thabo Mbeki is inaugurated as South African president

Abbreviations

AAC	All Africa Convention
ANC	African National Congress
APLA	Azanian People's Liberation Army
APO	African People's Organization
ARM	African Resistance Movement
AWB	Afrikaner Weerstandsbeweging (Afrikaner Resistance Movement)
AZAPO	Azanian People's Organization
BC	Black Consciousness
BOSS	Bureau of State Security
BPC	Black People's Convention
CA	Constitutional Assembly
CCB	Civil Co-operation Bureau
CI	Christian Institute
CLPP	Coloured Labour Preference Policy
CNETU	Council for Non-European Trade Unions
CODESA	Convention for a Democratic South Africa

COSAG	Concerned South Africans Group
COSATU	Congress of South African Trade Unions
CP	Conservative Party; Communist Party
CPRC	Coloured People's Representative Council
CPSA	Communist Party of South Africa
CUSA-AZACTU	Council of Unions of South Africa—Azanian Confederation of Trade Unions
CYL	(African National) Congress Youth League
DP	Democratic Party
DRC	Dutch Reformed Church
ECC	End Conscription Campaign
EPG	Eminent Persons Group
FAK	Federation of Afrikaner Cultural Organizations
FF	Freedom Front
GEAP	Growth, Employment, and Redistribution Policy
GNU	Government of National Unity
HNP	Herenigde Nasionale Party; Herstigte Nasionale Party
ICU	Industrial and Commercial Worker's Union
IEC	Independent Electoral Commission
IFP	Inkatha Freedom Party
ISCOR	Iron and Steel Corporation
LMS	London Missionary Society
LP	Liberal Party
MDM	Mass Democratic Movement
MK	Umkhonto we Sizwe (Spear of the Nation)
MP	Member of Parliament
MPLA	Popular Movement for the Liberation of Angola
NCOP	National Council of Provinces
NECC	National Education Crisis Committee
NEDLAC	National Economic Development and Labour Advisory Council
NGK	Nederduitse Gereformeerde Kerk

NNP	New National Party
NP	National Party
NRC	Natives Representative Council
NUSAS	National Union of South African Students
OFS	Orange Free State
PAC	Pan Africanist Congress of Azania
PFP	Progressive Federal Party
RDP	Reconstruction and Development Programme
RENAMO	Mozambique National Resistance Movement
SA	South Africa
SAAF	South African Air Force
SABC	South African Broadcasting Corporation
SACC	South African Council of Churches
SACP	South African Communist Party
SACPO	South African Coloured People's Organization
SACTU	South African Congress of Trade Unions
SADC	Southern African Development Community
SADF	South African Defence Force
SAIC	South African Indian Congress
SANDF	South African National Defence Force
SANNC	South African Native National Congress
SAP	South African Party; South African Police
SAR	South African Republic
SASO	South African Students' Organization
SSC	State Security Council
SWAPO	South West African People's Organization
TEC	Transitional Executive Council
TRC	Truth and Reconciliation Commission
TUCSA	Trade Union Congress of South Africa
UDF	United Democratic Front
UN	United Nations
UNITA	National Union for the Total Independence of Angola

UP	United Party
UWUSA	United Workers' Union of South Africa
VAT	value-added tax
VOC	Vereenigde Oost-Indische Compagnie

1

South Africa Today

This is the history of a large area of land in southern Africa. Because it begins with pre-human ancestors three and a half to four million years ago, it is the oldest history in this *Modern Nations* series. Because modern South Africa, with boundaries roughly as they are today, only came into existence in 1910, this book is also the history of a relatively new nation. And only since 1994 has South Africa's indigenous African majority regained dominion after nearly 350 years of rule over parts or all of the land by people of European ancestry. There are many threads here for the historian to weave, and they stretch a very great distance into the past.

LAND AND CLIMATE

South Africa has an area of 472,281 square miles, making it larger than California, Texas, and Indiana combined. Like much of Africa's topography, South Africa has a relatively narrow coastal zone that rises sharply to a great plateau region that makes up about two-thirds of the country. The stretch of land separating the coastal areas from the plateau is called the Great Escarpment, and it reaches its greatest heights in the Drakensberg Mountains along South Africa's southeastern edge. Across the plateau there are three areas described by the Dutch word *veld*: the High Veld, the Bush Veld, and the Middle Veld. *Veld* has several meanings in South Africa, but here it refers to (1) grazing or farming land, and (2) more generally, the landscape or countryside, flat or hilly, or nonurban land. Most of the interior region is High Veld, ranging in elevation from about 4,000 to 6,000 feet; it is level or slightly undulating terrain, reaching as far north as the gold mining region east and west of Johannesburg known as the Witwatersrand, or simply the Rand. The Bush Veld lies north of the Witwatersrand and averages less than 4,000 feet in height. The Middle Veld, the western section of the plateau region, ranges between 2,000 and 4,000 feet above sea level.

Where the plateau drops to the coast in both the south and southwest there are a series of steppes or sharp drops. In the east, from the interior seaward, are the Eastern Uplands and the Eastern Low Veld. In the south, traveling from the interior to the coast, one passes through the Great Karoo, the Swartberg Mountains, the Little Karoo, and the Langeberg Mountains before coming to a low-lying coastal plain. Towering over Cape Town to the south is Table Mountain, with a height of about 3,563 feet. To the southwest are a number of small mountain ranges stretching in various directions that separate the plateau from the sea. These include the Roggeveld, Bokkeveld, Piketberg, Hantam, Langberg, and Kamiesberg Mountains. The Kalahari Desert spreads across Namibia and Botswana into northwestern South Africa, and the Namib Desert runs along the western coast.

The Orange, Vaal, and Limpopo are South Africa's major rivers. The Orange River, the longest in the country (about 1300 miles), runs from Lesotho to the Atlantic and forms the border between South Africa and Namibia along the way. The Vaal River originates near Swaziland and flows in a southwesterly direction to the center of the country, where it joins the Orange River. The Limpopo River begins in the northeast and runs to the northwest and then east, bordering Botswana and Zimbabwe before entering Mozambique and continuing to the Indian Ocean. Rivers in the eastern Cape and Natal have played some role in South African history, but generally rivers were never of much importance because they are dry for much of the year and because the Great Escarpment makes upstream navigation very difficult. They have been tapped to some extent for agricultural irrigation and hydroelectric plants. There are important harbors at Durban, Cape Town, Port Elizabeth, East London, Richards Bay, and Saldanha Bay.

Although most of South Africa enjoys a mild, temperate climate, rainfall is always a matter of concern. Easterly trade winds blowing off the Indian Ocean reach most of the eastern and central parts of the country. Along the Transvaal and Natal coasts these winds are moisture laden and bring about 35 to 40 inches of rain annually. Rainfall amounts diminish rapidly as one moves west. The High Veld receives about 15 to 30 inches, and the northwestern Cape as little as 5 inches or less annually. This accounts for the desert-like conditions in the northwest and the semi-desert conditions in the Great Karoo. Rains usually fall between October and April, but the Cape peninsula and environs receive heavy winter rains (June to September) off the Atlantic Ocean of about 22 inches annually, which allows for intensive agriculture. Temperatures are the warmest around Durban and the southeastern coast, averaging 52° to 72° F in the winter and 69° to 81° F in the summer. Johannesburg averages 58° to 78° F in the summer and 45° to 63° F in the winter. Cape Town is the coolest, ranging between 60° to 78° F in the summer and 45° to 63° F in the winter. It rarely snows in South Africa except on some of the higher mountain ranges.

POPULATION AND RELIGION

South Africa's population in 1999 was 40.5 million. Of these, there were 31.1 million Africans, one million Asians, 3.6 million Coloureds (mixed-race), 4.4 million Whites, and 0.4 million others/unspecified. South Africa has eleven official language groups, with Zulu-speakers being the largest at 22.9 percent of the total population, followed by Xhosa (17.9%), Afrikaans (14.4%), Pedi (9.2%), English (8.6%), Tswana (8.2%), Sotho (7.7%), Tsonga (4.4%), Swazi (2.5%), Venda (2.2%), Ndebele (1.5%), and others (0.6%). Afrikaans, which evolved from Dutch, is the first language of nearly all Afrikaners (mainly of Dutch descent) and of many Coloureds. Afrikaners make up about two-thirds of the White population. English is the first language of about one-third of the White population and of the majority of Coloureds. English is also the most widely used language for all peoples. Most Indians speak English as well as one of the languages of India.

The majority of South Africans live in the eastern half of the country, where the high rainfall, good soil, and rich mineral deposits offer the most job opportunities. Four urban centers are home to nearly one-third of all South Africans: Johannesburg-Pretoria-Vereeniging in Gauteng province; Durban-Pinetown-Pietermaritzburg in KwaZulu-Natal; Cape Town and the southwestern Cape; and Port Elizabeth-Uitenhage in the eastern Cape.

Nearly 80 percent of the South African population is Christian, mainly Protestant. Most Afrikaners belong to the Dutch Reformed Church, whereas most English-speaking Whites belong to the Anglican, Congregational, Methodist, or Roman Catholic churches. Africans and Coloureds are also members of these denominations. Many other Africans attend syncretic churches that combine elements of traditional African religious beliefs with those of Christianity. The largest and most important of the so-called independent churches is the Zion Christian Church. Altogether there are about 6,000 independent denominations with about 9 million members. Many Africans continue to adhere to traditional African belief systems. The majority of Indians are Hindus or Muslims, and the extensive Malay population practices Islam. South Africa's Jewish community numbers about 100,000.

PROVINCES

South Africa's political system has undergone significant changes since the early 1990s, and the nature of these changes is the subject of much of the last two chapters of this book. Under the segregated apartheid system prior to 1994, South Africa was divided into four provinces (Cape province, Orange Free State, Transvaal, and Natal) and four "independent" *bantustans*, or homelands, and six nonindependent ones. The country's interim constitution, which took effect in April 1994, divided South Africa into nine provinces: Gauteng; Northern province; Mpumalanga; North-West Province; Free State; KwaZulu-Natal; Eastern Cape; Northern Cape; and Western Cape. All the former *bantustans* are once again part of the republic.

FLORA AND FAUNA

South Africa is world renowned for the variety of its natural flora. The Cape Floral Kingdom, which stretches from Cape Point north and east along the Atlantic and Indian Ocean coasts, contains more than twice as many species of flowers per acre than any other place on earth. There are over 8,500 species, 6,000 of which are found nowhere else. Kirstenbosch Gardens in the Cape Peninsula is one of the premier botanical gardens in the world. The country as a whole has over 23,200 different plants, 19,000 of which are particular to this region. South Africa's natural vegetation varies from region to region and is heavily dependent on amount of rainfall. There are rain forests in the Eastern Low Veld where rainfall is heaviest, and along the southern coast there are forests of yellowwood, stinkwood, ironwood, and cedar. The plateaus are predominantly grassland. The High Veld has few trees and resembles a prairie, whereas the Bush Veld is more like wooded savanna, having both trees and bushes. As the rainfall decreases to the west, so does the quality of the grasslands. The Great Karoo and the Little Karoo are semidesert and covered with dry scrub.

South Africa is home to many of the world's largest mammals, including hippopotami, rhinoceros, elephants, lions, zebras, leopards, monkeys, baboons, and antelope. As is true nowadays for most of Africa, these animals are generally found only on game reserves. The first and best known of South Africa's national game reserves is Kruger National Park (1926), occupying 7,523 square miles along the border with Mozambique. Within its boundaries it contains nearly every species of wildlife indigenous to the country. There are thirteen other national game reserves, including the Tsitsikamma National Park, Kalahari Gemsbok National Park, Addo Elephant National Park, Augrabies Falls National Park, and Table Mountain and Dongola national parks. Over 10 percent of the world's bird life, more than 900 species, are found in South Africa.

MINERAL RESOURCES

During the nineteenth and early twentieth centuries South Africa became a primary focus of British imperialists because of its extraordinary mineral riches. Gold, diamonds, platinum, and coal are its four most important mineral deposits. The Witwatersrand gold fields are the richest in the world. Gold and platinum group metals are now mined and produced almost exclusively for export. Most diamonds come from the Kimberley diamond fields. South Africa is one of the world's leading coal exporters, tapping the vast and easily worked coal seams in the northeast between Swaziland and Lesotho. Coal is South Africa's main source of energy. South Africa also has significant deposits of antimony, asbestos, chromium, copper, fluorite, iron ores, manganese, nickel, phosphates, platinum, tin, titanium, uranium, vanadium, vermiculite, and zirconium.

LIBRARIES AND MUSEUMS

Most South African cities have public libraries, some of which are Carnegie-endowed libraries from the early decades of the twentieth century. The largest library in South Africa is the Johannesburg Public Library, containing more than 1.6 million volumes. Legal deposit libraries are the Bloemfontein Public Library; the Library of Parliament, Cape Town; the Natal Society Library, Pietermaritzburg; the South African Library, Cape Town; and the State Library, Pretoria. There are also outstanding libraries connected with major universities, such as the University of Cape Town, University of the Witwatersrand, University of Stellenbosch, University of Natal, and Rhodes University.

South Africa has many fine museums, although several have only recently begun making space for exhibits that acknowledge Black contributions to art, history, and culture. Museums and galleries are in a critical stage of change and funding at the end of the 1990s. A large percentage of recent national budgets has funded various sites on Robben Island, including the prison where Nelson Mandela was held, as a museum and tourist attraction. Notable museums include the Michaelis Collection, the South African National Gallery, and the South African Cultural History Museum, all in Cape Town; the National Museum in Bloemfontein; and the MuseumAfrica (formerly the Afrikana Museum) in Johannesburg.

ECONOMY

South Africa, which occupies only 4 percent of the African land mass, has the largest gross national product (GNP) of any nation on the continent—larger than that of Egypt, Kenya, and Nigeria combined. South Africa has more than half the cars, telephones, automated bank machines, and industrial facilities of the entire continent. More than one-third of the nation's GNP is produced in the smallest province, Gauteng, which includes Johannesburg and Pretoria. However, this modern industrial nation also exhibits many signs of a developing economy, such as a severe disparity in the distribution of wealth, an overdependence on commodity exports, and a mass migration to urban areas where there are not enough jobs. South Africa in 1999 is classified as a middle-income country, with a per capita Gross Domestic Product (GDP) of about U.S. $3,000; but this number is deceptive because of the enormous differences between White and Black incomes.

CURRENCY

The rand, divided into 100 cents, is South Africa's basic unit of currency (about 6 rands equaled U.S. $1.00 in 1999). The South African Reserve Bank, founded in 1920, is the sole bank of issue. The country has numerous commercial, savings, and investment banks. Stock trading is done at the Johannesburg Stock Exchange (JSE), which ranks among the twelve largest in the world.

FOREIGN TRADE

South Africa's exports to industrialized countries are heavily dependent on primary and intermediate commodities such as gold, base metals, precious metals, and minerals. Gold accounts for about 20 percent of the annual value of South Africa's exports. The nation primarily exports manufactured goods to the other countries in Africa; in the late 1990s this made up about 20 percent of total exports. Major imports are machinery, petroleum, transportation equipment, chemical products, textiles, plastics, and metals and metal products. South Africa's leading trading partner and leading investor in 1998 was the United States. The European Union is South Africa's single largest trading bloc, followed by Asia; and Zimbabwe is the nation's largest trading partner in Africa.

TRANSPORTATION

Transportation systems are undergoing extensive changes that will carry into the twenty-first century. South Africa has over 13,000 miles of railroad tracks that link most major urban centers and that are operated through the state-owned Transnet. South African Airways, also state owned, is the largest airline in Africa. There are also several smaller carriers, and many of the world's major airlines fly into the airports at Johannesburg and Cape Town. South Africa has more airline passengers per year than all the countries of southern, central, and eastern Africa combined. The busiest airport is at Johannesburg. The government plans to privatize all airlines, ports, and railways by 2003.

There are some 117,000 miles of roads in the country, nearly 30 percent of which are paved. There are about 3.5 million passenger cars in use and several car rental companies. South Africa has the highest percentage of railway line and paved roads per 1,000 kilometers of land on the

African continent. Western-style taxi services operate in most cities, and there are many privately managed mini-bus or mini-taxi services as well.

MASS MEDIA

Radio and television broadcasting are operated by the Independent Broadcasting Authority, which took over from the state-controlled propaganda machine of the apartheid system in 1993. The South African Broadcasting Corporation provides radio services in eleven languages, as well as three television channels with programs in seven languages. Various satellite services are available, and video stores are found everywhere. Radio and television are funded through advertising and from licenses, although television piracy in South Africa is among the highest in the world, with over half the television audience refusing or failing to pay for annual licenses.

South Africa has about thirty daily, weekly, and financial newspapers, four of which are in Afrikaans and the rest in English. These include *The Mail & Guardian, Die Burger* (Afrikaans), *The Star*, and so-called Black newspapers: *The Sowetan, The City Press,* and *The Sunday World* (English).

2

The First South Africans, 4 Million B.C.E.–1488 C.E.

FROM THE BEGINNING

The creature probably fell down a shaft in the cave at Sterkfontein, north of Krugersdorp. It slumped face down, its head resting on its left arm, and it died. Three and a half million years later, in December 1998, Dr. Ron Clark found its remains—the complete skull and skeleton. Clark's discovery of one of humankind's earliest ancestors, called *Australopithecus africanus* ("the southern ape of Africa"), represents the most important fossil find in southern Africa since 1924. In that year Dr. Raymond Dart maintained that a small skull found at a site near the northern Cape town of Taung had some humanoid features, and he originated the name *Australopithecus africanus*. Clark's fossil and Dart's "Taung baby," so-called because it died at three or four years of age, were both pre-human relatives of man who lived in eastern and southern Africa one to four million years ago. *A. africanus* walked upright, had small human-like teeth, and may have used crude tools.

During the period between these two discoveries, many more excavations revealed southern Africa's rich human heritage and its possible location as the cradle of humanity. *Homo habilis* ("handy man") and *Homo erectus* ("erect man") both inhabited this region around one million years ago. The two oldest known fossils of modern man, *Homo sapiens sapiens*, who appeared approximately 100,000 years ago, were found on the Tsitsikamma coast in the Eastern Cape and at Border Cave in KwaZulu-Natal. In August 1997 David Roberts discovered the oldest known footprints of a modern human ancestor (called Eve) at Langebaan Lagoon north of Cape Town. They are believed to be 117,000 years old. Recent studies show that early humans roamed in hunter-gatherer bands across the South African subcontinent, developing tools and forms of social organization much earlier than previously thought. On 27 April 1999, researchers found a 2,000-year-old mummified body, probably of a Khoisan man, in the Kouga Mountains in the Eastern Cape. New research on the human gene pool continues to link these first South Africans to the modern population.

THE SAN

The San people, called Bushmen by Europeans, are the direct descendants of southern Africa's ancient inhabitants. Only a few thousand remain today, mainly in arid, desolate regions of the Kalahari Desert in Botswana and Namibia. For thousands of years, however, nomadic bands of these aboriginal hunters and gatherers moved across and lived within central and southern Africa, including the Kalahari. The San are smaller and have a lighter skin pigmentation than more recent African migrants into southern Africa. Their "click" languages are unique in the world, although during the last two thousand years of contact they passed on a few "clicks" to their African neighbors, particularly the Xhosa.

The San lived peacefully in small, egalitarian bands of nuclear families numbering between fifteen and one hundred people, depending on the carrying capacity of the local environment. Women and men had an equal voice in the group, although there was a gendered division of labor. Women took care of the campsite, the children, and the provision of edible plants, roots, nuts, and berries. Men also helped to collect food, but their main responsibility was hunting. Each band had a nominal chief who looked after the group's resources and performed rituals such as rain-making. The chief had little institutionalized authority, however; although he was respected, he was not elevated above other group members.

The San practiced no agriculture and kept no domesticated animals except dogs. They dwelt in caves, under rock shelters, or in temporary huts built out of reeds, saplings, and bushes—and always as near as possible to water. They ate a wide assortment of animals and plant food-stuffs, ranging from antelopes and elephants to wild fruits, berries, bulbs, and roots. They had no possessions except certain rights to sources of honey, ostrich eggs, and water. In some cases, bands inherited certain territory with springs and watering holes.

The San are most famous for their rock paintings. Using charcoal and natural dyes and pigments, they decorated the rock faces of their shelters and cave walls with images of the hunt. The highly respected eland and other game animals are portrayed with grace and simplicity of move-ment. Some paintings record the religious experiences of the San sha-mans, especially trance-dances. The earliest images, from about 27,000 B.C.E., are a historical record providing a glimpse of San life. They are also a witness to change, as more recent paintings portray contacts with Bantu-speakers and Whites.

Although frequently thought of as exclusively a hunter-gatherer soci-ety, San culture and economy changed over time as other Africans forced them out of their traditional habitats. Thus, over the last two thousand years, while most San continued foraging for food, some also domesti-cated goats, sheep, and then horned cattle. They exchanged foraged food and wild game for cereals and domesticated meat with their neighbors. Sometimes they lived in a subordinate relationship as clients to more powerful Khoikhoi, or Bantu-speaking neighbors. Sometimes, however, they warred with their pastoralist (livestock keeping) neighbors because they refused to recognize private ownership of livestock, hunting their neighbors' cattle and sheep as they did the wild eland.

THE KHOIKHOI

One San group that did domesticate livestock was the Khoikhoi pas-toralists, called Hottentots by the Europeans. The Khoikhoi were not Caucasoid as once thought, but Negroid like the San—and therefore Af-ricans. A common dictum of South Africa's former White rulers was that the Khoikhoi and San were not "Africans." At its extreme, this view denied Khoikhoi and San humanity by considering them as little more than animals. More commonly it justified White seizure of Khoikhoi and San territory because the land was not cultivated and therefore was not considered to be owned. "Africans," in the language of apartheid, were the Bantu-speaking agri-pastoralists (those who practiced both agricul-ture and pastoralism). Both Khoikhoi and San generally had lighter skin pigmentation than the agri-pastoralists and were physically smaller. These traits led early European visitors at the Cape to develop extravagant theories regarding Khoikhoi origins: from Jewish lost tribes, to "Hamitic" immigrants from north Africa, to pastoralists from the region between the East African lakes. Theories of Khoikhoi origins in north or east Africa are now discredited by South African scholars.

The Khoikhoi were a San hunter-gatherer group who domesticated livestock. Over time they took the name Khoikhoi, meaning "the real people" or "men of men," to distinguish themselves from those who did not own livestock and were therefore deemed inferior. The Khoikhoi called these people the San. The Khoikhoi probably began keeping domesticated sheep and cattle, acquired from pastoralist groups farther north, as early as 2,500 years ago. The Khoikhoi were somewhat larger in stature than the San, a dissimilarity that is now attributed more to the benefits of a richer diet, particularly regular access to milk and meat, than to genetic differences. They spoke a language closely related to the San dialect known as Tshu-Khwe that included click sounds, and the two shared a common religious tradition.

The Khoikhoi migrated into South Africa from a region around modern-day southern Zambia and northern Botswana at the beginning of the Christian era. They probably traveled south, skirting the eastern edge of the Kalahari Desert until they reached the junction of the Orange and Vaal Rivers. At that point one group headed west, following the Orange, and became the Kora and Nama branches of the Khoikhoi. Another group continued south from the Orange River to the Indian Ocean and then spread east and west. They traveled east perhaps as far as Natal, leaving their distinctive click sounds among Xhosa- and Zulu-speakers along the way. Westward they traveled to the Cape peninsula, where some turned north again, meeting with other Khoikhoi coming south along the west coast from the Orange River.

The environment dictated the daily pace of Khoikhoi and San life and shaped some of their most sacred religious and mythological beliefs. Archaeological evidence at gravesites, wall paintings, and observers' accounts indicate that the Khoikhoi and San had strong religious beliefs that sought to explain their relationship to the environment and to the supernatural. They recognized a supreme god, Tsui//Goab ("//" denotes a click sound), and an evil god,//Gaunab. Both these supernatural forces were believed to operate in the world, bringing rain, a good harvest, and fertility, or bad fortune, illness, and death. These peoples also recognized an ancestor-hero, Heitsi-Eibib, who watched over individuals and brought them good fortune. Their most important ritual was the trance, or medicine dance, which induced altered states of consciousness. During these trances the participants might commune with the animals of the hunt, be healed, or be assured of fertility.

The Khoikhoi adapted to the Cape environment and to their neighbors, the San and the Bantu-speakers, in several ways. Some who settled along Indian Ocean beaches in the eastern Cape region lived on shellfish and ultimately became known as *strandlopers* ("beach walkers") by the Dutch. Those Khoikhoi in the eastern parts of South Africa, where rainfall and rich pasture were plentiful, lived as pastoralists. Those in the western sections, nearer to the arid Kalahari Desert and dry Karoo, lived a mixed existence that was partly dependent on raising livestock and partly on hunting and gathering. For all Khoikhoi the dietary staple was milk obtained from goats and cattle. Many Khoikhoi also developed client relationships with their neighbors, either absorbing hunter-gatherers into their chiefdoms or being absorbed themselves into Bantu-speaking groups.

The Khoikhoi were organized socially and politically under chiefs into patrilineal clan groupings (chieftainship was hereditary, passing from father to son) of one or two thousand members. These chiefdoms—much larger than the San's small bands—consisted of several clans, each with its own headman, who in turn owed allegiance to the senior clan chief. Sometimes two men shared the chieftainship, but this arrangement occasionally led to groups splitting. Khoikhoi chiefs did not rule autocratically but with the advice of a council of clan heads. Subjects scorned chiefs who abused their authority. Chiefs displayed few outward signs of their special status, although they often practiced polygamy as an indication of wealth. With the introduction of private ownership and hierarchy of status and power, women lost the equality they had enjoyed in the hunter-gatherer societies.

Most Khoikhoi lived in knock-down huts made of reed mats fastened over bent saplings. (These mat houses, or *matjeshuise* in Afrikaans, were later used by early White livestock farmers.) They were easily dismantled and loaded onto cattle for transport. When the Khoikhoi stopped on their searches for water and pasture, they made a circular compound with these reed mat huts and placed their livestock in the middle at night for safekeeping.

Khoikhoi life centered around cattle and fat-tailed sheep. A man reckoned his status and wealth according to the number of sheep and cattle he owned, which he could pass on to his sons. Large flocks and herds made him an important member of the society. If he lost his livestock, he was reduced to serving another or perhaps returning to a hunter-gatherer existence. Before the Europeans arrived in 1652 the Khoikhoi traded sheep and cattle for iron, copper, and dagga (a type of narcotic plant) with their Bantu-speaking neighbors. After European contact the focus of Khoikhoi trading activity shifted toward the Cape Town market, where they traded cattle for tobacco, alcohol, salt, and other goods.

Neither the San nor the Khoikhoi ever practiced agriculture, but livestock gave the Khoikhoi a certain degree of self-sufficiency and mobility not possible for the San. Livestock also inspired a concept among the Khoikhoi that San hunter-gatherers found alien—private ownership of property. Thus, as the Khoikhoi left their ancestral home and moved south with their animals across southern Africa, they came into conflict with their San relatives in several ways. First, Khoikhoi livestock over-grazed and trampled pasture used by the San's traditional sources of meat—eland, zebra, and wildebeest. Second, because the Khoikhoi only slaughtered cattle in times of particular need or for ritual ceremonies, they depended, like the San, on the hunt as a source of meat and hides for clothing. Soon the depletion of wild game forced the San to raid Khoikhoi herds, thereby initiating a series of raids, counter-raids, and wars between the two groups that continued into the nineteenth century. Eventually many San left the favorable foraging areas. They moved into less hospitable regions such as the Kalahari Desert, which the San had already inhabited for thousands of years. Some fought back, however, raiding Khoikhoi and, later, White settler herds before retreating into wilderness hideouts. Still others abandoned their old ways and became Khoikhoi clients, working as herders or servants. Some San eventually acquired livestock, married Khoikhoi women, and were integrated into Khoikhoi society.

It is important to remember, however, that differences between the pastoralist Khoikhoi and hunting-gathering San were often hard to distinguish. San sometimes blended into Khoikhoi communities, and Khoikhoi sometimes lost their livestock and had to forage. For this reason, and because the Khoikhoi and the San shared many cultural, ethnic, and linguistic ties, they are often referred to collectively as the Khoisan.

Changes after European Contact

European contact caused many Khoikhoi to lose their independence and their identity. The late seventeenth and much of the eighteenth centuries were especially difficult times for them. Khoikhoi-Dutch wars, smallpox, theft or slaughter of livestock, alcohol addiction, and European settlement on their lands all took a toll. They were reduced to working as laborers and herdsmen on White farms alongside the slaves with whom they intermarried. White farmers often made little distinction between their Khoikhoi workers and slaves, treating them equally harshly.

Some Khoikhoi men and women served as intermediaries between the early Dutch colonists and neighboring Khoikhoi clans, and later with Bantu-speakers to the north and east. Autsumato, known as "Harry," was the interpreter for the first Cape governor. Krotoa, or "Eva," learned Dutch and Portuguese, married a Danish surgeon at the Cape, and was the first Christian convert. Doman was sent to Batavia in 1657 to become an interpreter. On his return he became angry at Dutch mistreatment of his people and took a leading role in the First Dutch-Khoikhoi War of 1659–1660.

The so-called Cape Coloured—a mixed people of Khoisan, European, African, and Southeast Asian ancestry—developed over time following decades of contact with the European community. They spoke a dialect of Dutch and wore European clothes. Many practiced Christianity or the Islam that arrived with slaves from Dutch colonies in Asia. Some married Europeans, and many children were born from illicit (and often forced) unions between European men and Khoisan and slave women. In fact, there was little difference between Coloured and White South Africans, particularly Afrikaners. They shared common languages, religions, cultures, and histories to the extent that Coloureds were called *bruin Afrikaners* ("brown Afrikaners"). The apartheid government went to great lengths, however, to legislate vague distinctions to justify Coloured disenfranchisement. As a result the term "Coloured" is now the subject of much debate in post-apartheid South Africa, particularly among the Coloured themselves.

When the somewhat more liberal British arrived in 1795, and Christian missionaries shortly thereafter, life for some Khoikhoi may have improved slightly. Many Khoikhoi went to live on mission stations, much to the displeasure of White farmers who employed them as farmhands and maids. Others headed north to the Orange River in the 1700s and 1800s. There they formed independent societies beyond the Cape government's reach. The most notable was the mixed race Griqua, who practiced a largely European lifestyle and would have been absorbed into the European community had race not already been a divisive factor in South Africa.

THE BANTU-SPEAKING PEOPLES

The first iron-workers and agri-pastoralists probably arrived south of the Limpopo River around the third or fourth century C.E. These so-called Bantu-speaking peoples remain the subject of considerable debate and investigation. Their travels south through central and southern Africa are commonly referred to as the Bantu Migrations, although scholars now question the appropriateness of this term. The process appears to have occurred more gradually, with small groups slowly expanding into new areas for grazing and cultivation, bringing their iron-working skills and agri-pastoral practices with them. Certainly no single mass migration of Bantu-speakers ever occurred.

A myth long held by White South Africans is that Bantu-speakers arrived in the Transvaal about the same time as the first Dutch ships sailed into Table Bay in 1652. South Africa was therefore regarded as "empty" before this time and free for the taking by the more powerful force. Although now fully discredited, this myth was long an official tenet of White rule in South Africa. Even though it is now possible to paint a broad picture of the Bantu-speakers' movements and lives over the past two thousand years, particular details still remain sketchy.

Much of what is known about the Bantu-speaking peoples comes from archaeology and linguistics. On the basis of evidence from iron and pottery remains, as well as language patterns, it seems the ancestors of these agri-pastoralists originated in the region of modern-day Cameroon, north of the equatorial rain forest. Beginning at least two thousand years ago, some emigrants advanced slowly southward through the rain forest and the region of modern-day Angola and then turned eastward toward what is modern-day Zambia and the Democratic Republic of the Congo (formerly Zaire). There they met other emigrants who traveled a route north of the rain forest toward the east African lake region and then turned to the south. By 500 C.E. these Bantu-speakers occupied settlements as far south as present-day KwaZulu-Natal.

Although they are called Bantu-speakers, there is no way of knowing what languages these people spoke in earlier times. The term simply acknowledges that societies throughout central and southern Africa belong to a related language group—like the Romance or Germanic language families of Europe. Also, no remnants of any other language families exist, other than Khoisan clicks and word borrowings. These people are always described as Bantu-speakers, however, and not merely as Bantu. There were no original Bantu people; the word itself simply means "persons." The apartheid government used "Bantu" as a label for all African "natives" and Bantu now is considered a racist term.

Linguists normally divide the mixed-farming Bantu-speakers in southern Africa into four main categories: Nguni, Sotho, Venda, and Tsonga. These fairly recent scholarly conventions, however, do not seek to deny the common heritage shared by the more than 100 million Bantu-speakers across central and southern Africa whose similarities are more significant than their differences. They are also not necessarily names that the various peoples used for themselves, particularly before about 1800.

The Nguni constitute the largest language category in South Africa. They occupy the southeastern coastal region between the interior plateau and the Indian Ocean, from the eastern Cape region to Swaziland. The dominant Nguni groups are the Zulu and Swazi of the northern Nguni, and the Xhosa, Mpondo, Thembu, Bhaca, Mfengu, Mpondomise, and Bomvana of the southern Nguni. These peoples settled the KwaZulu-Natal and eastern Cape region from the north. After arriving in the coastal zone, they moved in a southwesterly direction until Xhosa ancestors crossed the Fish River in the eastern Cape by at least the sixteenth century.

The Sotho constitute the other large language category in South Africa. These people inhabit the interior plateau running west to east from the edge of the eastern Kalahari Desert to the northern Transvaal, and south to north from Lesotho to all of modern Botswana. This category is commonly subdivided into three main groupings: the western Sotho, or Tswana, people; the northern Sotho, comprising the Pedi and Lobedu; and the southern Sotho, or Sotho, of the modern state of Lesotho and surrounding territory.

Two less populous language categories are the Venda and Tsonga. For many years scholars thought the Venda were recent Shona arrivals from across the Limpopo River who settled in the far northern Transvaal and absorbed non-Shona into their society. Scholars now believe the Venda settled in the far northern Transvaal at a very early date and absorbed Shona emigrants from the region of modern-day Zimbabwe into Venda society. Thus, although the Venda have close historical links to the Shona of modern Zimbabwe, Venda language and culture share several common features with the Sotho. Extensive archaeological evidence, particularly of mining activities, suggests that this region of the northern Transvaal has been occupied since the early Iron Age; details about Venda origins, however, remain speculative.

The Tsonga appear to have some Nguni roots, but their language and culture differ significantly from those of the Nguni in some important respects. They are fish-eaters, for example, which is a food strictly forbidden under Nguni taboos. The Tsonga live southeast of the Venda along the coastal strip and hinterland west of Delagoa Bay (modern Maputo, Mozambique). They used this strategic location in the past to play a dominant role in trade as middlemen between societies in Delagoa Bay and the hinterland.

Changes during the Late Iron Age

Important cultural and economic changes occurred throughout southern Africa around C.E. 1000. Archaeologists and historians identify the periods before and after this date as the early and late Iron Ages. Some of the major changes noticeable after C.E. 1000 include an increase in human and livestock populations, a subsequent growth in village size, and new patterns of land occupation. The most significant distinction is found in the introduction of new ceramic styles, possibly because women began to control pottery making (men had done so previously). A definite shift in land occupation also occurred. Early Iron Age societies generally settled in low-lying regions and river valleys, where the fertile soil supported subsistence agriculture. Late Iron Age societies settled in higher areas, particularly the Natal and Zululand uplands and the Transvaal and Orange Free State highveld. These settlements were much more diverse than earlier ones, ranging from (1) small, dispersed villages consisting predominantly of family homesteads, to (2) large, densely populated settlements.

Architectural styles also changed significantly, with an increased use of stone for building and circular stone walls serving as stock enclosures. Building with stone was more common among the Sotho and Tswana in the north, where stone was readily available. Their solid, beehive-shaped homes were normally made of cow dung and mud mixed into a hard, smooth plaster. Thatched roofs and stone placed around the bottom provided extra protection from rain. Floors were also a mixture of highly polished earth and cow dung that held down the dust. The Ndebele still construct homes like these, drawing elaborate, beautiful, brightly colored geometric designs on the walls with colored clay. The Nguni also had circular homes, called rondavels, but they were generally made from sapling poles or reeds with thatched grass mat walls. They kept their cattle in pens made from thorn tree branches.

Other late Iron Age changes include the emergence of complex, hierarchically structured political systems, perhaps owing to the increasing importance of livestock (particularly cattle) in agri-pastoral societies. Larger livestock herds may also account for the shift in settlement patterns from the more agriculturally suitable low-lying area to the higher elevations where soil conditions, rainfall, pasture, and the relative absence of disease favor pastoralism. As among the Khoikhoi, cattle were an indication of wealth. The agri-pastoralists south of the Zambezi River may have adopted pastoralism from the Khoikhoi, for unlike Bantu-speaking pastoralists farther north, they use the Khoikhoi words for "cattle," "sheep," and "milk."

Mining for South Africa's rich mineral reserves also appears to have intensified during the late Iron Age. Hundreds of ancient mines have been identified, particularly in the Transvaal, that produced copper, tin, gold, and iron, among other minerals, and employed remarkably sophisticated mining techniques for the time. Blacksmithing was a very specialized craft that accorded its practitioners high status. Iron for tools and copper for earrings, necklaces, and other ornamentation were particularly prized and served as principal trade items.

Trade on the Transvaal highveld also grew significantly during the five hundred years before the Europeans arrived. This growth was partially linked to the rise of Great Zimbabwe in the area of present-day Zimbabwe and to the market at Delagoa Bay. Pre-dating Great Zimbabwe, however, were important trading centers such as Bambandyanalo and Mapungubwe in the Limpopo Valley that originated sometime between C.E. 900 and 1200.

Changes after the Iron Age

Although a remarkable continuity of culture and economy existed among agri-pastoral societies from the late Iron Age to modern times, African societies were not static or unchanging. Bantu-speakers did not live in isolated villages, practicing only agriculture, only pastoralism, or only mining. Hunting remained an integral part of the economy until the nineteenth century, and all these pursuits were practiced in varying degrees according to the local environment and customs. What the people lacked they traded for, as when the Xhosa exchanged their cattle for Tswana iron and copper. Some products, such as ivory, beads, iron, and copper, were traded over great distances. Europeans found some trade items among the Xhosa in the eastern Cape region in the early nineteenth century that came from Delagoa Bay. Agri-pastoralists also constantly interacted with their Khoisan neighbors, often developing client or symbiotic relationships, and even intermarrying.

Most agri-pastoral societies in South Africa were chiefdoms, hierarchically and patrilineally structured and centered on clans. A clan consisted of all those descendants who traced their lineage back to a common (usually male) ancestor. The chiefdom was composed of many different clans, and the chief usually came from the most powerful clan. The clan, and often the chiefdom, was named after a common ancestor (as among the Xhosa and Zulu) or after a totem animal, such as the elephant or lion (as among the Tswana and Sotho).

Membership in the chiefdoms was quite flexible. Although kinship was a primary criterion for membership, political necessity also played a role. Essentially anyone swearing allegiance to a particular clan or clan chief could belong. Even some shipwrecked Europeans from the sixteenth century onward joined Nguni societies along the Indian Ocean coast. This flexibility explains how the Sotho king, Moshoeshoe, acquired a very large following in the mid-1800s. He gathered around him a number of refugees and members of broken clans and chiefdoms seeking shelter from the *Mfecane* wars of that period. The size of chiefdoms varied greatly, from a few hundred to fifty thousand or more. Until the nineteenth century, however, when access to unoccupied land and water became difficult, there was a tendency toward decentralization. Farmers constantly moved to new areas in search of rich pasture and arable land.

Chiefs were not all-powerful, they were subject to their subjects' will. They generally ruled with the help of advisory councils consisting of elders (both men and women), royal male relatives, or male commoners who earned their council seats by merit. Among the Sotho and Tswana, the chief called together all his male subjects when undertaking a new project or when needing to discuss news that affected everyone. These *pitso*, or meetings, were highly democratic gatherings of men. Every man was free to speak his mind and criticize the chief and his advisers in an open and safe setting, and to voice his support, or lack thereof, for the leader. Until land and access to water became scarce in the nineteenth century, discontent with a chief could be most effectively expressed by leaving him and joining another. A chief's wealth was measured by his cattle, but his power resided in the number and support of his subjects.

The availability of land and water sources, in the form of springs, rivers, and ponds, generally determined population density. In the southeast until the late 1700s the Nguni lived in dispersed farmsteads around a small, central village, usually the site of the chief's compound. Just north of the Nguni, the Sotho concentrated more in villages but tended to split and scatter quite frequently. In the nineteenth century the Sotho often located their settlements on mountaintops to defend against attack from White and African neighbors. The Tswana, in the northern Cape and the area of modern Botswana, occupied the most marginal zone for crop cultivation and usually lived in large towns with populations numbering in the thousands.

The homestead, comprised of a man and one or more wives, was the basic unit in most agri-pastoral societies. Polygamy was permitted but not common because of the costs involved. Bridewealth, or compensation to the bride's family, had to be paid for each wife; this usually took the form of cattle. Each wife and her children had a hut within the homestead compound. Some dependents, or clients, and members of an extended family might also reside there. These societies recognized private ownership of cattle but not of land. The chief held the land rights and allocated land to individual farmsteads for grazing and cultivation.

The agri-pastoral Bantu-speakers enjoyed an environment mostly free of mosquitoes, tsetse fly, and other vectors (disease carriers) that limit human productivity in the tropics. Disruptive factors included irregular rainfall, severe droughts, wars, and waves of locusts that ravaged crops. Grain was stored by the Nguni in pits, by the Sotho in woven baskets. Farmers preferred iron tools, especially hoes, but these were not always available, so they often used wooden implements such as digging sticks and spades.

Farmers cleared their land using the "slash and burn" method. They then rotated the fields, cultivating some for a few years, and leaving others to lie fallow. Sorghum and millet were the staple crops. Maize became important after the Portuguese introduced it through Delagoa Bay in the 1500s. Milk was the other important dietary staple. Most agri-pastoral societies also made a thick, rich beer from sorghum or other grains. They supplemented their diets by hunting, most commonly for various sorts of antelopes but also for larger game such as buffalo, elephants, hippopotami, and rhinoceros. Hunting provided a source of food, clothing, trade items, and sport. Meat, pumpkins, squashes, watermelons, gourds, a variety of green vegetables, and occasionally yams and beans supplemented the cereals, milk, and cereal beer to provide a generally healthy and nutritious diet.

South Africa's agri-pastoral communities shared a common set of religious beliefs, although practices, rituals, and names varied widely. They all recognized a supreme god, called Qamata by the Xhosa and Modimo by the Sotho. They communicated with this god through the ancestors, who were the primary foci of rituals and ceremonies. These "living dead," or superhuman beings, brought prosperity or bad fortune, depending on whether they received proper respect and attention. Individual farmstead heads, villages, and chiefdoms performed daily and annual rituals, frequently sacrificing sheep or cattle to propitiate the ancestors—for thanksgiving, healing, birth, initiation, marriage, death, rain, fertility, and military victory. Those performing the ceremonies had to invoke the ancestors in a proper and deferential manner, assisted by diviners who could interpret signs and omens. Lacking written texts, diviners passed on sacred beliefs and rituals through oral tradition, often during separate initiation ceremonies for men and women. Witchcraft, usually performed by women diviners known as *sangoma*, and sorcery were also practiced; these traditions survive today.

When Europeans first reached Africa's southern tip in the late 1400s, hunter-gatherers and pastoralists inhabited the generally arid Cape province. This western zone lay west of the Fish River and south of the Orange River. Pastoralists and agri-pastoralists occupied a middle borderland zone where adequate rainfall made sustained agriculture and livestock grazing possible. Agri-pastoralists dominated an eastern zone that included the interior plateau north of the Drakensberg Mountains and the southeastern coast. The agri-pastoralists and pastoralists normally interacted peacefully, sometimes in symbiotic relationships and sometimes as clients. In the borderland zone, agri-pastoral societies often fully incorporated pastoralists into their communities.

Relations with the hunter-gatherer San were not as peaceful. The San stalked cattle and sheep in the same manner as they hunted wild game. Pastoralists and agri-pastoralists considered the San pests to be destroyed, as did White settlers who arrived later. The San therefore lived a marginal existence, occupying desolate areas where no other peoples could or would live. By 1652 most San already lived on the fringes of the northern Cape, and nearly all ultimately migrated into the Kalahari Desert.

Changes after European Contact

European settlement after 1652 ended the independent existence that the Khoikhoi pastoralists enjoyed. Within a hundred years Khoikhoi society had been destroyed and most of those remaining in the Cape colony were reduced to poverty and working for Whites. By the late eighteenth century, mixed-race groups were fleeing the White colony and heading north across the Orange River to establish independent settlements.

In the seventeenth and eighteenth centuries the availability of fertile land and abundant water posed the most serious problems for the agri-pastoralists of the middle and eastern zones. For two thousand years Bantu-speakers had overcome these problems by expanding into new territory as their human and livestock populations grew. Toward the end of the eighteenth century, for the first time in their long movement southward, these iron-using, agri-pastoralists met a force that would check their advance—White colonists trekking east.

Sailov

3

European Invasion, 1488–1795

THE PORTUGUESE AND THE DUTCH

During the 1400s Europeans competed in voyages of discovery to find sea passages to Asia. They sought to avoid the Arab middleman sitting astride the land trade routes to the East. Portuguese sailors, not Columbus, won the race. They did so by traveling south and rounding Africa's southern tip. Beyond that point lay the Indian Ocean and the riches of Asia.

Bartolomeu Dias, the first Portuguese mariner to reach South Africa, rounded the Cape in 1488. He continued about 170 miles along the Indian Ocean coast before dropping anchor in February 1488 in Mossel Bay. When his men came ashore for water the local Khoikhoi herdsmen, seeing the pale, peculiarly dressed strangers emerge from the sea, misunderstood their intentions and threw stones. The sailors countered with crossbow bolts, killing one of the herders. Thus, the first encounter between White and Black in South Africa.

Dias eventually reached Algoa Bay, where he erected a wooden cross to the glory of God. At this point his crew, tired and fearful of the rough seas, forced him to sail home. One tradition has it that upon Dias's return the discovery of a sea route to India so pleased the Portuguese monarch,

weapon
(bolit.)
arrow

John II, that he renamed the Cape as Capo de Boa Esperanza—the Cape of Good Hope. With Dias as a pilot, Vasco da Gama made the next voyage around the Cape in July 1497. He traded a few trinkets with the Khoikhoi at Mossel Bay and named the lush tropical lands he sailed past along the southeastern coast on Christmas Day the Terra do Natal ("Land of the Nativity"). Da Gama continued northward along the east African coast as far as the area of present-day Malindi, Kenya, and then to Calicut and Goa in India.

The Portuguese controlled the maritime route to Asia around the Cape from 1498 to 1595. They monopolized trade in the Indian Ocean, driving out Arab merchants and capturing all the major trading cities along the east African coast. They built forts, established trading posts, traded in African slaves, and founded great landed estates (*prazos*) along the Zambezi River valley. But they had no interest in South Africa. It had nothing to offer compared to the riches of Asia, or even East Africa, and it had acquired a particularly disagreeable reputation. For example, the foul weather, stiff winds, and strong currents off the coast threatened every ship that passed. In fact, Dias himself died in a storm off the Cape in 1500. Moreover, in March 1510, Khoikhoi living near Table Bay killed Francisco de Almeida, the viceroy of Portuguese India, and fifty-eight of his men on their return voyage to Portugal.

In the late 1500s the English, Dutch, French, and Scandinavians all challenged Portugal for control of the Asian sea route. Ships occasionally anchored in Table Bay to take on fresh water and acquire meat from Khoikhoi pastoralists, but no country wanted a permanent settlement there. An English ship captain raised the issue with his government in 1620 but was ignored. The Dutch East India Company (Vereenigde Oost-Indische Compagnie, or VOC) heard a similar suggestion from a ship's crew wrecked in Table Bay in 1647. They listened.

A "Temporary" Colony of Freeburghers

The seventeenth century was the golden age of Dutch merchant activity and colonization. Their great ships required a safe harbor midway on their voyages to and from their huge colonial empire in Asia. They also needed a refuge where ships' crews, often fever-wracked and scurvy-ridden, could recover their health. The Dutch occupied the Cape five years after hearing of its mild climate and fresh water. On 6 April

1652, Commander Jan van Riebeeck landed at the Cape to establish a victualing, or refreshment, station for the VOC.

Van Riebeeck immediately erected an earthen fort, laid out a large vegetable garden, and constructed a freshwater reservoir. The Cape proved a perfect location, halfway between Europe and the East. Fresh vegetables grew abundantly in the Company garden (now the famous Gardens in Cape Town center). Ships sometimes left their sick crew members to recuperate because of Cape Town's temperate climate, the absence of tropical diseases, the ready availability of meat, and the plentiful supply of fresh water, fruit, cereals, and vegetables. But the VOC had no plans for a permanent colony at the Cape. Van Riebeeck viewed his assignment as a temporary one. He expected soon to take a more important post in one of the Company's great Asian colonies.

Initially only a few Company servants manned the tiny outpost at the foot of Table Mountain. It quickly became apparent, however, that employing Company servants and slaves to produce food for passing ships was neither cost effective nor efficient. Therefore, in April 1657 the Company released nine employees from their contracts, exempted them from land taxes for twelve years, and gave them farms in the area of present-day Rondebosch as freeburghers, or citizens. In exchange they agreed to remain in the colony and supply the Company's needs by raising wheat for bread, furnishing fresh meat, and serving in a burgher militia. They received no political rights and had to sell everything they produced to the Company, often at very low prices. Nevertheless, to the usually lower-class, poorly paid Company servants, this offered an opportunity for a new life.

The freeburgher population increased slowly but steadily, as Company employees—Dutch, Germans, Scandinavians, and other Europeans— took their retirement at the Cape. The Company also brought in some colonists, including orphan girls. Over 160 Huguenot (Calvinist Protestants) refugees arrived after 1688, fleeing persecution in France and increasing the White population by about one-sixth. Although the Huguenot settlers received land in the Franschhoek (French corner), near Stellenbosch, they were interspersed among other Dutch-speaking colonists and quickly became absorbed into Cape Dutch society. Being Calvinists and feeling comfortable in the Dutch Reformed Church to which most of the German and Dutch colonists belonged, they became integrated into the society quite easily. Today nearly all that remains of this episode are Afrikaans-speakers with French names, some architectural influences, and the world-renowned wines produced in vineyards originally planted by the immigrants.

The introduction of slavery also increased the colony's population. Van Riebeeck was under strict orders to preserve peace with the local inhabitants and was also forbidden from enslaving any of the Cape's indigenous people. He tried to persuade local Khoikhoi pastoralists to perform manual labor, but they refused. The Company possessed a few slaves but not enough to serve the growing colony, so Van Riebeeck tapped into the Atlantic slave trade. In 1658 two ships anchored in Table Bay carrying roughly four hundred enslaved Africans from west Africa and Angola, and they were brought ashore.

Although these first slaves were African, most of the colony's slaves came from Dutch colonies in Batavia, India, and Ceylon. A smaller number came from Madagascar, and fewer still from Mozambique. The Cape slave population increased through importation rather than natural reproduction. Male slaves always significantly outnumbered female slaves, at times by as many as four to one. Yet slaves consistently equaled, or even outnumbered, the White population.

The Beginnings of a Race-Based Society

A turning point in South African history occurred in 1717, when there were still only about 2,000 slaves in the colony. Company directors in Amsterdam asked the Cape Council of Policy (the local administrative body at the Cape) whether, on economic grounds, slavery should be continued. Only one Council member voted to end the institution. Thus, slavery continued, and a caste society developed based increasingly on race. The Cape slave population rose dramatically from the 1770s. By 1793 there were nearly 15,000 slaves and fewer than 14,000 freeburghers. By 1798 the slave population stood at more than 25,000.

The Cape slave economy was not a large-scale plantation system as in the Americas. The Company owned the most slaves, as many as 600. The majority of slaves were privately owned by senior Company officials and wealthy farmers, but few owned more than one hundred slaves, and most less than fifty. By the mid-1700s the colony had over 650 slave owners, but more than half owned six or fewer slaves. Yet slave owning was widespread enough to promote a dependency on slave labor rather than the development of intensive settlement and agriculture. This dependency lasted into the nineteenth century and encouraged a mentality among White settlers that certain work and occupations were "beneath" them.

Slaves performed a number of duties ranging from hard, manual construction labor and farming, to service as domestics, wetnurses, artisans, carpenters, fishermen, and gardeners. East Asian slaves were often highly skilled craftsmen, literate and totally reliable. Many were Muslims. Some were political prisoners, exiled in slavery to the Cape for rebelling against Dutch rule in their homelands. Their masters allowed them some freedom to practice their trades and to sell their goods for a profit. In return, they gave their owners a percentage of their earnings. Some slaves were able to purchase their freedom and become "free Blacks." Some free Blacks were also former slaves manumitted by their owners for religious or other reasons. The number of free Blacks was always small, however, and manumission became less common through the eighteenth century as racial prejudices hardened. Offspring of slave women and White freeburghers retained their mothers' slave status.

Growing Conflict

Before 1652 European ships often stopped to trade iron, copper, brass, and metal objects with Khoikhoi in return for fresh water, meat and other provisions. These meetings were seldom pleasant and frequently ended in violence, but they were random and the Europeans never stayed. After Commander van Riebeeck arrived, however, relations between Khoikhoi pastoralists and the Dutch worsened. Now there was a permanent European presence. Company servants and freeburghers seized the most fertile land and grazed their livestock on the best pasture. Because the local Khoikhoi pastoralists, numbering about 6,000, claimed all the land and pasture on the Cape peninsula and beyond, conflict was inevitable.

Initially these Peninsular Khoikhoi prospered from their proximity to the Dutch settlement and near monopoly of trade with it. They exchanged sheep and cattle for European copper, tobacco, cloth, liquor, and ornamental items. The growing number of ships calling at the Cape provided a constant market for fresh meat. The Khoikhoi, however, would never trade as many livestock as the Company required, so it increasingly turned to the freeburghers for meat.

The Peninsular Khoikhoi also acted as middlemen for the Dutch with Khoikhoi societies further inland and discouraged those peoples from coming to the Cape themselves to trade. As inland Khoikhoi began to encroach on Peninsular Khoikhoi land, however, and Europeans occupied their land from the Cape out, tensions increased between the Peninsular Khoikhoi and the White settlement. Wars broke out between the two sides in 1659–1660 and 1673–1677, which the Khoikhoi lost. Wars between the Peninsular Khoikhoi and powerful inland societies occurred as well.

As the White population grew and expanded farther north and east into the hinterland, the Peninsular Khoikhoi lost their trade monopoly, their power, and their influence. The Company sent expeditions of explorers and hunters inland to look for fertile lands, mineral wealth, and indigenous societies with which to trade. Illegal White traders also traversed the country, eventually making contact with the Xhosa west of the Fish River by 1702.

By the early 1700s wars with the Dutch, and among themselves, had taken their toll on Khoikhoi societies in the southwestern Cape. Their political and social systems had collapsed. Group members drifted away to work for Whites as cattle herders, shepherds, and common laborers. Even chiefs were reduced to servitude, as they had no more subjects. The Dutch were firmly in control and punished the local people for perceived wrong-doing with increasing severity—branding, beating, breaking on the rack, and exile to Robben Island. In 1713 a smallpox epidemic was the final disaster for Khoikhoi societies within 50 to 100 miles of the now well-established village of Cape Town.

Each succeeding Khoikhoi group opposed White encroachment into their territory. They fought wars, raided homesteads, drove off cattle, killed herders, refused to trade, and attacked trading expeditions. But in the end they could only delay, not stop, the European advance into the interior. By 1800 European expansion had destroyed nearly all Khoikhoi groups within the Cape colony. Individual Khoikhoi had few choices. They could go to work as servants and herdsmen on White farms, or they could flee to the edges of White settlement where they were squeezed between Whites on one side and Bantu-speakers on the other.

THE AFRIKANERS AND THE CAPE COLONY

In a conflict with the governor in 1707, the freeburgher Hendrik Bibault first called himself an Afrikaner (Dutch for "African"). With time, more freeburghers thought of themselves as Afrikaners, different from the VOC officials and servants who were Europeans. These first Afrikaners spoke Dutch, but Cape Dutch gradually evolved into Afrikaans.

In Dutch a farmer is called a *boer* and this term is sometimes used interchangeably with "Afrikaner," although the British tended to use *boer* in a derisive manner.

The VOC, not the States-General (state government) of the Dutch Republic, governed the Cape colony. The Dutch government gave the VOC monopoly trading rights in the Indian Ocean in return for a share of Company profits, and the VOC possessed more power than the largest multinational corporations do today. It could establish colonies, maintain an army, declare war, and sign treaties—all under the Dutch flag. The Cape was one tiny outstation in the great VOC empire based in Batavia. The VOC Chamber of Seventeen, or Lords Seventeen, in Amsterdam, and the Governor-General in Council at Batavia, ruled over this empire until 1732, when the Seventeen took total control.

From 1672 the Cape governor and a Council of Policy managed day-to-day affairs. The Council of Policy originally consisted of seven senior officials, called merchants, and the governor. It issued regulations affecting local government, such as setting local commodity prices, levying taxes, and appointing members to the Church Council. Two freeburgher councilors, in place of the governor, and the senior officials served on a Court of Justice that heard serious legal cases. Similar combinations of senior officials and freeburghers constituted a Matrimonial Court, an Orphan Chamber, and a Court of Petty Cases. The Independent Fiscal was a separate official who, after 1690, reported directly to the Lords Seventeen. He acted as public prosecutor in criminal trials and was charged with combating corruption and criminal activity, especially as it affected shipping. The Independent Fiscal was the only official whose power approached that of the governor. Individual Cape governors possessed varying degees of power. Few ruled without the advice and consent of their Council of Policy, but seldom were they overruled. Governors controlled local patronage, and their powers increased proportionally with their tenure of office, which averaged about thirteen years.

As the colony expanded, the Company established a local administration for outlying districts beyond the Cape: the Stellenbosch district (1682), Swellendam (1743), and Graaff Reinet (1785). A *landdrost* ("local magistrate") carried out official duties in each district. Four *heemraden* ("burgher councilors") assisted him. A third official, the *veldkornet* ("field cornet"), helped the *landdrost* in organizing local militia and checking on illegal livestock trade. All officials came from the local freeburgher population, and most were farmers.

One early governor, Simon van der Stel (1679–1699), is sometimes called the second founder of the Cape. When van der Stel became governor in 1679 there were only 87 freeburghers, of whom 55 were married with 114 free White children. But by that year, after recently fighting two bitter wars against the English and French, the VOC realized the strategic value of the Cape's location on one of the world's major shipping lanes. The Company ordered van der Stel to promote more immigration and thereby increase the number of freeburghers available for a burgher militia to defend the Cape against Holland's enemies. During van der Stel's tenure the French Huguenots and the European orphan girls arrived. Moreover, he encouraged so many Company servants to retire at the Cape that the Company worried about having enough crewmen for their ships. By the end of van der Stel's term the colonial population had grown to about 2,000 freeburghers, their wives and children, several hundred Company employees, and a significant number of slaves, political prisoners and exiles, freed convicts, Khoikhoi, and free Blacks. The colony was, if not prosperous, at least well established and a "tavern of the seas" for passing ships of all nations.

An Increasingly Stratified Society

White Cape society was becoming increasingly stratified, however. Company officials and a small number of prosperous burghers with large country estates and property in Cape Town occupied the top rungs of the social ladder. Together with military officers, members of the various boards and councils, and the Company's senior officials, they formed a social and economic elite in an increasingly complex caste society. They supported each other in their own best interests, including abetting illegal activities. Marriages between burgher daughters and Company officials often sealed the bonds between them. Company sailors and soldiers—and a growing number of poor, propertyless Whites—occupied the bottom rungs. Scattered in between were a few saloon and lodging house keepers, small traders and farmers, license holders, and farm overseers called *knechts*. Opportunities for education were almost nonexistent except for children of the elite. Levels of literacy and sophistication declined markedly the farther one traveled from Cape Town.

Simon van der Stel believed in the Cape's economic potential. By 1679 the colony had expanded somewhat, spreading east around False Bay to the mountain range known as Hottentots Holland and along the northern coast to Saldanha Bay. Van der Stel extended the colony even farther to the east. He founded a new village named after himself, Stellenbosch.

In 1688 the French Huguenots received land grants at nearby Fransch-hoek. By 1717 about 400 freehold farms had been granted and small settlements had been founded at Tulbagh, Wellington, and Paarl. Van der Stel promoted intensive agriculture when there were still few slaves. He encouraged vegetable, wine, and grain production. Like his predecessors, he sent out expeditions in search of gold. These expeditions found some mineral deposits, the most important of which was copper, but South Africa's real treasures of gold and diamonds were many miles, and many generations, away.

Willem Adriaan van der Stel succeeded his father as governor in January 1699. Willem Adriaan also promoted modern agricultural practices at the Cape, introduced new methods of wine-making, and experimented with wool production. However, the avarice of father and son was greater than this tiny colony and its poor, struggling population could support. The van der Stels owned one-third of the colony's most productive land, including their great estates; Simon's at Constantia, and Willem Adriaan's at Vergelegen. They were the colony's largest cattle and wheat farmers, wine producers, and slave owners. Their monopoly on the production and sale of grain and meat to the Company and Cape Town markets threatened to ruin the freeburgher population. The colonists finally protested this monopoly in a petition to the Lords Seventeen smuggled on board a homeward-bound ship. It led to Willem Adriaan's dismissal in 1707 and effected a fundamental shift in relations between colonists and Company officials. The White freeburghers, who considered South Africa their homeland, began playing a more influential role in the colony's development.

The VOC is sometimes accused of retarding the colony's development. The argument is that because the Company never intended to establish a permanent settler colony at the Cape, it had little interest in supporting the one that evolved there. Its only concerns were commerce, profit, and the well-being of its fleets. To guarantee cheap supplies of food staples it fixed prices, controlled retail licenses, and monopolized the trade in meat, grains, and wine with passing ships. This arrangement, scholars argue, encouraged smuggling, favoritism, corruption, and embezzling. Indeed, much of this is true. But from 1652 until the first British occupation of the Cape in 1795, the Company also brought the Cape within the orbit of the great Dutch East India empire and its infinite opportunities for commerce and trade.

The colony's natural limitations were the real source of the White settlers problems. The Cape had no raw materials or commodities of consequence; no large forests for timber; no rich, fertile soils for sugar, tobacco, or cotton plantations. There was no abundant rainfall. The quality of the items produced, particularly the meat and wine, was often poor and uneven. In these early days of European colonization of the Americas and Asia, there was no reason to invest in the Cape and few ways for the citizens to create wealth themselves. Furthermore, following the controversy over Willem Adriaan van der Stel, the Company ceased to support further immigration and the Cape had to increase its population naturally.

The VOC originally envisioned a densely populated community of farmers practicing intensive agriculture as in Europe, and entirely at the Company's service producing surplus crops for the Company's ships. But neither the environment nor the colonists' mentality were suited for this scheme. As the eighteenth century dawned, the settlers recognized that the Company's plan could not work. The western Cape's most arable land had too many people for its carrying capacity by the early 1700s. Sharp class distinctions had developed between a small minority of wealthy landed farmers in the grain and grape growing areas and the more numerous poor, landless Whites. These rich landowners had challenged Willem Adriaan van der Stel's power and monopoly. They were no longer poor, former Company servants living in crude daub-and-wattle hovels, but rural gentry who owned fine, substantial homes with gables in an architectural style known as Cape Dutch. They possessed the fertile land, slave labor, and considerable sums of capital needed to fund such enterprises. The remainder of the settler population looked for other ways to survive in their new homeland, farther from the Cape.

It is a commonplace to regard European expansion as a great scheme for domination carried out by kings and conquerors, but the actual, everyday process was much less organized and cunning. At the Cape, European expansion was carried forward by farmers and their wives and children, traders, adventurers, and even criminals, deserters, and vagabonds. They were waving no imperial flags. Certainly at the Cape these pioneers were often trying to escape Company, and later British, rule. In most cases they were simply common people in search of a new and better life. In South African history they are known as *trekboers*, or migrant farmers.

Migrant Farmers and Frontier Life

Farming became a less viable option the farther one traveled from Cape Town, the colony's only market. Even if one found fertile, well-watered land, enough to produce a surplus wheat crop year in and year out, there remained the problem of transportation. Indeed, transportation costs and hardships forced migrant farmers to produce goods that offered a high return per pound conveyed, such as ivory, hides, soap, aloe, butter, and ostrich feathers. But the most profitable produce were the cattle and sheep that could walk to market on their own.

The Company intended to control the meat trade with local Khoikhoi by sending out trade expeditions and by selling monopoly licenses to butchers. There was never enough Khoikhoi meat, however, to satisfy the needs of the settlements and the passing fleets. Nor could the Company prevent freeburghers from trading illegally with the Khoikhoi and, later, the Bantu-speakers. Prohibitions on trade between Whites and Blacks only angered the freeburghers and encouraged more illegal traffic. As the eighteenth century progressed, the Company relied increasingly on the freeburghers' herds for its meat supplies.

The *trekboers* migrated out from Cape Town in two directions, north and east. When the barren semi-desert checked the northern migration 300 or so miles to the north, the migrants turned eastward parallel to the Orange River. The larger, eastern migration followed the line of greatest rainfall, moving along the southern coast for about 450 miles, as far as Algoa Bay, before Bantu-speakers blocked its advance. This migration then turned northward. Eventually both migrations came together and traveled northeastward until the Khoisan stopped them. In this manner, migrant farmers defined the colony's general borders by 1770.

Migrant livestock farmers in the interior enjoyed many advantages. There were seemingly endless expanses of land with no significant obstacles—such as wide rivers, thick forests, harsh climates, or tropical diseases—for hundreds of miles. Individual Khoikhoi could be kept as servants and livestock herders much more cheaply than as slaves. Because this was some of the richest game country in the world, elephants, wildebeests, rhinoceros, and other large animals provided food, and their tusks and hides were valuable trade items. Migrant farmers were not lazy and unwilling to do the hard labor required for intensive agriculture. They were simply successfully adapting to the economic conditions. Grazing land was cheap and virtually unlimited, whereas capital, land, and labor for grain and grape production were scarce. Hunting, trade, and livestock farming afforded the only means to make a living in the interior. Consequently many migrant farmers soon developed an economy, and even a way of life, similar to that of the neighboring Khoikhoi and Bantu-speaking pastoralists.

Livestock farming thus became the one occupation at which poor Whites could make a new beginning with little capital. Cattle and sheep farming in the relatively arid environs of the Cape interior, however, required extensive amounts of grazing land. The Company's system of land tenure actually favored colonial expansion by allowing for just such large acquisitions of land. A farm's size was determined by the farmer walking east, west, north, and south a half-hour's distance from a fixed point, resulting in a circular farm of roughly 6,000 acres. The migrant farmer received rights to his loan farm in return for a small annual rent. Although in theory the farm was on loan, in practice the farmers bought, sold, and passed on the properties to their heirs as if they owned them. For nearly the first 150 years of European settlement, migrant farmers occupied land almost wherever they pleased—and as much as they could measure off—as long as they did not encroach on their neighbor's 6,000 or 10,000 acres. The colonial border expanded very quickly when taken in such large chunks, especially by large families with many sons in need of new land.

Government was far away and rarely affected the livestock farmers' daily lives. The Company would not supply the necessary administration and troops to control this colonial expansion, and local government in the interior tended to be lax. The *landdrosts, heemraden,* and *veldkornets* belonged to the communities over which they governed. They were generally unwilling to enforce unpopular laws relating to illegal trade, hunting without a license, or improperly treating Khoikhoi servants and slaves.

The Cape colony of the eighteenth century consisted of two worlds. The southwestern Cape contained the seat of government and commerce, as well as what little cosmopolitan life an outpost on the distant fringes of the Dutch empire could offer. Here were large grain and wine estates and relatively wealthy citizens in their fine Cape Dutch homes. Here was the harbor catering to the needs of the great ships. Here were a few schools, churches, and stores. Enlightenment ideas came via European ships to the southwestern Cape, but seldom did they radiate into the interior. The new villages founded in the eighteenth century, such as Stellenbosch and Swellendam, remained small and inconsequential. The colony's only true market was in Cape Town; all the colony's exports and imports passed through it, from cloth to ivory, coffee to gunpowder.

In the interior the migrant farmer's pastoral existence gradually replaced that of the Khoikhoi. Although they lived much like their African neighbors, few Whites lost complete contact with Cape Town. Usually once a year the farmers hitched up their wagons and journeyed with their families, sometimes for several hundred miles, into Cape Town to trade livestock and produce for coffee, tea, sugar, gunpowder, cloth, and other items. While in Cape Town they married, baptized children, caught up on news, and visited relatives. Then they returned to their frontier homes.

Frontier families lived fairly self-sufficiently. They provided for nearly all their daily needs, making their own clothes, tools, food, and shelters. Many young couples lived in tents or tented wagons; some couples spent their entire married lives this way. Some built Khoikhoi "mat houses," to be taken down and transported as they wandered in search of richer pasture and more plentiful water. Travelers generally saw fewer signs of a European lifestyle—furniture, fashions—the farther they traveled from Cape Town. Schools were nearly nonexistent. A wealthy farmer might hire an occasional itinerant schoolmaster for his children, but frequently the schoolmaster was almost as illiterate as his charges. Learning rarely rose above the elementary level. At the extreme edge of European settlement, White settlers lived much like their African neighbors. Beyond that edge went some few White men who married African women and became part of their adopted African society.

The migrant farmers were Calvinists, a people of the Old Testament. They took their law from the Bible, not the government. In this patriarchal world the Bible defined proper relationships between husband and wife, parent and child, master and servant. Religion was important but perhaps more so in the ideal than the practice, and the migrant farmers practiced what was agreeable. Ministers were scarce, and great distances separated villages and farms. Religious observances were usually confined to individual homesteads. Each morning the patriarch gathered all his family, servants, and slaves to hear him read from the Bible and to pray. Every three months families came together at a predetermined site to hold a *nagmaal*, or holy communion service, for several days. It was a solemn religious occasion but also one for socializing. Dances were held, and many couples first met at these gatherings. The literate among them read mostly religious tracts and the only book that mattered, the Holy Bible. It taught that they were God's newly chosen people and that Africans were the children of Ham blocking the way to the promised land.

Expansion inland increased significantly from the middle of the eighteenth century, as growing numbers of White settlers looked for land. As they traveled north and northeast, they entered the arid Karoo, which had few streams or sources of permanent water. The land was only good for seasonal grazing when the rains came and pasture was sweet. Livestock farming by Whites thus became even more extensive. Farmers used vast areas for seasonal communal grazing while continuing to settle individual 6,000-acre tracts.

In 1778 Governor van Plettenberg set out to inspect the colony's borders. East along the coast he found White farmers living alongside Xhosa farmers in the area known as the Zuurveld ("sour grazing fields") between the Sundays River and the Great Fish River. Van Plettenberg fixed the Great Fish River as the boundary between the White colony and the Bantu-speakers beyond. Traveling to the northeast, he marked the colonial boundary with a beacon near the area of modern Colesberg. The boundary for the great stretch of land west to the Atlantic coast remained undefined. Despite the governor's best intentions, however, he could not enforce his decrees. The White migrant farmers disobeyed them, and he had no authority over the Africans.

Limits to Colonial Expansion   G-B, France

The final years of the eighteenth century witnessed the VOC's decline owing to debts, competition from the British and French, and mismanagement. The American Revolution and republican movements in Holland sparked some republican protests in the western Cape in 1778. A Cape Patriot movement, patterning itself on the patriot party in Holland, asked the Dutch States-General to take over the colony from the Company. When the Prince of Orange overthrew the patriot party in Holland, the Cape Patriots lost their allies in the States-General and their movement died out.

By century's end as well, colonial expansion had been halted in the northwest, mainly by the arid semi-desert, and even today it is thinly inhabited. In the north and northeast to the Orange River, the migrant farmers' movements had been checked by the San. When the White settlers reached the northern borders, they found themselves under fierce attack by bands of San and by some destitute Khoikhoi, who killed their herdsmen, drove off their livestock, and sometimes burned their homes. Settlers used their home militia to defend themselves against these raids. When a particular locale came under attack, the *landdrost* summoned parties of men, called commandos, to bring their guns and horses and mount a defense. These commando units were often quite large, sometimes including men from one or two frontier districts.

First employed in the early 1700s, by century's end commandos no longer waited for Khoikhoi and San attacks but went on search-and-destroy missions, sometimes without government authority. As frontier settlements pushed deeper into the northern and northeastern frontiers, San resistance intensified. San destroyed settlers' homesteads and forced Whites to abandon already settled territory. By the 1770s the commandos were waging a war of extermination against the San, killing them in great numbers. Captured San became life-long servants on White farms. Children were seized, ostensibly to receive a "civilized" and "Christian" upbringing but actually to become "apprentice" laborers on White farms. By 1800 Whites controlled the prime grazing lands.

WHITE CONTACT WITH THE SOUTHERN NGUNI

White traders first came face to face with the Xhosa in the eastern Cape around 1702. The Xhosa, the largest and most powerful of the Bantu-speaking southern Nguni, inhabited the area of present-day southern Natal, the Transkei, and the Ciskei. By 1702 some Xhosa grazed their herds along the Great Fish River, the southernmost point of settlement by Bantu-speakers. By this date as well the Xhosa had had many years of contact with the Khoisan, as evidenced by the presence of click sounds in the Xhosa language. The name "Xhosa" comes from a Khoikhoi word meaning "to destroy," and no doubt it signifies the nature of the initial contacts between the two. By the 1700s, however, the agri-pastoral Xhosa were the regional power, and their relationship with the pastoralist Khoikhoi was mutually reciprocal. Some Khoikhoi were absorbed into the Xhosa, such as the Gqunukwebe, a half-Khoikhoi, half-Xhosa chiefdom. Others became Xhosa clients, hunting and working for Xhosa in return for agricultural products and protection. Khoikhoi also acted as middlemen for trade between the Cape and Xhosaland and served as interpreters for White expeditions.

Xhosa society tended toward segmentation; that is, households consisting of families or lineages initially lived in proximity with other households to form a chiefdom. After a time, as families grew and fertile land became scarce, some households broke away to find less crowded land with better soil and water resources. Here they established a new chiefdom. The Xhosa paramount chief had little authority to prevent this, as his main function was ceremonial. Sometime in the late 1600s, however, a strong paramount chief named Tshawe interrupted this tendency toward decentralization and unified the Xhosa. He destroyed the independence of the individual clans and established a royal lineage. Little is known about the paramount chiefs who followed Tshawe except for Phalo, who ruled from 1730 to 1775 and whose death marked the end of Xhosa unity. Two of Phalo's sons, Gcaleka and Rharhabe, fought over the succession even while Phalo was alive. Gcaleka forced Rharhabe to move west of the Kei River, creating two Xhosa polities: the Gcaleka of the Transkei, and the Rharhabe of the Ciskei.

When Gcaleka died in 1778, his ineffectual son, Khawuta, assumed the chiefdomship. In the meantime, Rharhabe consolidated his power in the west while trying unsuccessfully to overthrow Khawuta and regain paramountcy. He brought Khoikhoi and San groups under his control but died in a war with the Thembu in 1782, together with his son and successor, Mlawu. Mlawu's son Ngqika was next in line of succession but still a minor. Mlawu's brother, Ndlambe, became regent.

Ndlambe further strengthened Rharhabe's chiefdom during his regency from 1782 to 1795. He either subjugated surrounding chiefdoms with his own forces or drove them further west, where Afrikaner settlers attacked them. The imiDange were one such group, defeated by the frontier farmers in the First Frontier War of 1779–1781. Ndlambe also attacked the mixed Khoikhoi-Xhosa Gqunukhwebe and defeated them with White settler help in 1793. In 1795, however, Ngqika reached the age of majority and challenged his uncle for the chiefdomship. Ngqika took Ndlambe prisoner in battle and forced him to live at his Great Place. He then set about concentrating power in his own hands.

Ngqika enjoyed initial success, but beginning around 1800 he faced challenges from both east and west. In 1800 Ndlambe escaped, taking his followers west across the Fish River and settling in the Zuurveld. At roughly the same time, Hintsa, a new paramount king, emerged among the Gcaleka. The Xhosa were now divided in three, with Ndlambe, Ngqika, and Hintsa all seeking to increase their power and territory at the others' expense. In the long term, however, these internal divisions did not pose as great a threat to Xhosa society as did the increasingly large number of Afrikaners settling on their western border. And even these White farmers did not affect the Xhosa people's future to the extent that the arrival of British imperial rule did in 1795.

4

The British and the Cape Colony, 1795–1870

The Cape lay thousands of miles from Europe, but political, economic, and social revolutions occurring in England, France, and Holland in the late eighteenth century had immediate and far-reaching consequences for the tiny Dutch colony. Enlightenment ideas promoting human equality, equal rights, and the abolition of slavery had significantly affected social relations across Europe and had inspired the French Revolution of 1789. In England, Enlightenment ideas generated significant humanitarian, anti-slavery, and evangelical movements. The evangelicals formed several new mission societies that embarked on missionary activity in Africa and Asia. New economic theories, particularly those of Adam Smith, changed the way in which the major commercial nations, such as France and Holland, did business. They effected the most change in Britain, where they were linked to the Industrial Revolution and made that nation a nineteenth-century superpower.

England and France had spent the previous two centuries warring with each other. In February 1793, two weeks after the execution of Louis XVI, revolutionary France declared war on monarchical Britain. By this time France was at war with nearly all of Europe. France overthrew the Dutch Republic in 1795 and established the pro-French Batavian Republic in the Netherlands. The Batavian Republic then took charge of the

Dutch East India Company (VOC). Britain quickly realized that a French occupation of the Cape would threaten trade with India and East Asia. Consequently, British troops, with the support of gunfire from four British sloops-of-war, forced the tiny Dutch garrison to surrender the Cape colony in September 1795.

THE CAPE COLONY, 1795–1834   — GB

The British occupied a tiny enclave of about 25,000 slaves, 20,000 White colonists, 15,000 Khoikhoi, and 1,000 free Blacks. By comparison, London's population alone was about 700,000 at this time. Cape Town was the only significant town in the colony. There was not a single major export product of any significance, nor any mineral deposits to attract investment. Sparse rainfall, an absence of suitable coastal harbors, a lack of navigable rivers into the interior, a reliance on primitive agricultural practices, and a shortage of cheap labor made economic ventures risky. The Cape was too tiny to provide a profitable market for the colony's few commodities, such as wine, wheat, hides, and aloe; and major markets in Europe and the Americas lay thousands of miles away. The sea voyage from England to Cape Town took about three months.

Thus, Britain begrudgingly occupied the Cape as a temporary expedient to prevent it from falling under French authority and to guarantee provisions and a safe harbor for Britain's great Asian fleets. The British had little interest in colonization and no interest in investing large numbers of troops or great sums of money to foster a stable and economically viable colony there. The early British governors, mostly military officers drawn from the English landed aristocracy, were instructed that the colony must pay for itself.

The First British Occupation of the Cape, 1795–1803

The first British occupation brought little immediate change to the Cape. To service and supply their Asian fleets the British needed the Dutch colonists' support and trust, which they immediately set out to win. They allowed slavery to continue, and they guaranteed religious freedom and the continued use of Dutch. They retained the Roman-Dutch legal system but banned torture. The British also abolished the hated trading monopolies held by the Dutch East India Company and a few privileged freeburghers.

Of primary concern for the colony's new rulers was unrest in the

Cape's eastern frontier districts that threatened Cape Town's supply of fresh meat. For some time Ndlambe's Xhosa had been settling in the Zuurveld region west of the Great Fish River, the colony's eastern boundary. The Xhosa presence angered the Afrikaner settlers who also coveted this land. In July 1795, the Graaff-Reinet burghers rebelled and declared themselves an independent republic. The Swellendam burghers followed suit: They wanted the Xhosa to be pushed back across the Fish, permission to recover stolen livestock, and the right to keep captured Xhosa women and children as farm laborers. In 1796 the rebels forwarded their demands to the leader of the British occupation forces, General J.H. Craig. He flatly denied them and quickly ended the rebellion by cutting off all supplies to Graaff-Reinet, including precious gunpowder.

In 1798–1799 White frontier farmers rebelled again. This time the British responded swiftly and forcefully, sending troops by land and by sea. The troops included some of the Cape Regiment, consisting of armed Khoikhoi. This rebellion also quickly collapsed, although some Afrikaner rebels escaped into Xhosaland. In the confusion following the rebellion, Khoikhoi servants ran away from their Afrikaner employers, carrying stolen arms and ammunitions. The Zuurveld Xhosa prepared to defend themselves against government forces, which they believed intended to drive them back across the Fish River. When the British forces withdrew, eastern frontier commandos were left to defend against united, armed Khoikhoi and Xhosa bands that attacked White farms and caused widespread devastation.

During this Third Frontier War (1799–1803; the first two were in 1779–1780 and 1793), burgher commandos proved unable to prevent combined Khoikhoi and Xhosa raids, and the British refused to pay for permanent forces to contain the conflict. Raids and commando counterattacks continued until a treaty temporarily suspended them. The hostilities pushed the settlers back toward Cape Town rather than driving the Xhosa back across the Fish River. Roughly one-third of the 8,000 White inhabitants fled the region, leaving behind more than 500 burned farmhouses and thousands of dead cattle, sheep, and horses. The extent of Xhosa losses is not known. Despite these heavy losses, none of the underlying frontier problems had been resolved.

Christian missionaries also arrived in the 1790s. The commercially oriented Dutch East India Company had displayed little interest in advancing Christianity at the Cape. Although Dutch colonists called themselves Christians, the term often referred as much to social distinctions as to religious ones. Some few slaves and Khoikhoi were converted in the colony's early days, but as racist attitudes hardened, White Christian affinity weakened. Owners were particularly reluctant to baptize slaves who, some believed, ought to gain their freedom with their new faith. Islam flourished in the Cape's Malay community.

During the entire Dutch period, Georg Schmidt, a German Moravian missionary, made the only significant effort to evangelize indigenous peoples in South Africa. In 1737 he established a Khoikhoi mission at Baviaanskloof, east of Cape Town. The mission was quite successful but also foreshadowed the controversies surrounding missions in the nineteenth century. Local burghers resented the freedom enjoyed by Khoikhoi mission residents. And the Dutch Reformed Church, the established church of the colony, refused to recognize Schmidt's baptisms, on both religious and racial grounds. Schmidt abandoned the mission in 1744. Moravian missionaries returned to Baviaanskloof, which they renamed Genadendal, in 1792 and found some of Schmidt's converts still holding Christian services. The Moravians later founded missions at Elim, Mamre, and Pella and established the Moravian Hill church in District Six in Cape Town.

The interdenominational London Missionary Society (LMS) came to South Africa in 1799. It was founded in 1795 by Protestant churches that were challenging the dominance of the established Anglican Church in England. They were revivalist, evangelical, militant dissenters who, in Anglican eyes, were "irregular" in their beliefs. Their missionaries usually came from the upper levels of the working class and, although literate, had little formal theological education. Dr. J.T. van der Kemp, who led the first group of LMS missionaries, was atypical and one of the more famous and controversial figures in South African history. Van der Kemp was a former Dutch military officer who went on to study theology and then became a medical doctor. After his arrival in South Africa he went to work among Ngqika's Xhosa, but the Third Frontier War doomed his mission. He then tried to form a Khoikhoi congregation in 1801 and hold services in the White church at Graaff-Reinet. This angered the White settlers, who destroyed his mission station near Graaff-Reinet. They viewed it, and all missions, as refuges for runaways and vagrants. Van der Kemp's marriage to a former African slave, as well as his lifestyle (he lived in an African hut like his charges and went about barefoot and unkempt), further alienated him from White society. His unorthodox views on the religious and "civilizing" mission (he did not require manual labor as a precondition for religious conversion) lost him his fellow missionaries' support. He finally established the Bethelsdorp mission station among the Khoikhoi near Port Elizabeth.

The Batavian Republic, 1803–1806

The Treaty of Amiens (1802) between Britain and France bought a temporary truce in Europe and stipulated that Britain return the Cape to the Batavian Republic in February 1803. The two Batavian officials sent to run the colony, Commissioner-General J.A. de Mist and Governor J.W. Janssens, were intelligent, hard-working, and tolerant. Unlike the British, de Mist and Janssens expected to stay and immediately set out to reform government and improve Cape society. During their brief three-year rule, however, little significant change occurred, although the colony remained relatively peaceful.

British Rule Returns, 1806–1834

The Treaty of Amiens broke down in 1805 with Napoleon's victory at Austerlitz over combined Austrian and Russian forces. The British quickly reoccupied the Cape in January 1806 but once again assumed their presence was temporary. Only after defeating Napoleon at Waterloo nine years later did they begin to consider the Cape a colony.

As the British resumed their occupation, two actions taken in London significantly affected the small colony. In 1808 the British Parliament abolished the slave trade, thereby making the Cape's labor shortages even more severe. Parliament also gave the Cape preferential tariffs for its export goods, particularly wine. The period from 1813 to the mid-1820s, when the preferences were withdrawn, was one of unprecedented economic prosperity. Wine became the Cape's leading export.

As the new British governor, the Earl of Caledon (1807–1811) faced two critical problems in the frontier districts: large numbers of Khoikhoi desertions from White farms, and continuing bad relations between White settlers and the Xhosa living in the Zuurveld. In 1809 Caledon issued the Caledon Code, a proclamation requiring all Khoikhoi in the colony to have a permanent address either on a mission station or with a White employer. He also introduced a pass system by which Khoikhoi traveling outside their district of residence were required to carry a pass from the local magistrate. These regulations effectively bound most Khoikhoi to lives of labor on White farms and were partly a response to the labor shortage created by the ending of the slave trade.

In 1809 Caledon asked Colonel Richard Collins to report on conditions in the eastern Cape. Collins's subsequent report made three major proposals. First, Whites and Africans should have no contact with each other, particularly for trade, until Whites were dominant in the region. Second, the Xhosa should not only be driven out of the Zuurveld area, but pushed back all the way to the Keiskamma River. Third, at least 6,000 European immigrants should be settled along the Fish River, forming a protective barrier against Xhosa incursions.

Sir John Cradock replaced Caledon in September 1811 and immediately set to implement Collins's proposals. On Christmas Day, 1811, Colonel John Graham led a force of British regular troops, settlers, and the all-Khoikhoi Cape Regiment into the Zuurveld. In a ruthless and brutal campaign unlike any previous frontier wars, Graham's forces attacked Xhosa men and women indiscriminately, burned villages, destroyed corn and other crops, and confiscated thousands of head of Xhosa livestock. This Fourth Frontier War ended in 1812 when colonial forces drove Ndlambe, other lesser Xhosa chiefs, and 20,000 of their people from the Zuurveld into Ngqika's territory east of the Fish River. For Graham's efforts, Cradock named the little garrison camp in the region Grahamstown. Cradock also erected a string of outposts to guard against further Xhosa incursions, from the mouth of the Fish River northward to another new village called Cradock. This victory marked a turning point in South African history. Although the Xhosa continued to raid and wage war for another fifty years, the balance of power now shifted to the Whites.

Cradock introduced regular circuit courts in 1811 that soon became the object of Afrikaner wrath, as Black employees, even slaves, could now testify in court against their masters. Khoikhoi workers, aided by British missionaries, sued farmers for abusive treatment, even murder, and sometimes won. Afrikaners called these courts the Black Circuit, and they indirectly led in 1815 to a minor episode in frontier history known as the Slagtersnek Rebellion, near Graaff-Reinet. It began when Khoikhoi soldiers killed an Afrikaner farmer named Frederik Bezuidenhout who resisted arrest for mistreating a servant. Johannes Bezuidenhout, Frederik's brother, declared war on the colonial government, but local authorities quickly put down the rebellion, killing Johannes and hanging five ringleaders. Although the incident was relatively insignificant at the time, during the twentieth century Afrikaner Nationalists depicted the Slagtersnek rebels as early martyrs in the struggle against British cruelty and oppression.

Governor Cradock also revised the land tenure system. Prior to 1813 farmers could occupy 6,000 acres on loan for a nominal fee. This system worked when land was plentiful and frontier farmers practiced extensive livestock farming. When the San in the north and the Xhosa in the east blocked further White expansion, however, land became scarce and more intensive farming practices were required. To encourage these practices and denser settlement, Cradock introduced a perpetual quitrent system that substantially raised loan farm rental fees and required proper land surveys. In return, farmers could buy their land, thereby ensuring more permanent ownership and heritability. The farmers disliked the new system, however, because they did not have the cash to make the rent payments and because it made land more expensive. Many refused to participate in it. In the long term, though, these changes placed agriculture on a more sound economic basis and promoted more progressive, intensive farming methods.

The reform-minded Cradock also presented a plan in 1812 to establish English language schools throughout the colony. He opened a free school for the needy of all races and both sexes in Cape Town in 1813. During the following decade English-speaking teachers, who received bonuses for teaching in the interior, started free public schools for Whites in Stellenbosch, Graaff-Reinet, Tulbagh, and elsewhere. These were part of a local effort to socially and culturally anglicize the colony. From 1795 Afrikaners could hold public office if they declared their loyalty to British rule. Many became anglicized, and their children learned English. After 1814 English was required for anyone seeking employment in the civil service.

In 1814 Lieutenant-General Lord Charles Somerset (1814–1826) replaced Cradock as governor. Somerset was the most autocratic of all British governors and was closely identified with the wealthy, western Cape wine and grain farmers. He spent a substantial sum of public money to build himself a country estate, called Newlands, to rival theirs. During his first six years in office, Lord Charles maintained the existing legal and administrative systems. These systems were especially agreeable to an aristocrat of his temperament because they placed all important powers in his hands. He also made full use of the political and financial patronage system that had characterized Dutch rule. Somerset made several important contributions to the colony's social, cultural, and economic life. He established a South African Turf Club and imported thoroughbred horses at his own expense. He established the South African Public Library, the South African Museum, the Commercial

Exchange, and the Somerset Hospital. He also promoted progressive techniques in arable farming and introduced new breeds of cattle and sheep. Like Cape governors before him, however, his primary concern was the eastern frontier.

Colonel Graham's brutal expulsion of Ndlambe from the Zuurveld resulted in Xhosa overcrowding and conflicts over grazing land east of the Fish River, made worse by a severe drought in 1815. Political tensions increased between Ngqika, his uncle Ndlambe, and the Xhosa paramount chief, Hintsa. Hintsa was the nominal superior of both Ngqika and Ndlambe, although he lived with his people east of the Kei River. In the midst of this turmoil there arose two Xhosa prophets, Nxele and Ntsikana. Ndlambe appointed Nxele (also called Makana) as his chiefdom's official diviner. Christian missionaries had influenced Nxele in his youth, and at one point he called himself Christ's brother. In 1817, however, he proclaimed that a strict adherence to Xhosa beliefs would bring back the great ancestors, who, with the help of a mighty wind, would drive the Whites from the Zuurveld. Nxele's call struck a responsive chord among young Xhosa men. Ngqika lost many of his followers because of his supposed colonial sympathies, and they joined his uncle Ndlambe. The other prophet, Ntsikana, served Ngqika. Unlike Nxele, Ntsikana believed in peace and accepting God's will. Nxele and Ntsikana represent the two choices available to Africans in response to White rule through the end of the twentieth century: violent resistance and protest, or peaceful resistance and protest.

Ndlambe's men used guerrilla tactics to recapture the Zuurveld after their defeat in 1812. They burned farmsteads and stole cattle on such a scale that few colonists would settle there. As Xhosa attacks increased following the drought of 1815, so too did settlers' calls for government action. In 1817 Somerset rode to the frontier and forced Ngqika to meet with him. He offered the Xhosa chief a trade monopoly with the colony if Ngqika would agree to stop all cattle raiding. The British bribed him with presents and cajoled him by naming him principal chief of all the Xhosa. The other Xhosa chiefs angrily protested the agreement, and in 1818 an anti-Ngqika coalition under Hintsa, and led by Nxele, inflicted on Ngqika a devastating defeat at the Battle of Amalinde. Ngqika complained to colonial authorities that the attack had been motivated by his efforts to stop cattle thefts. Ignoring pleas for peace from other Xhosa chiefs, Governor Somerset sent a colonial force to Ngqika's aid, and it recaptured most of his cattle.

Somerset's actions set off the Fifth Frontier War (1818–1819). On 22

April, as many as 6,000 Xhosa led by Nxele swooped down on Grahamstown from the surrounding hills. They approached without fear because Nxele had promised he would turn the British bullets into water. He did not. The devastating musket and cannon fire killed scores of Xhosa. Colonial forces drove the Xhosa back across the Fish River and hounded them for three more months. Finally Nxele voluntarily surrendered in an effort to stop the bloodshed. Imprisoned on Robben Island, he drowned in 1820 while trying to escape. In his death Nxele took on mythological proportions, and later Xhosa generations expected him to return as their savior. The Xhosa expression "waiting for Nxele" means having a forlorn hope.

The colonial victory over Ndlambe and Hintsa ushered in fifteen years of relative peace on the eastern frontier. The Cape government continued to play off different chiefdoms against each other, exploiting old rivalries to prevent the Xhosa from uniting against the colony. After the war Somerset informed the faithful Ngqika that he must also surrender all the lands between the Fish and Keiskamma Rivers. This area constituted much of Ngqika's chiefdom, including his birthplace. Somerset planned to make it a neutral zone, free of colonists and Africans alike. Although no colonial forces came to force them out of this neutral zone, the threat remained, particularly as colonists took to calling the area the "ceded territory." It remained for the next generation of Xhosa leaders to combat White expansion.

The British Settlers, 1820

Somerset now instituted Collins's third recommendation, the importation of European settlers. Colonial officials had long recognized that the colony's settlement patterns and extensive pastoral economy were obstacles to a diverse economy, efficient land use, and a dense population capable of defending itself against attack. Huge livestock ranches spreading across vast stretches of land also impeded the growth of towns, thereby limiting commercial activities and employment opportunities. Somerset aimed to use British settlers (1) to create a more dense settlement pattern along the colonial border as a barrier against Xhosa aggression, and (2) to provide a new model for colonial land settlement and agriculture. Somerset's plan was part of a much larger effort by the British government to export its excess population and thereby ease unemployment and social unrest at home. In July 1819 the British Parliament voted £50,000 to transport citizens from the British Isles to the

Cape, where each adult man would receive about one hundred acres of Zuurveld land. About 4,000 men, women, and children eventually reached the Cape, beginning in April 1820. Another 1,000 wealthier citizens paid their own way in return for a land grant.

The scheme was doomed from the beginning. First, the British government hid the fact that the British (or 1820) settlers were going to a volatile frontier zone where they would have to serve as part-time soldiers. Second, the settlers came from all walks of life, but few were farmers. The majority came from the urban artisan class, but there were also merchants, ministers, discharged sailors, schoolteachers, and representatives of various professions. Third, the land west of the Fish River was of poor quality, received irregular rainfall, and was ill suited for intensive agriculture. During their first three years the settlers experienced crop disease, drought, and a memorable flood. Most settlers soon abandoned their farms and took up their former vocations in Grahamstown and other villages in the eastern Cape region. Many became frontier traders. The few who remained on the land followed Cape tradition and demanded larger farms. In the 1830s they introduced merino sheep farming, and soon wool became the colony's major export item.

The British settlers actually made the frontier situation more difficult. They still required colonial troops for their protection. They made the land shortages even more acute. And they did not assimilate into the Afrikaner community as previous European immigrants had; instead they maintained their cultural differences. They considered themselves more civilized and culturally superior not only to Africans but also to Afrikaners. This division between Afrikaner and English has lasted through the twentieth century. Only their common need to stand united against the much larger African population has brought them together.

MISSION SOCIETIES

Mission societies significantly influenced Cape politics and labor relations and alienated much of the Afrikaner community. The London Missionary Society was the most influential and powerful of these organizations. The Wesleyan Missionary Society and the Glasgow Missionary Society arrived in 1816, and the Church Missionary Society in 1821. They established missions among the Xhosa in the east and among the various African societies across the Orange River, including the Khoikhoi, Griqua, and Tswana. In 1833 the Paris Evangelical Mission Society established a Sotho mission in modern Lesotho.

At first, missionaries simply appeared at a village and requested permission to stay and preach. Over time, as Africans realized that a resident missionary brought certain benefits, they invited them to come and settle. Africans were often more interested, however, in the material goods and firearms that missionaries might provide than in the missionary's Christian message. Resident missionaries served as shields against attacks by White settlers and other Africans. Missionaries also brought European medical practices and literacy. Perhaps most important, missionaries served as advisers, suggesting how to deal with White officials and settlers most appropriately.

Most British missionaries possessed the evangelical spirit of the day, seeking to "convert the heathen." At the same time, their own middle-class backgrounds emphasized hard work, industry, and commerce. In their minds, Christianity and their own nineteenth-century British "civilization" were one and the same. "Progress"—as represented by private ownership of land, the learning of crafts and trades, literacy, and surplus production for the marketplace—accompanied the Bible into these "dark" lands. The "pagan" cultivator, scratching out a subsistence existence on commonly held land, could only become a Christian if he or she also spoke English and adopted English clothes, manners, and customs.

Missionaries received the support and encouragement of the British commercial classes, as well as that of many local merchants and traders who provided cloth, ironware, and other items for the expanding African market. Missionary relationships with local government officials were more ambiguous. They required government permission to enter the colony and to establish mission stations beyond the colonial boundaries. But many missionaries preferred that government not interfere with their work and only intervene when the mission was threatened. Many sought to isolate their missions from the outside world in an effort to create ideal Christian villages. They tried to prevent their converts from having contact with Africans, who might tempt them to return to their former "pagan" ways. They also tried to keep them away from "ungodly" White soldiers, settlers, and traders.

Most missionaries believed Africans were inferior to Europeans, but given time and a proper example, Africans could become "civilized." These relatively liberal and humanitarian views placed them at odds with the settlers, who regarded Africans simply as beasts of burden for the Whites and disliked all missionary activity. Agricultural commodities produced on missions competed with those of White farmers. Missions gave shelter to potential African laborers. The missionary view that Africans could become equal to Whites threatened the entire social and economic fabric of Cape society.

One missionary who particularly aroused Afrikaner anger was Dr. John Philip. He arrived at the Cape in 1819, the newly appointed superintendent of LMS missions in southern Africa. The son of a Scottish weaver, Philip was a self-taught and exceptionally brilliant Congregational minister. Until his death in 1851, he struggled unceasingly for legal equality between Khoikhoi and Whites. He was responsible for the rapid expansion of LMS missions across southern Africa and the promotion of education. He also encouraged other missionary societies within the region.

In 1826 Philip traveled to London to make a case for Khoikhoi equality before his influential friends in Parliament and the abolitionist movement. While there, he published *Researches in South Africa*, a two-volume propaganda piece that blatantly supported his cause and outraged White colonists. Meanwhile, however, in 1828 Acting Governor Burke outmaneuvered Philip by issuing Ordinance 50, which sought to improve "the condition of the Hottentots [Khoikhoi] and other free persons of color at the Cape." It abolished all discriminatory practices against Khoikhoi and other free Blacks. On paper it afforded the Khoikhoi freedom of movement and legal equality with Whites; they no longer had to carry passes, they could own land, and they could have more freedom "in bringing their labor to a fair market." Ordinance 50 had the immediate effect of disrupting the Cape labor market, as many Khoikhoi left White farms in search of better opportunities. Some settled at the Kat River Settlement, a community founded in 1829 where Khoikhoi could own land. Whites now paid more for Khoikhoi workers but had less control over them.

An even greater shock to the Cape's system of racial inequality soon followed. By the early 1830s the abolitionist movement was one of the most powerful political forces in Britain. In 1833 their years of lobbying came to fruition when Parliament passed an Emancipation Act freeing all slaves throughout the British Empire. Slaves were to begin a four-year apprenticeship starting in 1834. In the Cape at the end of that period, the freed slaves would have full legal equality with Whites under the provisions of Ordinance 50. The Emancipation Act provided for compensation to slave owners—but only payable in London and only at about one-third of the slaves' actual market value. Many Cape slave owners never received any compensation.

POLITICAL AND SOCIAL CHANGES

Governor Somerset's agricultural improvements made him many friends among the wealthy farmers. He was much less popular with the British settlers, who blamed him for their miserable circumstances. Somerset branded as "radicals" those settlers who petitioned for redress of grievances and publicly voiced their concerns. Unlike the Afrikaners, however, some British settlers could challenge Somerset's autocratic rule because they had influential friends in England. In 1822 a British Commission of Inquiry arrived to investigate all matters relating to Cape administration and to suggest improvements. Its recommendations eventually led to sweeping changes, including the adoption of the British legal system, its court procedures, and trial by jury. In 1828 a Charter of Justice established a Supreme Court with a Chief Justice and three other judges independent of the executive branch. The Charter made no reference to color or class, so theoretically the courts were now available to everyone. English-style resident magistrates replaced the old Dutch local *landdrost, heemraden,* and *veldkornet.* The British abolished the Burgher Senate and created a Council of Advice. Judges rode circuit until the 1860s, setting up court in small villages, often in conjunction with the *nagmaal* (or quarterly Holy Communion Service). In July 1828, Parliament guaranteed press freedom at the Cape, officially recognizing the right of individuals to publish freely, subject only to general libel laws. Parliament also ensured the right to open debate of public policy and to reporting on government without prior censorship.

Anglicization also gained momentum in the 1820s. This was never a specific goal of British rule; it resulted more from the desire of local officials to make the Cape British. Sir John Cradock initiated some anglicization policies in the 1810s, but the real impetus came from Lord Somerset after 1822. He brought in Scottish schoolteachers to teach in free public schools. Students were given incentives for using English, which alienated many Afrikaner parents. In 1824 English became the official language of government. Afrikaners particularly resented the anglicized legal system, which they considered not only too liberal (because slaves could testify against masters) but also nearly unintelligible. Anglicization continued throughout the nineteenth century, as education, architecture, government, social and leisure activities, and the economy all adopted a more distinctly British character. The Afrikaner community in the western Cape interacted more frequently with British officials and merchants and adapted more easily to British ways. Other Afrikaners, however, especially those in the interior districts, deeply resented this subversion of their society, culture, and Dutch language.

A shortage of labor remained one of the nineteenth-century Cape's most pressing problems. The British government attempted, through Ordinance 50 and the abolition of slavery, to free laborers from forced working conditions. These measures met only limited success in opening the labor market, however. First, they went against the racist structure of Cape society. Over time, local officials passed laws, such as the Cape Masters and Servants Acts of 1841 and 1856, that controlled farm and domestic labor and undermined the equality guaranteed for Khoikhoi and former slaves by Ordinance 50. Second, as long as Cape capitalism revolved around agriculture and trade, Khoikhoi and former slaves could farm their own, or mission, land as easily as work for the Whites. Only after the discovery of diamonds and gold later in the century, and the beginnings of industrial capitalism, did the South African labor market undergo dramatic changes.

A shortage of labor led to representative government in South Africa. Pressure by British settlers had forced minor concessions for representation in the 1820s and 1830s. Colonists were still dissatisfied with this limited representation, however, and pressed for elected assemblies, as in Canada. The issue came to a head in 1849 when the British government attempted to deport convicts to the Cape as it had to Australia. Cape colonists rose up in protest and forced the British to reverse their decision. This victory emboldened them to ask for their own legislative body. In 1854 the Cape colony received a constitution providing for a representative bicameral parliament, with officials appointed from London continuing to control the executive branch. A liberal franchise guaranteed the vote to all men, regardless of race, who owned property worth at least £25 or earned a minimum salary of that amount. Qualified Africans retained the right to vote in the Cape until 1936, and Coloureds until 1956.

THE XHOSA WARS

Lord Somerset's efforts in the eastern Cape region provided a few years of relative peace between the Xhosa and the colony. Both sides took advantage of the calm to trade. Large, government-sanctioned trade fairs were held at Fort Willshire on the Keiskamma River and elsewhere.

In the late 1820s the colonial government permitted a few licensed White traders to cross the border and trade privately with Africans. Many African and colonial traders traded illegally.

For both White and African alike, however, there still remained the persistent need for more land and water. Ngqika died in 1829, and his nine-year-old son Sandile succeeded him. Sandile and his brother Maqoma, who served as regent until 1840, were more militant than their father. In 1829 colonial officials forced Maqoma off his lands in the neutral zone along the Kat River in order to establish a Khoikhoi settlement there. This harsh treatment of Maqoma, the public humiliation of other chiefs by colonial officials and settlers, and constant commando raids on their cattle herds convinced the Xhosa that the Whites intended to take all their land. The Xhosa had watched Khoikhoi societies disintegrate and did not want the same to happen to them. The Xhosa were also under pressure from the northeast. Devastating wars among the Zulu and other northern Nguni in the 1810s and 1820s drove many refugees, called Mfengu, into Xhosaland, putting even greater strain on limited water and land resources. The Mfengu occupied a subordinate position in Xhosa society—the Gcaleka Xhosa called them "dogs"—and turned to colonial officials and missionaries for assistance. They later prospered and took the colony's side in three frontier wars.

By December 1834 Xhosa anger and indignation were so great that the Gcaleka and Rharhabe Xhosa put aside their differences. Maqoma and another of Ngqika's sons, Tyhali, led about 12,000 Xhosa warriors in a surprise invasion across the entire eastern frontier, as far west as Algoa Bay, igniting the Sixth Frontier War (1834–1835). They attacked in small guerrilla bands. Hundreds of settlers abandoned their farms and fled to Grahamstown. The colonial forces counterattacked, led by Colonel Harry Smith. He attacked Hintsa, the Xhosa paramount chief, beyond the Great Kei River. En route his forces destroyed Xhosa food supplies and drove off all their cattle. In April 1835 Smith invited Hintsa to peace talks, pledging the chief's safety, but it was a trap. After several days of threats and bullying by Smith and the colonial governor, Benjamin D'Urban, Hintsa tried to leave. Soldiers shot him dead and cut off his ears as souvenirs. The war ended in September when the remaining chiefs made peace, but they did not surrender. After all the destruction and bloodshed, relations between the two sides remained as unsettled as before. Efforts were now made to bring peace to the frontier through treaties, rather than by force. This policy worked for a while, although few colonists supported it. Eventually both the treaty system and the peace failed because the British refused to provide the troops, manpower, and resources necessary for their success.

The eastern frontier experienced two more frontier wars, each more devastating than the last, before Xhosa society collapsed. The Seventh Frontier War (1846–1847) began in March 1846 when Whites arrested a Xhosa man for stealing an ax from a colonial shop. In what became known as the War of the Ax, colonial troops once again destroyed Xhosa crops and grain reserves and took their cattle. As their people starved, Xhosa chiefs surrendered. The peace lasted for only three years. The new Cape governor, Sir Harry Smith, initiated the Eighth Frontier War (1850–1852) by his arrogant behavior. He deposed the Ngqika Xhosa chief, Sandile, and established a new British colony, British Kaffraria, in Xhosa territory between the Keiskamma and Kei Rivers. Humiliated by this and other actions on Smith's part, the Ngqika Xhosa, some Thembu, and even some Kat River Settlement Khoikhoi attacked the colony. They were spurred on by another Xhosa prophet, Mlanjeni, but the same pattern prevailed. The Xhosa were initially successful in driving deep into colonial territory. They were soon forced to surrender, however, after colonial troops destroyed their food supplies and cattle.

By now Xhosa resistance had been crushed. Land in the Kat River Settlement and British Kaffraria became available for White settlement. Scores of Xhosa were forced to relocate. Sir George Grey became governor in December 1854 and implemented a system of indirect rule he had used with the Maori in New Zealand. He set about to "civilize" the Xhosa, undermining their beliefs through European institutions (schools, missions, hospitals). He also sought to instill among them a western work ethic through wage labor on public works. Xhosa chiefs received salaries for enforcing colonial laws but were answerable to colonial magistrates. Grey justified the establishment of White settlements across Xhosaland as models of White civilization. The Xhosa were a beaten people, impoverished and humiliated. And then matters became worse.

In 1855 lung disease attacked Xhosa cattle herds and spread quickly, with some Xhosa losing more than 80 percent of their livestock. With their world turned upside down, the Xhosa experienced a period of psychological trauma during which they sought answers from within their indigenous belief system and from outside their own traditions in missionary teachings. Several prophets arose, including an adolescent girl named Nongqawuse who lived east of the Kei River in the still independent territory of the Gcaleka paramount chief, Sarhili. In April 1856 she announced that ancestors had appeared to her in a vision and given her a message. All cattle must be slaughtered and grain stores destroyed, after which the ancestors would return with healthy cattle and fresh grain. White people and unbelievers would be swept into the sea by a great wind.

Tragically, Sarhili supported Nongqawuse and the Great Cattle Killing began. For months the Xhosa killed their cattle and destroyed their crops. When the first date promised for the prophecy's fulfillment came and passed, unbelievers were blamed for the ancestors' failure to return. Pressure increased for everyone to participate, and most Xhosa eventually did in a societal suicide lasting fifteen months. It ended in July 1857 when Sarhili renounced all belief in the prophecy, but by then the Xhosa had destroyed an estimated 400,000 head of cattle and perhaps 40,000 Xhosa had starved to death. As many as 35,000 more fled into the colony, where they took work on farms and in towns.

Governor Grey took advantage of the calamity to advance his "civilizing" plans. Magistrates' powers were extended at the expense of local chiefs, some of whom were banished. British Kaffraria's boundaries were expanded to include all territory west of the Kei River between the mountains and the Indian Ocean. This area, later known as the Ciskei, now became part of the Cape colony. It included remnants of the Ndlambe, Ngqika, and Gqunukhwebe societies, as well as the Mfengu. Starving Xhosa found work in the colony or jobs in Grey's public works projects in Kaffraria. Some, particularly Mfengu, were settled in closely controlled villages administered by Whites. German legionnaires and north German peasant immigrants were settled west of the Kei. Only the Gcaleka Xhosa, east of the Kei River in the area of present-day Transkei, retained some degree of independence.

Xhosa society was now divided. One group, called the "red" people because they wore cosmetic red clay, continued their traditional ways. The other group, the "school," or mission, people, were Christian converts. One of the most famous of the "school" people was the Reverend Tiyo Soga (1829–1871), a Xhosa commoner born on a mission station. He served first as a missionary, then as a translator, then as an ordained Xhosa minister, and finally as a Presbyterian Church minister. He studied in Scotland and married a Scotswoman, Janet Burnside. He anticipated the teachings of the African American leader Booker T. Washington by encouraging vocational training and economic self-reliance.

5

African States, Afrikaner Republics, and British Imperialism, 1770–1870

THE NORTHERN FRONTIER

While Cape governors concerned themselves with the eastern frontier, the north and northeast also underwent dramatic change. Long occupied by the San and Southern Sotho, new groups entered the region in the late eighteenth and early nineteenth centuries. First came the Griqua, mixed-race descendants of Europeans, Khoisan, and slaves, belonging mainly to two clans, the Barendses and the Koks. They roamed the land along the Orange River with their livestock from the area of modern Namibia to the Orange Free State. In the early 1800s LMS missionaries convinced them to settle north of the Orange near Griquatown. In the 1820s political rivalries, population pressures, and missionary meddling split the Griqua community. One group of Koks and Barendses, led by Adam Kok III, settled at Philippolis on the middle Orange River. A second group, under Cornelius Kok II, settled at Campbell, northeast of Griquatown. With missionary encouragement, the Griquatown community elected Andries Waterboer, of San descent, as their leader.

White frontiersmen and farmers followed closely on the Griquas' heels. Blocked by the Xhosa in the east and the arid regions to the northwest, colonial expansion shifted to the north and northeast. Migrant livestock farmers *(trekboers)* ignored official boundaries and pushed across the frontier, driven by an insatiable need for land and water. British colonial officials, like their Dutch predecessors, did little to stop them. During the severe drought and locust years of the early 1820s, many migrant farmers grazed their livestock on temporary farms north of the Orange River. Most returned to the colony during good years, but some settled permanently beyond the Orange. These Afrikaner *trekboers* remained loyal to the British colonial government, petitioned it to annex the new territories, and even offered to pay taxes. In the mid-1830s, however, Afrikaners of a different mindset flooded through this northeastern passage, leaving the colony forever.

LMS missionaries crossed the Orange River in the early 1800s and settled among the Griqua, Sotho, and Tswana. Robert Moffat established the Kuruman mission among the Tswana in 1817. It became one of the most famous missions in southern Africa, where newly arrived European missionaries received instruction on African mission work and on simple survival. The missionary and explorer David Livingstone came there in 1841, married Moffat's daughter, and then headed off to great adventures in central Africa.

UPHEAVAL AND CHANGE AMONG THE NGUNI

Change also occurred among the northern Nguni in southeastern South Africa in the late eighteenth and early nineteenth centuries. Events there during this period redirected the course of southern African history. The extent and nature of these events are the subject of heated debate among South African scholars. In histories written after the 1920s, the term *Mfecane* (Zulu) or *Difaqane* (Sotho) refers to a period of wars and social change from roughly the 1770s to the 1830s. There are several translations of the word: "time of troubles," "crushing," "forced migration," "total war." The term probably dates back to a Xhosa word used by colonial settlers for homeless Africans who entered the colony during this period, the Fetcani. By the end of the nineteenth century writers used it to describe the period, and from there it passed into the history books.

Little is known for certain about the *Mfecane*. The Bantu-speaking societies in southern Africa were pre-literate and left no written records. Some English traders settled at Port Natal (modern Durban) in 1824, and it is their generally biased records that give us our earliest picture of the Zulu king Shaka and the *Mfecane*. These traders served as Shaka's advisers and accepted his overlordship in return for trading privileges.

Racial prejudices, and the myth-making needed to justify White domination, influenced subsequent descriptions and interpretations into the late twentieth century.

What can be said about the events and changes occurring during this period? Why did they happen? One theory links the changes to White labor demands converging from east and west. That is, slaves were needed for the slave trade through the Portuguese port at Delagoa Bay (modern Maputo) and on to Brazil. The Cape colony always needed more African laborers. But the human bodies required for both the Portuguese slave trade and the Cape labor market increased only toward the end of the *Mfecane*. They did not cause it. Another theory suggests that African societies in the region began to compete more intensely for control of the commodities trade, particularly ivory, with the Portuguese through Delagoa Bay. Guns received in this trade made the competition more violent. Perhaps this was a contributing factor. Most historians, however, agree that the primary causes for these events were climate change, population pressures, and the role of the cow in Nguni society.

At the end of the eighteenth century the land in the area of modern KwaZulu-Natal—roughly between the Phongolo River in the north, the Tugela River in the south, and the Buffalo River valley in the west—experienced several decades of good rainfall and mild climate, making it green and fertile. Cattle populations increased significantly as a result. Young men could acquire cattle easily to provide bridewealth for a wife. More young men could also afford more than one wife. Earlier and more numerous marriages led to a population explosion that put tremendous pressure on the land's carrying capacity and significantly affected social and political relationships in northern Nguni society.

Cattle had always been the main unit of wealth. Large livestock herds gave kings, chiefs, and local homestead heads prestige and power. As cattle became more plentiful, the simple economics of supply and demand caused their value to drop. Now even commoners could acquire large herds, and many did. Possessing power of their own, they broke away from their chiefs and formed new settlements. This was not difficult while there was still plenty of grazing land and water. As human and animal populations continued to grow, however, land shortages developed and chiefdoms fought over the remaining unoccupied land.

Weaker, smaller chiefdoms allied themselves with larger chiefdoms for their mutual defense. By the 1790s there were three dominant political formations in the region: in the north along the Phongolo River were (1) the Ngwane under the leader Sobhuza and (2) the Ndwandwe under the leader Zwide, and in the south were (3) the Mthethwa under the leader Dingiswayo. In 1802 a drought settled over the land, leading to a horrible famine. The people called this time *Madlathule*, meaning "when we were obliged to eat grass." Marauding bands preyed on isolated homesteads, and refugees fled in search of food and protection.

The *Madlathule* famine led to war between Zwide and Sobhuza in the north. The leader Sobhuza lost and retreated inland, where he incorporated several smaller Sotho and Nguni groups with his own people to form the present-day kingdom of Swaziland. Zwide headed south around 1817–1818 and met Dingiswayo's much stronger forces. Zwide, however, tricked Dingiswayo into coming to peace talks, where he had him assassinated. Zwide then drove Dingiswayo's leaderless army back almost to the Tugela River and became the most powerful ruler in the region. But his supremacy was short-lived.

Among the many client chiefdoms in Dingiswayo's Mthethwa confederacy were the Zulu under Senzangakhona. Around 1787 Senzangakhona fathered an illegitimate son named Shaka. Shaka joined Dingiswayo's army in 1809 and rose rapidly through the ranks. Soon he was supreme commander of the most powerful military force in southern Africa. Following Senzangakhona's death in 1815, Shaka seized the Zulu chiefdomship and approximately three years later assumed leadership of the Mthethwa confederacy after Dingiswayo's assassination.

Shaka revolutionized warfare in southern Africa. Dingiswayo had begun a military draft whereby men of roughly the same age were placed into regiments, or *amabutho*. Women were organized according to this age-grade system as well. Because they could not marry until released from their regiments (for men in their thirties and women in their twenties), this system caused birth rates to drop. Under Shaka the *amabutho* became highly disciplined regiments. In previous Nguni wars, opposing forces stood facing each other across an open stretch of land and threw spears back and forth. Shaka's troops employed an *assegaai*, or short stabbing spear, instead. Although the Ndwandwe and Ngwane appear to have used it earlier, Shaka's men were more skilled in its use and now fought hand-to-hand, protected by body-length cowhide shields. Shaka also developed an innovative strategy for attack known as the bull-and-horns formation. This crescent-shaped maneuver consisted of several densely packed regiments in the center, or head, and one regiment on each side forming the horns. As the head advanced, the horns enclosed the enemy, trapping all inside. Finally, when Dingiswayo defeated an enemy, he generally left the ruler in power and spared the people. Shaka sometimes destroyed his enemy completely, killing the royal families, massacring their followers, including women and children, and destroying their crops. Shaka incorporated the survivors into his kingdom, under lesser chiefs, and demanded annual tribute of grain and cattle. By the 1820s Shaka's own people were living in fear and terror. His reign came to its own bloody end in September 1828 when two half-brothers stabbed him to death. One of these half-brothers, Dingane, replaced Shaka as Zulu king.

Shaka's wars of conquest from 1818 to 1828 both united and divided the northern Nguni people. His incorporation of other chiefdoms into his Zulu state created the largest and most powerful African society in southern Africa in the nineteenth century. On the other hand, people who were unwilling to live under Shaka's rule fled from his armies. The Ngoni, for example, traveled north to Tanzania, under their leaders Zwagendaba and Nxaba, where they formed important kingdoms in Malawi, Tanzania, and Zambia. Many refugees moved south, including Madikane and his son Ncaphayi, who formed the Bhaca chiefdomship in the northern Transkei. One of Shaka's own lieutenants, Mzilikazi, rebelled against him in 1821 and retreated with his regiment to the northwest, establishing a small state between the Vaal and Limpopo Rivers. Mzilikazi and his followers were called the Ndebele (Zulu) or Matabele (Sotho) and were feared only a little less than the Zulu. They fought a series of battles with the Griqua, Sotho, Tswana, and Afrikaner farmers. Mzilikazi and his people eventually settled in southern Zimbabwe, where the Ndebele now form the second largest ethnic group in that country.

As the war's shockwaves spread north across the Drakensberg Mountains, a Sotho leader named Moshoeshoe organized his own people and refugees from other chiefdoms in the Caledon River valley. There he built his headquarters on a flat-topped, impregnable mountain fortress called Thaba Bosiu. From this elevated position, his warriors could fend off attacks from below. Moshoeshoe was a skillful diplomat and ruler who managed to hold his kingdom (modern Lesotho) together for several decades, despite repeated attacks from both Whites and Africans.

White mythology to the contrary, these wars did not depopulate the eastern half of southern Africa, but they did cause massive political reorganization, much havoc, and extreme suffering. The Zulu, Swazi, Sotho, and Ndebele formed large, highly centralized states. The citizens of these states, who had previously belonged to various small chiefdoms, now developed common, national identities under powerful kings. The remainder of the nineteenth century saw each of these nations fight to protect its independence against invading Afrikaner and British forces. The wars also produced thousands of refugees. Some entered Xhosaland and placed increased pressure on land and water resources there. Scores of refugees fled to the Cape colony, where they worked for White employers. Slave traders captured other refugees and channeled them as slaves through Delagoa Bay. Many survivors hid away in isolated valleys and mountain caves. The widespread death and destruction, massive migration, and concealment of those who remained made the country appear "empty" to advancing White farmers and traders; they thought the land was free for the taking.

THE GREAT TREK

In history books the roughly 15,000 Afrikaner men, women, and children who left the Cape colony in the 1830s and 1840s are called *voortrekkers* ("pioneers"), and their mass migration is known as the Great Trek. In the twentieth century the Great Trek attained mythological proportions in Afrikaner historiography. The people at the time, however, called themselves emigrants, and in some ways this movement was nothing new. Since the earliest days of European settlement, Dutch-speaking *trekboers* had migrated out from Cape Town. They ran into obstacles that halted their expansion in the late 1770s. By the 1830s, due to extensive livestock practices, the land's limited carrying capacity, the Afrikaners' large families, and the arrival of British settlers, the Cape frontier was overpopulated. It could not support the White and African pastoralists. The urge grew to trek again.

There were other factors as well that spurred the Great Trek, such as the abolition of slavery, although this only significantly affected the wealthiest men. Afrikaner farmers despised the Black Circuit courts and Ordinance 50 for denying them the almost total control they had previously enjoyed over their Khoikhoi workers. British promotion of land reform and intensive farming upset Afrikaner notions about land ownership and use. The British settlers' arrival, and the introduction of merino sheep, caused land prices to rise significantly. Missionary liberalism and humanitarianism, and Afrikaner perceptions that the government sided with the Africans against them, threatened their way of life. They resented the anglicization policy that demeaned their language and their culture. Changes in local government denied Afrikaners a political voice and their wealthier and more ambitious leaders political office. Finally, cattle raids and heavy losses during the Sixth Frontier War (1834–1835) proved the Cape government would not protect them against African attacks. Thus, many frontier Afrikaners believed they had no choice but to leave. They disliked British rule but could not challenge it. The loss of the Black labor force meant some Whites might have to work for other Whites, which was totally unacceptable. Their exodus from the colony was infused with an Old Testament fervor grounded in their Calvinist faith. They believed they were a chosen people heading into the promised land.

Two important distinctions must be made. First, the earlier livestock farmers, or *trekboers*, generally supported the Cape government and only migrated in search of grazing and hunting land. They continued to pay taxes and expected—even asked—the government to extend the colonial boundaries. The *voortrekkers*, on the other hand, were escaping British rule and went searching for land to establish an independent Afrikaner republic. Second, the *voortrekkers* were not heading into a great unknown. Xhosa blocked their way eastward across the Fish River, so *voortrekker* parties turned to the northeast to Natal, Transorangia, and the Transvaal. They generally knew where they were going, what routes to take, and what to expect. *Trekboers*, traders, and informal reconnaissance parties had been crossing the Orange River for years. Some Whites had already settled beyond the border by the 1830s. Colonists also knew something about the *Mfecane* through excursions across the border with their live-stock and through refugees, missionaries, and the English traders at Port Natal. In 1835 a reconnaissance party *(kommissie-trek)* reported from Port Natal that the land was fertile, well watered, and apparently unpopulated. It also noted that Port Natal, with its excellent harbor, would make an ideal capital for a new state. Other reconnaissance parties journeyed to the north and northeast and returned with positive reports as well.

Two prominent Afrikaner leaders, Gert Maritz and Piet Retief, advocated a mass migration in early 1834, but serious preparations began only after the Sixth Frontier War. The Great Trek began in late 1835 when separate parties under Louis Trichardt and Janse van Rensburg crossed the Orange River and headed toward the Transvaal. Parties led by Hendrik Potgieter, Gert Maritz, and Piet Uys soon followed. The emigrants, mostly livestock farmers from the eastern districts, were organized into parties of relatives and neighbors under recognized local leaders. A large party might have a hundred wagons and thousands of sheep and cattle. Khoikhoi servants and former slaves accompanied their masters. In July 1835 van Rensberg's party was destroyed in a conflict with Soshangane's warriors. West of the area of modern-day Pretoria, Mzilikazi's Ndebele attacked Potgieter's party in October 1836, killing many livestock and some emigrants. The migrants survived by circling and lashing their wagons together to form a tight enclosure, called a *laager*, as a barricade against attack. In early 1837, Maritz and Potgieter joined forces to attack Mzilikazi's settlement and inflicted heavy losses. Dingane's Zulu attacked Mzilikazi shortly thereafter. A final *voortrekker* attack in October 1837 forced Mzilikazi to gather his followers and move across the Limpopo River into the area of modern Zimbabwe.

Potgieter and Maritz organized a government consisting of a seven-member burgher council (the *volksraad*, or people's assembly council), with Maritz as president and judge and Potgieter as military leader. When Piet Retief arrived with his large party in March 1837 the emigrants elected him governor and supreme military commander. A disagreement now arose over the migration's future direction. Retief favored Natal. Potgieter preferred the Transvaal highveld, believing the British would not allow an independent Afrikaner republic in Natal. In October 1837 Retief left to seek permission of the Zulu king, Dingane, to settle in Natal. Meanwhile, after defeating Mzilikazi, Potgieter claimed a large area of the Transvaal, although the emigrants had neither the firepower nor the manpower to rule over such a vast region and the Africans who lived there. They established small settlements at Winburg and Potchefstroom.

Retief's visit to Dingane's capital, Mgundgundlovu ("the place of the great elephant"), proved disastrous. The small but growing English community at Port Natal was already challenging Dingane's authority, and he feared the arrival of more Whites. Dingane also knew about the Xhosa wars and the Whites' efforts to seize Xhosa land. After preliminary negotiations, during which Retief bragged about the emigrants' defeat of Mzilikazi, he and Dingane purportedly signed a treaty in which the Zulu king ceded to Retief all the land between the Tugela and Mzimvubu Rivers. On 6 February 1838 Retief's party was invited inside the royal courtyard for drinks and dancing but had to leave their guns outside. Once inside, Dingane signaled for his soldiers to attack. Retief and his men were clubbed to death.

On 17 February, before the remainder of Retief's party could recover from this crushing loss, Zulu regiments attacked two emigrant *laagers*, killing about 500 (half of whom were servants) and capturing large numbers of livestock and horses. When an April counterattack failed and a cold winter set in, the entire emigrant movement seemed in danger of collapsing. The arrival of Andries Pretorius (after whom Pretoria is named) saved the day. Elected commandant-general, Pretorius moved against the Zulu with five hundred men, more than fifty wagons, and two cannons. As Pretorius approached the Ncome River he learned that a Zulu army was nearby. He immediately drew his wagons into a fortified *laager* by the river. Early on the morning of 16 December approximately 10,000 Zulu warriors attacked and suffered a crushing defeat. Three thousand Zulu died under the blistering fire of musket ball and cannon grapeshot, whereas the Whites suffered only three minor injuries. The Whites called it the Battle of Blood River, because so many Zulu died that the waters of the Ncome River turned red with blood. Before the battle, the *voortrekkers* supposedly made a vow to God to commemorate the day if they were victorious. Afrikaner Nationalists in the twentieth century venerated 16 December variously as Dingaan's Day, the Day of the Covenant, or the Day of the Vow, and it became a national holiday (celebrated by Afrikaners) under the apartheid regime. In 1995 the Black majority government declared it the Day of Reconciliation.

Following the battle, Pretorius and his commandos moved on to Dingane's capital at Mgundgundlovu but found it deserted. They did uncover the bodies of Retief and his men and reported finding the land treaty with Dingane's mark on it. If this document ever existed—and some historians doubt it did—it is now lost. Real or not, the Afrikaner emigrants claimed Natal based on Dingane's treaty. They formed the Republic of Natalia, with their capital at Pietermaritzburg. They drew up a constitution, elected Pretorius as president, created a people's assembly, or *volksraad*, and reinstituted the former Dutch system of local administration by appointing *landdrosts, heemraden*, and *veldkornets*. In 1841 Potgieter became chief-commandant of an adjunct assembly at Potchefstroom.

The emigrants also tried to duplicate the racial privileges and relationships they had enjoyed in the Cape under the Dutch. The Natalia franchise was limited to Dutch-speaking adult male emigrants of European descent, and it became the model for all subsequent Afrikaner governments. Blacks were denied all political rights, reduced to servitude, racially segregated, and generally mistreated. Commandos kidnapped African children and forced them to work for their food, clothing, and accommodation under an "indenture" system. When this failed to satisfy their labor requirements, each farmer was allowed to have five African families living on his land. "Surplus" Africans were driven off to southern Natal.

While Natalia struggled to survive, Dingane's half-brother, Mpande, turned against him in 1839 as a result of the Blood River defeat and forced him to flee to Swaziland, where he was killed. Mpande then began a long reign (1840–1872) as Zulu king. Mpande consolidated his power by murdering his rivals and enlarging his army. He rarely went to war, however, and never challenged either Afrikaner or British rule in Natal, even after Natalia annexed the southern part of his territory south of the Tugela River.

The Great Trek had caught the British off guard. Lieutenant Governor Andries Stockenstrom believed the emigrants were simply carrying on the *trekboer* tradition. The Cape governor, Sir Benjamin D'Urban, thought the emigrants were making a mistake but took no action to halt the exodus. The British also had no interest in extending their colony and had repeatedly refused to annex Natal. Yet they worried that the emigrants might stir up trouble among Africans on the colony's eastern border. They also wanted to maintain control of the excellent harbor at Port Natal and were concerned not so much with the Afrikaners but that a foreign power might ally itself with the Afrikaners and seize the port.

Reports of Afrikaner abuse of Africans and the kidnapping of African children reached the Cape by the early 1840s, often through missionaries. The expulsion of "surplus" Africans to southern Natal, near the Transkei, finally prompted Governor Napier, D'Urban's successor, to intervene. He sent a force of 250 men to raise the Union Jack over Port Natal in 1842, effectively denying the Afrikaners free access to the harbor. After minor skirmishes between the colonial forces and Pretorius's commandos, the Afrikaners abandoned armed resistance to British rule in June 1842. On 15 July the Natalia *volksraad* in Pietermaritzburg submitted to conditions making Natal part of the British Empire. As evangelical and humanitarian lobbies still helped to shape British colonial policy, the conditions guaranteed equality for all regardless of color, origin, race, or creed. In 1843 Natal became a separate district of the Cape colony, and the first Afrikaner republic came to an end.

THE BRITISH NATAL COLONY, 1843–1870

Britain's annexation of Natal caused most of the roughly 6,000 Afrikaner men, women, and children who had settled there to migrate back north across the Drakensburg Mountains. The British were left with a colony they did not want, with a declining White population and a growing African one. To correct this imbalance, they transported around 5,000 men, women, and children from Britain to Natal between 1849 and 1851.

These were part of the Great Emigration between 1847 and 1851 during which more than a million people left Britain, mostly headed to North America. Like the earlier British settlers, these new arrivals were mainly middle class, with few farming skills and little idea of the dangers or hardships they faced. Many soon returned to England after failing at farming. Some left Natal for the Cape or highveld, and others resumed their trades in Natal's two major settlements: Durban on the coast, and Pietermaritzburg in the interior. Natal's White population grew steadily thereafter, reaching about 18,000 by 1870, of whom about 3,000 were Afrikaners. This number was minuscule, however, in comparison to the African population that was perhaps fifteen times as large. Natal's African population increased significantly during the early 1840s when wars of succession in Zululand caused thousands there to flee. To handle this situation, the British gave authority over Zulu relations to a Wesleyan missionary's son, Theophilus Shepstone. Raised in the eastern Cape, Shepstone spoke Zulu and Xhosa. He immediately established a good, albeit paternalistic, relationship with Mpande that preserved peace between the Zulu and Natal for many years.

Within Natal itself, Shepstone implemented dual policies of segregation and indirect rule that served as models for future South African governments. First he demarcated several large areas of Natal land as African reserves and convinced about half the African population to relocate onto them. By the 1860s there were over sixty government and mission reserves, comprising about 16 percent of Natal's total land area. The remaining 84 percent was either privately owned by Whites or held by the government. The remaining African population worked these lands. They paid rents to White landowners and produced large quantities of agricultural and pastoral products. To rule over the large African population, Shepstone instituted a governing policy of "indirect rule" whereby local chiefs retained authority over their own people, according to African law and custom, but were ultimately answerable to colonial officials. In disputes between Whites and Africans, the latter deferred to European law.

Shepstone also tried to provide Natal's African population with opportunities for a western education and support for their economic endeavors. These efforts generally failed because he received inadequate financial and administrative support from the colonial authorities. The predominantly English White population became increasingly racist as the African population grew. They also opposed Shepstone's schemes and resented African successes; by 1870 African peasants were producing the great bulk of Natal's agricultural produce. Mission societies felt the White animosity as well, in particular the American Board of Commissioners for Foreign Missions, which arrived in 1835. They received 175,000 acres of Natal land for mission stations, set up schools and medical clinics, and eventually helped to create a significant westernized African middle class. Whites complained that by helping Africans maintain an independent existence as agriculturists or pastoralists, Shepstone and the missionaries were denying White employers access to cheap African labor.

Those White English settlers who continued to farm experimented with a wide range of commercial crops along the warm, humid Natal coast. The most viable new crop was sugar, but it is very labor intensive to produce. Independent African farmers, accustomed to less demanding grain or livestock farming, refused to work on sugar plantations. In 1860, therefore, Natal began importing indentured Indian labor—6,000 workers altogether over the next six years. Their contracts ran for five years, after which they were free of their obligation and could settle permanently. Many did, and because twenty-five Indian women were imported for every one hundred men, a substantial Indian community soon evolved. By the 1890s Indians outnumbered Whites in Natal. Some Indians continued to work on sugar plantations beyond their initial five-year contract. Some took up service work as cooks, house servants, and tailors, whereas others developed small fruit and vegetable gardens in Pietermaritzburg and Durban. Eventually Indians moved into trade and opened small shops. Some became quite wealthy and extended their commercial activities throughout South Africa. The indentured Indian labor system continued until 1911.

AFRIKANER REPUBLICS

Constant dissension among various leaders, particularly between Pretorius and Potgieter and their followers, divided the White *voortrekker* communities on the highveld in Transorangia and the Transvaal. There was also a group of *trekboers* who settled in the region before the Great Trek and remained loyal to the British-ruled Cape colony. This put them at odds with the republican *voortrekkers*. Britain's annexation of Natal and its recognition of African sovereignty, however, eventually brought the various Afrikaner groups together. Potchefstroom and Winburg declared their independence and laid claim to the entire Transorangia territory between the Vaal and Orange Rivers.

Adam Kok and his Griqua followers already occupied the southwestern part of Transorangia. Moshoeshoe claimed the territory from the Orange River to the fertile land north and west of the Caledon River. The British viewed the Griqua and Sotho states as buffer zones on the northern Cape border and worried that the Afrikaners' claims would threaten the peace. In November-December 1843, Governor Napier signed treaties with both Adam Kok and Moshoeshoe making them allies of the Cape colony. They were to extradite criminals, even Whites, back to the colony and promote peace and order. These treaties aroused Afrikaner indignation. No Afrikaner, even one who remained loyal to the colony, would live under African rule. Hendrik Potgieter, in his determination to escape British rule, now led his followers even further to the northeast. He established settlements at Ohrigstad (1845) and Schoemansdal (1848). Those Afrikaners who remained behind in the western highveld looked to Andries Pretorius for leadership. They refused to recognize Kok's authority when he tried to arrest one of them, forcing the British to take action.

In June 1845 a new Cape governor, Sir Peregrine Maitland, met with Adam Kok and declared that Griqua territory would be divided between "alienable" and "inalienable" lands. The Griqua had absolute authority over the "inalienable" part to the south of the Riet River, and no Whites could settle there. Whites could purchase or lease land in the "alienable" territory north of the river. Authority there rested with Major Henry Warden, who Maitland appointed as British Resident. Warden received little support from Cape authorities, however, and Afrikaners viewed him as a symbol of British rule and resented his presence. He failed to resolve the conflicting land claims among the Whites, the Africans, and the Griqua. The Seventh Frontier War in the eastern Cape in 1846–1847 served as the catalyst for one final attempt to resolve the Transorangia conflict. In February 1848 the newly appointed governor, Sir Harry Smith, met with Moshoeshoe, Pretorius, and others at Bloemfontein. Smith issued a proclamation annexing the entire territory between the Drakensburg Mountains in the east, the Vaal River to the north, and the Orange River to the west and south. This territory would be called the Orange River Sovereignty, and it included Adam Kok's lands and nearly all of Moshoeshoe's Sotho kingdom. The Afrikaners within the Sovereignty once again had to decide whether to live under British rule or migrate northward. Pretorius and his followers moved north of the Vaal River to Potchefstroom and the Magaliesberg region. From there Pretorius continued to interfere in Transorangia politics, however. Even Moshoeshoe sought an alliance with Pretorius in 1851 against the British officials in the Sovereignty.

Moshoeshoe is justly recognized as one of the most skillful African kings and diplomats of the nineteenth century. Having created a stable kingdom following the *Mfecane*, he now faced Afrikaners who threatened to seize his lands. Choosing the lesser of two evils, he placed himself under British protection and accepted British overlordship of the Orange River Sovereignty, but the British then turned against him. Warden drew a new boundary for the territory—the infamous Warden's Line—that took away much of Moshoeshoe's land. Warden's Line favored White land claims and effectively removed Moshoeshoe's authority over the Rolong, Kora, and Tlokwa who lived in his kingdom. When Warden tried to enforce the boundary his small forces were defeated by the Sotho king, but Moshoeshoe tactfully withdrew before inflicting a crushing defeat. Warden's actions placed Moshoeshoe in an untenable position, having lost significant and fertile parts of his kingdom and authority over his subjects.

Harry Smith's successor, George Cathcart, visited the Orange River Sovereignty in July 1852. He concluded that without a substantial increase in troops and civil servants, abandonment of the area was the only viable option. In a fit of imperial arrogance, Cathcart decided to humble Moshoeshoe before the British departure. He ordered the Sotho king to pay some Afrikaner farmers compensation for earlier losses of livestock and horses. When Moshoeshoe failed to meet the ultimatum's terms, Cathcart sent in troops. Sotho forces met the advancing British forces at Berea Mountain, and the resulting battle ended in a standoff. The British captured over 4,000 head of cattle, but the Sotho killed 38 British soldiers. Ever the skillful diplomat, Moshoeshoe offered Cathcart a face-saving exit. He asked that Cathcart take the captured livestock as just compensation, and he reaffirmed his allegiance to Queen Victoria. Cathcart withdrew, anxious to get away without further losses. In the long run, Moshoeshoe knew the British were still his best bet. Thus, he fought when attacked but avoided beating the British so badly that they might seek revenge.

The British now abandoned the highveld, leaving the territory's governance to the local White population. Accordingly the British first sent a two-man commission to the Transvaal. The commissioners met with Pretorius and other Transvaal officials on the Sand River in January 1852. In the subsequent Sand River Convention, Britain renounced all territorial claims beyond the Vaal River, effectively granting the Afrikaners there their independence. A decline in missionary and humanitarian influence in Britain in the early 1850s left no one to argue for African rights against Afrikaner aggression. Where British sympathies lay by this time is apparent from that part of the agreement allowing the Transvaalers access to gunpowder through the Cape, but denying such access to Africans.

Another British commission negotiated the Orange River Sovereignty handover. It met strong opposition to British withdrawal from missionaries, loyal Afrikaner farmers, and British traders, merchants, and other professionals. The commissioners eventually found some Afrikaners who agreed to accept responsibility for the sovereignty's governance. They signed the Bloemfontein Convention in February 1854. For the first time the British withdrew from a previously annexed territory. They renounced all authority north of the Orange River and revoked all treaties with African rulers there, other than with Adam Kok. They simply ignored the land disputes between Moshoeshoe, Adam Kok, and the White farmers.

In the Sand River and Bloemfontein Conventions the Afrikaner emigrants realized their long cherished dream—independence. They now controlled two republics, the Orange Free State and the Transvaal. For many years, however, independence was essentially all they had because internal dissensions continued to divide the small community. They left behind established institutions in the Cape but failed for many years to establish new ones in their republics. They were unable to provide the protection and security from African attacks they had demanded from the Cape colonial government. They relied on itinerant traders from the Cape, often English, to provide many of their needs. Most remained simple livestock farmers well into the twentieth century.

THE ORANGE FREE STATE

Free of the British imperial presence, the White settlers between the Vaal and Orange Rivers immediately formed a republican government. They adopted a constitution incorporating aspects of local administration from the Cape, a legislature similar to Natalia's, and human rights provisions from the U.S. Constitution. White men elected the president, the legislative body (the *volksraad*), and the *veldkornets*, whereas the *landdrosts* were government appointees. The two main problems facing the government were (1) extremely fragile loyalties to the republic, and (2) strained relations with the neighboring Sotho kingdom.

Although the Free State White population included English-speaking missionaries, traders, merchants, hunters and artisans, the majority were Afrikaners. Some still dreamed of a single Afrikaner nation to the north and south of the Vaal River. In the first years after Free State independence in 1854, Martinus Wessels Pretorius, Andries's son, made several unsuccessful attempts to overthrow the Free State president and unite the two Afrikaner communities. Despite this shaky beginning, the Orange Free State constitution worked, and a stable (albeit racially segregated) society evolved with its capital at Bloemfontein.

Problems with the Sotho were more serious. The British had left the border problem unresolved, giving rise to continual disagreement and conflict over boundaries and land ownership. Tensions rose as populations grew on both sides. After mediation failed, the Free State declared war on Moshoeshoe's kingdom in 1858 and commandos attacked Thaba Bosiu. They were unable, however, to storm the heights. Meanwhile, mounted Sotho parties raided White settlements deep inside the Free State. The Free State commandos were forced to withdraw, and nothing was settled.

When war broke out again in 1865, Moshoeshoe, who was now nearly eighty years old, appealed for British help. The British took no immediate action but watched as White commandos destroyed Sotho crops and food stores and took Sotho livestock. This new strategy proved so devastatingly effective that it appeared the Sotho kingdom would completely collapse. The British worried that this would cause further problems for the eastern Cape frontier. Just when it seemed all was lost, the Cape governor, Sir Philip Wodehouse, annexed the kingdom in March 1868, with permission from authorities in London and from Moshoeshoe. The "Basutoland" kingdom became a direct British dependency. The Sotho surrendered a large area of rich, fertile land to the Free State in the final agreement but retained enough to survive as a viable state.

Basutoland did not have adequate land, however, to support its growing population, and many Sotho migrated to other parts of South Africa to work for Whites. The country has remained a source of labor for South African farms, mines, and industries to the present day. In 1871 the British persuaded the Cape colony to administer Basutoland, which it did until 1884 when Basutoland returned to British control. It became the independent African state of Lesotho in 1966, finally realizing Moshoeshoe's dream. He died in 1870 and was buried at Thaba Bosiu.

THE SOUTH AFRICAN REPUBLIC

In 1858 citizens of Potchefstroom, Lydenburg, and Soutpansberg adopted a single constitution for the entire Transvaal and formed the new South African Republic (SAR), with its capital at Pretoria. They elected Martinus Pretorius the first president. Most Transvaalers put aside their differences for a while and accepted the new government. Pretorius made one more attempt to unite the two Afrikaner republics in 1860 when he ran for the Orange Free State presidency and won. His independent-minded opponents, however, forced the SAR *volksraad* to demand that Pretorius choose between the two presidencies. He chose the Orange Free State but continued to keep his hand in Republic politics, and it remained divided between his supporters and his opponents. This internal squabbling, even civil war, among the various factions continued throughout the 1860s and 1870s and contributed to Britain's annexation of the Republic in 1877.

By the late 1860s Whites had carved out two British colonies and two Afrikaner republics in southern Africa. Their economies were still based on agriculture, and only the Cape's wool and ostrich feathers were viable exports. Altogether there were only about 250,000 Whites, and they still obtained most of their basic commodities—such as sugar, flour, coffee, clothing, ironware, and firearms—from abroad.

By this period Khoikhoi and Xhosa societies had lost their independence. The other major African societies, however, had endured the *Mfecane* and Afrikaner and British expansion and still challenged White supremacy. All the new areas of White expansion, in Natal and the two Afrikaner republics, were bordered by large, well-organized African communities. The Zulu, the Venda, the Tswana, and the Swazi far outnumbered the Whites and constantly threatened the fragile new White states. One will never know how this all might have turned out, for the discovery of diamonds and then gold changed South African history forever.

6

The British Imperial Age, 1870–1910

THE MINERAL REVOLUTION

For over three hundred years the great powers of Europe had little interest in South Africa except for its strategic value and ability to service their passing fleets. Then, in April 1867, two children playing along the banks of the Orange River found a shiny pebble. That pebble transformed South Africa into one of Britain's most valuable possessions. The pebble was a diamond, the first evidence of a deposit of mineral riches unrivaled anywhere in the world.

More diamond discoveries along the Orange and Vaal Rivers soon attracted over 10,000 diggers from southern Africa, Europe, and the United States. In 1872 the miners moved away from the riverbanks to dig in open farm fields, and their numbers increased to 20,000 Whites and 40,000 Coloureds and Africans. The richest of these farms sites was at Colesberg Kopje (Colesberg Hill), modern Kimberley today. There miners dug the world's largest man-made hole, the "Great Hole" at Kimberley. What they uncovered were ancient diamondiferous lava pipes yielding unparalleled concentrations of gem diamonds.

Problems arose as the number of miners grew and the mining conditions changed. The first miners needed little capital to simply scrape off topsoil and commence digging. But as excavations sank deeper, collapsing walls and seeping water caused frequent delays, additional expenses, and perilous working conditions. The large quantity of diamonds produced, and the unregulated market for their sale, precipitated a dramatic price drop. Making a profit became difficult without investing huge amounts of capital. Steam power, mechanization, underground tunnels, and the amassing of claims by a few individuals replaced individual claim owners working above ground with picks, shovels, wires, and pulleys. Cape officials initially tried to protect the small, independent miners. They also enforced laws guaranteeing Coloured and African claims, which caused bitter resentment among White miners. Some small-scale White miners formed a Defense Association to protest these developments. In June 1875 imperial troops suppressed an open revolt at Kimberley. Soon thereafter officials instituted a color bar to prevent Coloureds and Africans from making claims, and they lifted the limitation on the number of claims an individual might have. Small-scale mining quickly came and went.

Three individuals eventually emerged from the competition for control of the diamond mines: Barney Barnato, Alfred Beit, and Cecil Rhodes. Barnato and Rhodes were rivals who formed large companies by amassing smaller claims. Beit was a German diamond buyer who allied himself with Rhodes and gave Rhodes access to the enormous financial resources of the European Rothschild family. This massive financing gave Rhodes an advantage and forced Barnato to join his holding with Rhodes's in 1888 to form De Beers Consolidated. After this union and the purchase of the remaining diamond-producing companies of any significance, De Beers possessed a near monopoly on diamond production in the region and diamond sales worldwide.

In 1886 Frederick and Henry William Struben discovered gold along the Witwatersrand (White Water Reef) 30 miles south of Pretoria. This crescent-shaped, gold-bearing reef stretched 40 miles east and west along the watershed between the Limpopo and the Orange river systems. The gold deposits were generally of a much lower grade than those in Australia and Canada. Moreover, gold extraction in South Africa was an expensive process in which small flakes of gold had to be separated from crushed rock. The gold reef's southern portion also tilted downward, making these mines some of the world's deepest. What made South African gold mining commercially viable was the immense, unequaled quantity of gold ore. Gold eventually had a far greater impact on South Africa than diamonds did, transforming its economy from agricultural to industrial and its society from rural to urban. Gold also became the underlying cause for war between the British and the two Afrikaner republics, and the eventual unification of the country.

When Rhodes and Beit realized the gold fields' potential value they moved their operations to the Witwatersrand, bought up claims, and created a new company, the Consolidated Gold Fields Limited. By the mid-1890s the Witwatersrand gold fields, or simply the Rand, contained the world's largest mining operations. As in the diamond fields, individual miners could not afford the enormous capital investment necessary to mine far below the surface and to extract gold from ore. The large-scale mining operations required for this were initially funded by capital transfers from the diamond mines, but investments soon flooded in from overseas, as did foreign immigrants. An initial speculative boom saw the creation of over 140 companies, but by century's end a few large holding groups backed by European financiers controlled everything. These groups formed the Johannesburg Chamber of Mines, which regulated such issues as wage levels, job reservations, and labor recruitment. A single giant monopoly company, like De Beers in diamonds, never evolved in the gold industry because the products were marketed differently. Diamonds were sold according to supply and demand. When a monopoly, such as De Beers, kept diamonds off the market, prices rose. Gold prices, on the other hand, were fixed in London, no matter how much gold was available.

Making a profit in the gold mining industry therefore depended entirely on producing gold as cheaply as possible, which, in turn, directly affected labor conditions and race relations on the mines. Given a fixed gold price, labor costs became a critical variable. The Rand adopted the Kimberley color bar, which not only prevented Africans and Coloureds from staking claims but also created a racially divided labor force. Whites took the skilled, supervisory, and other high-paying positions, whereas Africans performed all the unskilled and semi-skilled tasks for low wages. Well-paid Whites moved about freely, lived with their families, and received subsidized housing. Africans came to the mines alone, lived in all-male compounds, and slept in dormitories with dozens of men to a room. They had to carry passes and were closely watched by their supervisors. They could advance only so far before encountering a color bar. White protests led to higher wages, job protection, and better working conditions. African protests were violently crushed.

The discovery of diamonds and gold also created secondary industries, such as railroads, ports, and various public works, to support mining.

The enormous infusion of people and new capital into the country also bolstered economic activity in other areas. Agricultural production, for example, increased to feed the growing immigrant population and provided African farmers with enough income that for a while they could continue to live independently and not work for Whites as wage laborers. But the greatly expanded need for mine, railroad, and farm laborers put even greater strains on the always limited African labor supply. The two Afrikaner republics competed with the Cape and Natal, and the farming sector competed with the mines and railroads for African laborers. Some Whites were opposed to independent African farmers leaving the land and going to work as wage laborers. These included missionaries, White landowners who rented to Africans, merchants who traded with African peasants, and White farmers with African share croppers. The labor shortage soon forced White employers to draw in migrant African workers from areas in South Africa that were not under White control, and from neighboring regions in the area of modern Botswana, Mozambique, and Zimbabwe. A migrant labor system thus developed at an early date, with Africans leaving their families and working as contracted laborers for periods ranging from several months to a year or more.

THE SCRAMBLE FOR SOUTHERN AFRICA

The discovery of South Africa's enormous mineral wealth came just as Europe began its great age of colonization and imperialist acquisitions. European powers scrambled for some of what King Leopold II of Belgium called "that magnificent African cake," and Britain took the biggest slice. In South Africa the British, with some Afrikaner help, conquered one African people after another, culminating in the defeat of the last independent African society, the Venda, in 1897. Britain then conquered the two Afrikaner republics and brought all of South Africa into the empire.

By the 1860s the Xhosa had already lost their independence. The Griqua, on the Cape colony's northern border, lost their independence in the 1870s following a dispute as to what government had jurisdiction over the diamond fields. The Griqua chief, Nicolas Waterboer, Andries's son, claimed the fields and other nearby sites as part of Griqualand West, but the Orange Free State and the Transvaal claimed them as well. An arbitration court awarded the lands to the Griqua in 1871, which greatly angered the Afrikaner republics, particularly when the Cape governor,

Sir Henry Barkly, then declared British authority over all Griqua lands. In 1876 a land court ruled Waterboer's claims invalid, and the Orange Free State and Transvaal renewed their efforts to seize the land. To avoid annexation by the Afrikaner states, Waterboer asked for and received British protection. Britain formally annexed Griqualand West, and all the mineral wealth it contained, to the Cape colony in 1880.

The Zulu Wars

The Zulu possessed the strongest African military force in southern Africa but were troubled by internal factionalism and segmentation of royal families. Despite the *Mfecane*, Shaka's assassination, Blood River, and a subsequent civil war, the Zulu had managed to hold together and maintain their independence under Mpande. A civil war in 1856, however, between two of Mpande's sons, Cetshwayo and Mbulazi, threatened to tear the kingdom apart. In the end, Cetshwayo won and became heir apparent. Because Mpande had never been an effective administrator, Cetshwayo unofficially held much of the power. He became king following his father's death in 1872.

One of Cetshwayo's principal concerns was the encroachment by Afrikaner farmers on Zulu land from the Transvaal. For years Cetshwayo tried to live at peace with his White neighbors, even offering to submit land disputes with the Transvaal Afrikaners to British arbitration courts. John Dunn, an English trader from Natal, advised the king to form an alliance with Natal to block further Afrikaner expansion. Cetshwayo and the Natal secretary of affairs, Theophilus Shepstone, worked out an agreement in which Shepstone officially recognized Cetshwayo as the Zulu king. In return for his counsel, as well as firearms, Cetshwayo made Dunn a Zulu subchief. In the late 1870s, however, as the British attempted to unite all of southern Africa under a British-controlled confederation, both Shepstone and Dunn turned their backs on Cetshwayo. Shepstone convinced the British high commissioner, Sir Bartle Frere, that the Transvaal's territorial claims against the Zulu were legitimate. Frere did not need much persuasion. He believed the Zulu stood in the way of peace and stability in southern Africa. The destruction of their armies would free thousands of Zulu to work for Whites. It would also lessen White anxiety about Zulu attack, lower defense costs, earn Afrikaners' gratitude for land claims settled in their favor, and confer considerable prestige on British rule, thereby enhancing the possibility for confederation.

In December 1878 Frere supported the Transvaal in a land case against Cetshwayo, but an arbitration court found in the king's favor, granting him even more land than he originally claimed. Frere then used a minor border incident as an excuse to issue Cetshwayo an ultimatum. The Zulu king had thirty days to disband his army and permanently abandon the Zulu military system. Cetshwayo offered to settle the matter peacefully, but his overtures were refused. The Anglo-Zulu War began on 11 January 1879 when about 7,000 British regulars, an equal number of conscripted African troops, and some 1,000 colonial volunteers entered Zululand in three separate columns. The invasion began as the Zulu celebrated their First Fruits festival, and Cetshwayo's entire army of about 30,000 men were assembled at Ulundi. The king decided to attack the center column, defeat it, and then ask for peace. So the British would not seek revenge for their defeat, he ordered his forces only to kill soldiers, not civilians, and not to enter Natal.

The British marched into Zululand with the same arrogant sense of racial and military superiority American Colonel George Custer had against the Sioux at Little Big Horn only three years before, and they fell victim to a similar fate. The center column camped the night of 21 January on a hillside called Isandhlwana. Having failed to scout ahead of their line of march or to secure their encampment at night, the 1,600 British soldiers awoke the following morning surrounded by several Zulu regiments. The Zulu attack caught the British unaware, poorly prepared, and badly deployed, and the British were decimated. At Isandlwana the British suffered their worse defeat since the Crimean War. The Zulu inflicted the greatest defeat on an European army by an African force in African history, killing nearly every soldier. They followed their victory at Isandlwana by attacking a British outpost just inside the Natal border at Rorke's Drift, but the small garrison held them off until reinforcements arrived. The devastating defeat at Isandlwana shocked the British public and severely tested the British troops' confidence. Most important, it destroyed Frere's credibility and forced the British to reconsider their southern Africa policy. First, however, they had to finish off the Zulu and salvage British military honor.

When the British became serious about winning the war, their superior military technology and more efficient supply systems gave them the advantage. After reinforcements arrived, the British resumed their march on Ulundi. Cetshwayo repeatedly sued for a negotiated peace, but his offers were ignored. The war culminated in a final battle in July 1879. The British burned Ulundi, the royal homestead, and captured Cetshwayo, exiling him to Cape Town. Having defeated the Zulu army, the British tried to destroy the Zulu nation. They split Zululand into thirteen separate chiefdoms under thirteen appointed chiefs, including the White man John Dunn and descendants of pre-Shakan rulers Zwide and Dingiswayo. They appointed a British judge to settle disputes between the chiefs, who were not to have armies.

Over the next twenty-five years, the Zulu kingdom underwent many changes. The British allowed Cetshwayo to return for a time but with very limited powers. He eventually died under British protection after losing a civil war. His son, Dinuzulu, negotiated land deals with a group of Afrikaners and handed over the northern third of the former kingdom. The British annexed the remainder and imposed a tax on African huts. They arrested Dinuzulu when he tried to resist the tax and exiled him to St. Helena Island. After the British defeated the Afrikaner republics in the early 1900s, they incorporated Zululand into Natal and established a number of Zulu reserves (land reserved for Zulu habitation) equaling about one-third of the former Zulu kingdom. The remainder they opened to White settlement.

The Sotho and the "Gun War"

The British annexed Basutoland and made it a direct British dependency in 1868, two years before Moshoeshoe's death. Letsie (1870–1891) succeeded his father as paramount chief. The Cape colony took control of Basutoland in 1871 and instituted a system of governance by magistrates. In 1878 a Sotho ally, Moorosi, the Phuthi chief, complained that a White magistrate's rulings were threatening his traditional authority. The British told Letsie to handle the problem, and he forced Moorosi to pay a fine. Later that year a new magistrate arrested Moorosi's son on an apparently trumped-up charge and sentenced him to four years of hard labor. When the boy escaped from jail and Moorosi refused to return him, the British sent troops to stanch the rebellious act. Letsie supported the colonial forces, over his senior chiefs' objections, to demonstrate Sotho loyalty. Moorosi took refuge with his armed followers on a fortified mountaintop. He survived a siege from April to November 1879, but a combined colonial and Sotho force finally scaled the summit and killed him, his senior sons, and councilors. The colonial forces cut off Moorosi's head and mutilated his body. The colony took possession of all Phuthi cattle, abolished the Phuthi chiefdom, and distributed individual Phuthi as laborers to Cape farmers.

Moorosi's brave and defiant act might have been nothing more than an isolated incident had it not occurred when it did. In 1878 the British became alarmed that migrant laborers were returning to Basutoland with large numbers of firearms purchased in the diamond fields. The Cape Parliament therefore passed the Peace Preservation Act calling for the disarmament of all Africans falling under the Cape's authority. In October 1879 Cape prime minister Sprigg visited Basutoland to announce the government's intention to disarm the Sotho. Several colonial officials, as well as the French missionaries working among the Sotho, opposed this action. They knew, as did the Sotho, that without weapons to defend themselves, the Sotho would lose all their land to White encroachment. The guns also represented substantial investments in money, and gun possession was a sign of Sotho manhood. To take them away reflected British distrust of Sotho loyalty and rendered the Sotho powerless and dependent. Letsie had sided with the British against Moorosi, hoping his show of loyalty would persuade the colonial officials to allow loyal Sotho to keep their guns. When it did not, Letsie, the French missionaries, and some other Sotho called for obedience to the decree; but Letsie's son, Lerotholi, and Moshoeshoe's son, Masupha, called for resistance—and theirs was the majority opinion. Most Sotho now united to resist the gun prohibition and attacked those Sotho who surrendered their weapons.

The "Gun War" lasted a little over a year, with neither side gaining an advantage. British forces were busy in 1879–1881 with wars against the Zulu and the Afrikaner republics. Guerrilla tactics by the Sotho quickly exhausted the Cape's willingness to fight and to pay for this war, which cost the tiny colony about three million British pounds sterling. When the rebellion spread from Basutoland to the neighboring Thembu and Griqua, the British decided to end the conflict. In April 1881 the British high commissioner, Hercules Robinson, ruled that the Sotho could keep their weapons, provided the guns were registered and the Sotho made reparations payments to the Cape.

The colony's defeat in the "Gun War" brought a change in policy. The Cape no longer looked to administer African societies on its borders. For their part, the Sotho retained possession of their weapons, but the old chief Letsie now ruled over a deeply divided territory in which traditional order had broken down. The kingdom was threatened with anarchy. With the support of most Sotho chiefs, the Cape called on the British government once again to exercise direct administration of Basutoland. The British restored direct rule in 1884, and Basutoland remained a British protectorate in southern Africa until it gained independence in 1966 as Lesotho. Though politically independent, the Sotho remained economically dependent on work in South Africa to the end of the twentieth century.

The Tswana

In the 1880s the British worried that the Transvaal's westward expansion would threaten the economically and strategically important "missionary road," or "Road to the North," running from the Cape to the area of modern Zimbabwe and right through Tswana territory. Missionaries, traders, and merchants traveled north along it to reach Kuruman and beyond, and by century's end it was the primary access route into central Africa. In 1885 the British annexed the Tswana territory south of the Molopo River as the British Bechuanaland crown colony. In 1895 it was transferred to the Cape colony. The southern Tswana rose in rebellion in 1878 and again in 1896–1897 against this seizure of their land, but they were incapable of stopping White expansion. In 1977 the apartheid regime declared parts of it the Bophuthatswana homeland, but after 1994 they were incorporated back into South Africa. The Tswana north of the Molopo fared much better. The British annexed their territory as the Bechuanaland protectorate in 1885. It remained a High Commission territory until gaining independence in 1966 as Botswana. All the Tswana were hurt by the severe rinderpest (a virulent, highly infectious cattle disease) epidemic that struck southern Africa in 1896–1897, killing large numbers of livestock. As a result many Tswana were forced to work in South African mines and for White farmers.

The Pedi and the Swazi

Two African communities east of the Transvaal, the Pedi and the Swazi, experienced very different fates. The Pedi suffered severely during the *Mfecane*. They revived in the 1850s under Sekwati and his son, Sekhukhune I, who succeeded him in 1861. The Pedi settled north of the Zulu, where they faced attacks from Swazi to the southeast and from Afrikaners to the west. Berlin Missionary Society missionaries divided Pedi society as well through their conversions and by allying with Afrikaner farmers against them. Pedi men successfully adapted to the economic opportunities of the 1860s and 1870s, however, by working on White farms and becoming the major labor force in the diamond mines. The Pedi resisted White demands for land, labor, and taxes from Pedi migrants. Transvaal farmers felt threatened by Pedi independence, and White fears led to rumors of a Pedi invasion of the eastern Transvaal. A Transvaal army consisting of 2,000 burghers, 2,400 Swazi warriors, and 600 Transvaal Africans attacked the Pedi in July 1876 but could not defeat them. When the British annexed the Transvaal in the following year, the Pedi remained independent.

After defeating the Zulu in 1879, the British went after the Pedi. They sent an invasion force against the Pedi in November 1879 that included 8,000 Swazi and 3,000 Transvaal Africans. This massive force inflicted a crushing defeat and captured Sekhukhune. The Pedi lost their independence, and over the next two decades the Pedi state collapsed as various rivals fought over the kingship. The Transvaal government expropriated a large area of Pedi land and forced many to work on White farms or on building the Delagoa Bay railway line.

The Swazi emerged from the *Mfecane* as a kingdom of Sotho subjects ruled over by a Nguni aristocracy. In the mid-1800s this ruling elite established a unified nation, complete with an army organized on the Zulu model. Because the Zulu were their major enemy until 1879, the Swazi also maintained good relations with Natal and the Transvaal. After the Anglo-Zulu War, however, White farmers, gold prospectors, and others pressured the Swazi king Mbandzeni and his ministers to sign away various rights in return for gifts. By 1889 the Swazi had handed over nearly their entire kingdom to Whites, including most trading, land, grazing, and mining rights. The South African Republic then seized Swaziland to have an outlet to the Indian Ocean. Swaziland became a Republic protectorate in the mid-1890s but without Swazi consent. The British acquiesced in this seizure but immediately blocked Transvaal's access to the sea by annexing a strip of Indian Ocean coast. Swaziland became a British High Commission territory in 1907, and it gained its independence in 1968.

THE BRITISH AND THE AFRIKANERS

In the 1870s, British officials attempted to unite all of South Africa into a confederation. Lord Carnarvon, the colonial secretary of Disraeli's Conservative government in London, tried in 1875 to arrange a joint meeting of representatives from the Cape, Natal, the Orange Free State, and the Transvaal to discuss confederation. He sought the creation of a White-ruled federal government—somewhat like the British dominion established in Canada in 1867. Carnarvon's efforts, however, met with little success. Official representatives from the Cape, Transvaal, and Natal did not even attend the London meeting, and the Orange Free State president came specifically to oppose confederation. Carnarvon then switched tactics. Whereas Whites in the Cape, Natal, and the Orange Free State all generally opposed British interference in their affairs, Whites in the Transvaal were deeply divided—among the various Afrikaner factions, and between the Afrikaners on one side and the English-speakers and *uitlanders* ("foreigners") on the other. All of them feared attacks from the Zulu and Pedi, and many had a profound dislike for the president, T.F. Burgers. The Pedi defeat of Republican forces in 1876 gave Carnarvon an excuse to annex the Republic. He sent Theophilus Shepstone there in 1877 to accomplish this goal in any way he could. Shepstone succeeded by skillfully playing one faction against another, and the British annexed the Transvaal in April.

Transvaalers initially welcomed British protection, but as the Zulu and Pedi threat diminished after 1879, Transvaal Afrikaners turned against British rule. Mismanagement and arrogance also caused the British to lose whatever support they originally enjoyed. Paul Kruger led Afrikaner resistance to the annexation. A farmer's refusal to pay taxes touched off a war in 1880. Afrikaner commandos soon seized the advantage by blocking reinforcements from reaching besieged British garrisons and by invading Natal. After the Afrikaners destroyed a force of 280 British soldiers at Majuba Hill in February 1881, a new liberal government under Prime Minister William Gladstone agreed to negotiate with Kruger. The Pretoria Convention, signed in August 1881, ended the Anglo-Transvaal War. Kruger was elected the president of the new South African Republic. The British agreed to allow the Afrikaners complete internal independence. Reluctantly, the Afrikaners accepted British control over the Republic's foreign relations and over some rights of Africans.

In 1884 Germany annexed South West Africa (Namibia) and called a conference of European nations in Berlin that same year to establish guidelines for the seizure of African territory, setting off the "Scramble for Africa." The British were concerned the Afrikaner republics would ally themselves with the Germans in South West Africa and block British access to the "Road to the North." Throughout most of the nineteenth century the British had simply reacted to events as they happened in southern Africa without formulating any long-term goals. At century's end, gold, the scramble for colonies, and increasing international challenges to Britain's economic and military power forced it to formulate a colonial policy for southern Africa.

Yet Britain remained reluctant to invest adequate money and manpower to occupy and control South Africa outright. After its confederation scheme failed, the British turned to Cecil Rhodes to represent their interests and promote British imperial policy in southern Africa. Rhodes not only controlled both the diamond and gold industries but also became prime minister of the Cape colony in 1890. He was the quintessential British imperialist, who envisioned a British imperial Africa stretching from the Cape to Cairo. Rhodes's interest in British control of southern Africa was not simply tied to imperialist ambitions, however. He was concerned about his massive investments in the Transvaal gold fields and also about the Germans or Afrikaners blocking his access to greater mineral discoveries in the areas of present-day Zimbabwe, Zambia, and Malawi to the north.

The new spirit of nationalism popular in western Europe in the late nineteenth century also touched the Afrikaners. The Anglo-Transvaal War provoked a wave of pan-Afrikaner nationalism. A Cape Dutch Reformed minister, S.J. du Toit, founded a newspaper, *Die Afrikaanse Patriot*, and wrote a book, *Die geskiendenis van ons land in die taal van ons volk* (The History of our country in the language of our people), which gave expression to this new spirit. Du Toit published these works in Afrikaans, the language of the common people, rather than High Dutch. In them he argued that the Afrikaner *volk* were a unique people, chosen by God to rule over the "heathen" peoples of southern Africa. Du Toit garnered little support for his views at the time, but National Party ideologues adopted his nationalist philosophy in the 1930s and 1940s.

Du Toit also formed a pan-Afrikaner political organization, the Afrikaner Bond, but it received little support in the Transvaal or Orange Free State because Afrikaners there were more interested in independence than unity. An Afrikaner journalist in Cape Town, Jan Hofmeyr, took control of the Bond to advance his own, more pragmatic political ideals. Hofmeyr sought cooperation and compromise between the British and Afrikaners and was willing to work within the colonial system to mold a unified South Africa. He formed a political alliance with Cecil Rhodes and helped Rhodes get elected as prime minister. Hofmeyr supported Rhodes's plans to expand his mining operations north of the Limpopo. In return, Rhodes promised to help Afrikaner farmers and workers, especially the wealthy Cape wine farmers who formed Hofmeyr's power base.

Following the discovery of gold in 1886, the Transvaal became the center of commercial wealth. Thousands of *uitlanders*, or foreigners, flooded into the republic to work in the mining industry. These mostly English-speaking, urban male adventurers from the British Isles, Europe, Australia, and North America outnumbered Afrikaners by the mid-1890s. Paul Kruger and other members of the Transvaal *volksraad* now ruled over a much different country than the Transvaal of only a decade earlier. Kruger had come there as a boy on the Great Trek. Although he was an extremely adept politician, like most Transvaal Afrikaners he was relatively uneducated and held to a strongly conservative form of Calvinist protestantism. And, like most of his supporters, his deepest love was for the land and livestock, not for cities and industry. The Transvaal leaders wanted to assist the mining industry, however, recognizing that gold wealth could ensure their independence. They worried, though, that as the *uitlander* population grew, Afrikaners would lose control. They developed a number of schemes to break their ties with the Cape and Natal, including completing a rail link to Delagoa Bay (Maputo) in 1894. They also sought to profit from the mining industry by granting monopolies to concession companies for the manufacture of dynamite and rail transportation to the coast. Efforts by the Republic to maintain independence, however, frustrated the mine owners, infuriated the *uitlanders*, and gave the British an excuse for war.

The mine owners were unhappy with the high prices the monopolies charged for dynamite and rail transport. They were troubled by the Transvaal's poorly educated, unsophisticated leadership, whose administration of the increasingly modern industrial state was inefficient and bureaucratic. Perhaps most important, they wanted the Afrikaners to do more to assist the recruitment of African miners, to enforce a pass system, and to forbid liquor sales in the mines. Kruger angered the *uitlanders* by raising residency requirements for voting in presidential and *volksraad* elections from five to fourteen years.

During the 1880s and 1890s southern Africa became a great chess board, with the two Afrikaner republics and the British making move and countermove. Britain's annexation of Sotholand and Bechuanaland, as well as their control over Zululand, prevented the republics from expanding into these territories. In 1885, Rhodes's British South Africa Company traveled north of the Limpopo River and occupied a large territory in modern Zimbabwe. When Swaziland became a Transvaal protectorate in 1894, Britain countered by annexing a coastal strip between Zululand and Mozambique in 1895, cutting off the Transvaal's access to the Indian Ocean except through the rail line to Delagoa Bay. The Transvaal also allowed a rail line in from the Cape in 1892 and a

Natal line in 1895. These three lines satisfied the mining industry's need for railroad lines to transport materials in and minerals out. They also forced the Cape and Natal to compete for freight, to the Transvaal's advantage.

When Lord Salisbury's Conservative government replaced the Liberals in the English general election of 1895, it made the Transvaal a top priority. Larger geopolitical issues such as the European scramble for African colonies, Germany's recognition of the Transvaal government, the decline of British industrial might relative to other world powers, and increased jingoism all bolstered Britain's desire to make the Transvaal British. Locally it was Cecil Rhodes, the imperialist, capitalist Cape prime minister, who forced the issue.

In late 1895, with the support of Joseph Chamberlain, British secretary of state for the colonies, Rhodes plotted the overthrow of the Transvaal government. He planned to send an armed force of British South Africa Company police into the republic from Bechuanaland under the command of Dr. Leander Starr Jameson. Meanwhile, the *uitlanders* were to mobilize in the Transvaal. The joint forces would then capture Johannesburg and establish a provisional government. Rhodes realized too late that the plan had little support among the deeply divided *uitlander* community and tried to stop the invasion, but Jameson ignored Rhodes's message. When the expected *uitlander* uprising failed to materialize, Transvaal commandos easily captured Jameson and his five hundred men on 2 January 1896. The Jameson Raid became a political and public relations nightmare for Rhodes and the British.

In London, Chamberlain denied any involvement in the plot but was forced to convene a Committee of Inquiry. At the Cape, Rhodes resigned as prime minister, lost much of his Cape Afrikaner support, and faced questions about his South Africa Company. As the victor in this little affair, Kruger magnanimously commuted the death sentences of the *uitlander* conspirators to £25,000 in fines and sent Jameson and his men back to the Cape. Critical British public opinion of the government soon reversed itself, however, when it was learned that the German kaiser had sent Kruger a congratulatory telegram. Rhodes was once again the imperial hero, his personal reputation restored in England and South Africa. After threatening Chamberlain with disclosures about the secretary's involvement, Rhodes also received assurances of support for his British South Africa Company.

PRELUDE TO WAR

Following the Jameson Raid, Kruger immediately took action to guarantee Transvaal independence and weaken *uitlander* influence. He rearmed the Transvaal forces with modern weapons, mostly imported from Germany. He strengthened the alliance between the Transvaal and the Orange Free State in 1897 by renewing their existing treaty of mutual assistance. Kruger reduced the powers of the judiciary, thereby strengthening the executive and legislative branches. Finally, he placed tighter restrictions on *uitlander* political activities. With his popularity at its zenith, Kruger won a landslide majority in the republic's 1898 presidential election.

Having barely survived the clandestine Jameson affair with his office and government still intact, Chamberlain decided that direct British intervention was necessary to curb Afrikaner influence in South Africa. In mid-1897 he chose Sir Alfred Milner as high commissioner for South Africa. Milner was a dedicated British imperialist who believed the Social Darwinian myths of the age that the "British race" was superior to all others and was destined to rule the world. Milner's racial views led him to think that the members of the "Boer race" must believe they had a similar destiny. He wrongly envisioned them plotting to secure a single Boer nation that brought together the Transvaal, Orange Free State, and the Cape. He arrived in South Africa, therefore, with a deep distrust of all Afrikaners, including the Transvaal reformers and even the Cape Afrikaner loyalists.

Milner initially thought internal opposition within the Transvaal would bring down Kruger's government. Kruger's sweeping election victory in 1898 convinced him, however, that a military confrontation was the only way to preserve and expand the British imperial presence in South Africa. He now found fault with every action taken by Kruger and the *volksraad*. In May 1899 he compared the plight of thousands of British subjects in the Transvaal to that of slaves. He refused any compromise and rejected every concession the republic offered. Meanwhile, the British cabinet prepared for war. It ordered troop reinforcements to South Africa and moved units already there nearer to the Orange Free State and Transvaal borders. The Afrikaner republics realized the British would accept nothing less than the complete surrender of their independence. Hoping to strike at the outnumbered British forces before reinforcements arrived, Kruger issued his own ultimatum. The South

African War began when Kruger's ultimatum expired at 5 P.M. on 11
October 1899.

THE SOUTH AFRICAN WAR

The British called it the Boer (or Anglo-Boer) War, and the Afrikaners
referred to it as the Second War of Freedom (the first being the Anglo-
Transvaal War). The British fought to bring all of South Africa under
imperial rule and to gain total control over South Africa's mineral
wealth. The Afrikaners fought to defend their independence. Initially a
war between Afrikaner and British, all South Africans were eventually
pulled into it, White and Black. It divided families, pitted region against
region, and left a legacy of animosity that continues to the present. It
was an imperialist war but also a civil war. For these reasons, many
historians today call it the South African War.

Kruger's hurried ultimatum gave the Afrikaner forces an early advantage, and they quickly took the offensive. They attacked British positions
in British Bechuanaland and Griqualand West. They invaded Natal, hoping to occupy Durban before British reinforcements could arrive at the
port. They sent commandos into the Cape Midlands, trying to raise popular support among local Afrikaners. They defeated British forces in mid-
December 1899 at Colenso, Stormberg, and Magersfontein, during what
the British later called Black Week. They then laid siege to British garrisons at Kimberley, Mafeking, and Ladysmith. The British had expected
a quick end to Afrikaner resistance, but this rapid succession of Afrikaner
victories forced them to rethink their strategy. Such a challenge to the
British Empire could not be allowed to succeed, no matter the cost.

The Afrikaner forces had a slight numerical advantage in October
1899, but British reinforcements soon arrived and kept arriving until they
outnumbered Afrikaners nearly five to one. The British eventually committed nearly 450,000 troops to the war, drawn from the British Isles,
Canada, Australia, New Zealand, and South Africa. Afrikaner forces,
made up of commando units from the Transvaal and Orange Free State
and volunteers from the Cape, Natal, and overseas, never numbered
more than 90,000. Few were professional soldiers, even among the officers. The Afrikaners had managed to acquire a large arsenal of weapons
and artillery before the war, but the Royal Navy quickly blocked their
supply routes from Europe when war began. Nor did the Afrikaners
receive any significant material assistance from Europe or America, despite widespread public support for their cause. The only true advan-

tages Afrikaners enjoyed over the British were an instinctive knowledge of their home terrain and climate, and their extraordinary riflery and equestrian skills. These won the Afrikaners their initial victories and held the British at bay for two and a half years. However, they were not enough to win the war.

The war's first phase ended in December 1899 when the Afrikaners failed to take advantage of their early successes and became bogged down in sieges. The British forces began the year 1900 with a new commander, Field-marshal Lord Roberts, and a new second-in-command, Lord Kitchener. Under Roberts the British seized the offensive and drove the Afrikaners back on all fronts. They lifted the sieges and then advanced into the Orange Free State and Transvaal, capturing 4,000 Afrikaners at Paardeberg. They occupied Bloemfontein in March, Johannesburg in May, and Pretoria in June. The latter victory forced President Kruger, now age seventy-five, to flee into exile to Europe, where he died in 1904. The British proclaimed British sovereignty over the "Orange River Colony" and the "Transvaal Colony." Roberts returned to England a conquering hero at the end of 1900, convinced he had won the war.

Roberts was wrong. Boer commando units still held the rural areas, and they began an intensive guerrilla war. Highly mobile commandos living off the land blocked rail lines, attacked weary British troop columns, raided supply depots, and always refused to stand and fight as the British preferred. Commandos under Afrikaner generals Jan Smuts, Louis Botha, Christiaan de Wet, and Barry Hertzog rode deep into the Cape and Natal, rallying sympathizers to their cause.

Lord Kitchener responded to this guerrilla warfare in a manner that makes the South African War the twentieth century's first "total war." He ordered his troops to wage war against the entire Afrikaner population, not just its army. They adopted a scorched earth policy, destroying an estimated 30,000 farmsteads, burning the crops and confiscating the livestock. They sent captured commandos into exile and imprisoned White civilian women, children, and the elderly in concentration camps. These were not extermination camps like those of a later war (World War II). Nonetheless, the British were incapable of attending to the simple daily needs of thousands of prisoners. Consequently an estimated 28,000 White prisoners, more than three-fourths of them children, died from amoebic dysentery, measles, and other diseases. More than 105,000 Africans were detained in separate camps, and at least 14,000 of them died. Kitchener also strung 3,700 miles of barbed-wire fences and built

8,000 blockhouses, mostly along railroad lines, to stop commando guerrilla activities. Meanwhile, the British tried to return the occupied republics to some degree of normalcy. They reopened the gold mines. They allowed Afrikaners who surrendered, derisively called joiners or hands-uppers by republican Afrikaners, to return to their farms. About 1,800 hands-uppers joined the British forces as Volunteers and National Scouts. Lord Kitchener's tactics, particularly the camps, stirred a humanitarian outcry in Britain and left a bitter memory in the Afrikaner community.

An initial peace effort failed in February 1901 when Milner refused Afrikaners' demands for continued independence and pardons for Afrikaner forces. The war dragged on for another year. By 1902 only about 22,000 hungry, exhausted, and demoralized Afrikaner soldiers remained in the field. These were the so-called bitter-enders, who despised the hands-uppers and continued to fight on. Most White South Africans recognized the war was over, however, and peace committees began to form. "Stop the war" and "Pro-Boer" movements in Britain reflected an increasing war weariness there as well. Finally, in May 1902, at Vereeniging in the southern Transvaal, commando leaders agreed to Milner's terms. The Treaty of Vereeniging required that the republics surrender their independence. In return, they were promised eventual political autonomy, the right to maintain their language in schools and courts, and massive economic assistance for postwar reconstruction. Afrikaner prisoners-of-war were to be released. Bowing to Afrikaner sensitivities, the British turned their backs on South Africa's African population and left open the African franchise question until the former republics were restored to self-government.

This conflict began as a White man's war. Africans were to sit on the sidelines while Afrikaners and British fought to determine who would rule South Africa. In reality, Africans could not avoid the war. Although they did not fight with Afrikaner commandos, Africans and Coloureds provided support services such as driving wagons, tending horses, and collecting firewood. They also cared for Afrikaner farms while their masters were away. Most Africans and Coloureds, however, supported the British, who used them in the same ways as the Afrikaners but also as scouts, spies, and guards. The British also gave firearms to Africans, for example, to chief Kagama of the Ngwato Tswana. Zulus, Tswana, and others spontaneously took revenge on Afrikaner commandos when opportunities arose. Afrikaner leaders at Vereeniging cited African military activities in support of the British as a primary reason for their ending the war. Africans could properly take credit, therefore, for their contributions to the British war effort and fairly expect their rights and land to be restored following the British victory.

By giving Africans the vote, Milner could have ensured the consolidation of British control over the former Afrikaner republics that he so desired. But giving Africans rights and freedoms was not an option Milner considered. He viewed South Africa as a White man's country and Africans only as cheap labor for White farms and mines. The Afrikaner republics' failure to fully exploit the Black labor supply to the mine owners' satisfaction had been a leading cause for the war. Allowing Africans the franchise would also set a bad precedent for Britain's other colonies in Africa and Asia. Thus, Africans were the real losers in the war. In rural areas the British relocated Afrikaner farmers on their prewar farms, pushing aside Africans who had worked the land during the war. The British also provided White farmers with millions of pounds sterling in financial assistance and set about modernizing agricultural production. Little was done to aid African farmers.

Conditions were worse for urban Africans. After the British occupied Johannesburg, they forced Africans to work on rail lines and roads and tightened the pass laws. When Africans returned to the reopened mines, they found their wages reduced. When they balked at working for such low wages, creating a severe labor shortage, the British imported Chinese mine workers. By 1906 there were approximately 51,000 Chinese working in the mines, together with 18,000 Whites and 94,000 Africans, and South Africa controlled 32 percent of the world's output of gold. The Chinese laborers thus made a significant contribution to the revitalization of the South African mining industry, but they also undercut African leverage and helped to perpetuate a racist system of low wages, job reservations, and limited workers' rights.

POSTWAR RECONSTRUCTION AND CONSOLIDATION

Since the 1870s the British had placed South Africa in the same category as their neo-European colonies of Australia, Canada, and New Zealand, where Whites were in the majority. But South Africa was more like some of Britain's Asian and tropical African colonies, where Europeans represented a small minority of the total population. But neither the Conservative government that Milner served, nor the Liberal government that replaced it in 1906, believed Britain's South African interests could be preserved without White support. Moreover, the war's price in money and lives had exhausted much of the imperial spirit in England. In the

Treaty of Vereeniging the British simply imagined a White-ruled South Africa that would, like Canada or Australia, maintain imperial ties with the mother country, and they ignored the majority Black population. By leaving the question of the political status of Blacks to be decided by White South Africans after they obtained self-rule, the British abandoned their century-long humanitarian effort to control race relations in South Africa. Thus, the Afrikaners lost the war but won in the peace their independence and long-desired right to rule over Blacks as they chose.

Milner's main objective after the war was to unite the two British colonies and the two former Afrikaner republics into a federation within the British Empire. To help him formulate laws and policies that would bring about a reconstructed and unified South Africa, Milner recruited a group of young Oxford University graduates who became known as Milner's "kindergarten." Before returning to England in 1905, Milner established a customs union of all the British colonies in southern Africa. He also united the two railways of the former Afrikaner republics in the Central South African Railways. Most important, Milner appointed the South African Native Affairs Commission (1903–1905) to investigate the treatment and status of African labor prior to the granting of self-government. The Commission was to construct a plan to ensure Blacks were "well-treated" and "justly governed." The Commission's report significantly influenced social policy throughout the twentieth century. Its most consequential proposal was the territorial segregation of Blacks and Whites through the creation of native reserves in the rural areas and separate locations for urban Blacks.

Before returning to England, Milner also made English the primary medium of instruction, with instruction in Dutch limited to a few hours per week, but his attempts to anglicize the Afrikaner population failed. The horrible experiences of the war had only heightened Afrikaner nationalism. The Afrikaners countered Milner's English medium schools by creating private Dutch "Christian National Education" schools. Though not very successful, these Dutch medium schools did promote Afrikaner nationalism and illustrate the Afrikaners' determination to defend their traditions and language. In the Transvaal, former Afrikaner generals Louis Botha and Jan Smuts formed the Het Volk ("The People") Party. In the Orange River Colony, former president Steyn and J.B.M. Hertzog established another Afrikaner political party called the Orangia Unie ("United Orangia"). Afrikaner solidarity was also reestablished between Afrikaners in the former republics and the Cape Afrikaners. By the time Campbell-Bannerman's Liberal Party won the British elections of 1906, Afrikaner leaders were ready for the British to fulfill their pledge of self-government.

The Liberals were prepared to offer self-government but mistakenly misread the electorates in the former republics. In February 1907 the Transvaal received self-government, and the Orange River Colony four months later. To Britain's surprise, Het Volk won in the Transvaal, and the Orangia Unie Party in the Orange River Colony. British miners in the Transvaal had turned their backs on the mining magnates' Progressive Party and voted for the Transvaal National Association, which had ties with Het Volk. Thus, five years after the war's end, the two former republics were again ruled by Afrikaners. John X. Merriman and his anti-imperialist South Africa Party, supported by the Afrikaner Bond, won Cape elections in February 1908. Only Natal remained to wave the British imperial flag.

The formation of these four separate, self-ruled British colonies was not a positive step forward. Rather, it was nearly a step backward to prewar conditions. Milner's Customs Union was collapsing as the different communities quarreled over tariffs. Prewar disputes over railroad traffic to and from the gold mines resurfaced and deeply divided the territories. Questions about international jurisdiction were raised when Mohandas K. Gandhi, a young Indian lawyer, led a nonviolent campaign against efforts by the Natal and Transvaal governments to enforce pass laws and curtail Indian immigration. It took the last armed rebellion organized by a traditional ruler in South Africa, however, for Whites finally to see the value of a political union.

The insurrection was provoked by issues of land, taxes, and labor. Tensions in Natal had increased after the South African War as agriculture became more commercialized and African tenants and squatters were driven off the land. Higher taxes were levied on Africans, including a new poll tax in late 1905 on top of existing hut and dog taxes. Many Africans refused to pay, and scattered acts of violence occurred. The Natal authorities declared martial law and called out the militia after two White policemen were killed in February 1906. When a Zulu chief named Bambatha tried to organize a revolt against the taxes, the Natal militia ambushed and killed him in June. The rebellion then spread to other parts of Natal and lasted into 1907 before the militia ruthlessly suppressed it, killing more than 3,000 Africans while losing only 30 men themselves. A year later Natal officials arrested the Zulu paramount chief, Dinuzulu, and accused him of high treason for instigating the rebellion, although they presented no evidence of his guilt. By 1909 as many as 80 percent of adult Zulu men worked as migrant laborers. For White South Africans, however, the rebellion sounded an alarm: they must unite against the African threat to their dominance.

The four colonies all agreed that some form of centralized federal government was necessary, but for different reasons. Remaining members of Milner's "kindergarten" wished to strengthen Britain's imperial influence in South Africa. Most Afrikaner leaders, on the other hand, wished to weaken it. All parties, however, wanted a central government that would regulate railroad, trade, and tariff issues and legislate country-wide laws guaranteeing White supremacy. An intercolonial conference in May 1908 recommended that a National Convention draft a constitution for a united South Africa.

The four colonies sent thirty White male delegates to the Convention's first meeting in Cape Town in October 1908. The sixteen delegates of British ancestry and fourteen Afrikaners had to find solutions to four important issues: (1) whether to have a unitary or federal form of government, (2) who should have the franchise, (3) how to draw electoral divisions, and (4) the status of the English and Dutch languages. In May 1909 the delegates completed a draft constitution that became the South Africa Bill, which the British Parliament enacted without alteration. The South Africa Act, or Act of Union, received the royal assent in September. It profoundly shaped South African politics and society for the rest of the century.

The constitution provided for a strong central government with the four colonies reduced to provinces possessing local powers only. There was a two-house Parliament, with the upper house, the Senate, having more limited powers than the lower House of Assembly. Executive powers fell to a governor-general representing the British Crown and a cabinet of ten ministers headed by a prime minister and accountable to Parliament. All cabinet ministers were to hold seats in Parliament. The final locations of these various branches of government represented an ungainly compromise following a contentious debate. The Parliament would be in Cape Town; the Executive Branch and Civil Service in Pretoria, a thousand miles away; and the Supreme Court in between at Bloemfontein. There was no Bill of Rights, and any article in the constitution, except for two, could be amended by a simple majority in both houses, thereby negating the judiciary's power. (This winner-take-all system of law making, in which the majority's power goes unchecked, allowed the National Party to implement the racist apartheid system with almost a free hand after 1948.)

The Convention delegates settled the franchise issue fairly easily. Before the war, Africans, Indians, and Coloureds could not vote in the Transvaal and Orange Free State, and only a few could vote in Natal. The Cape allowed all adult men, regardless of race, to vote and hold office provided they could pass property or earnings tests. It was clear that Natal, the Transvaal, and the Orange Free State would not support any Black enfranchisement and the Cape would not abandon Black voting rights. The delegates reached a compromise whereby each province retained its existing franchise laws, but only Whites could hold seats in the Union Parliament. Cape liberals and African, Indian, and Coloured political organizations protested vehemently against this arrangement. To blunt this criticism, the delegates agreed to an "entrenched clause" in the constitution requiring a two-thirds majority of both houses sitting together to reduce or remove the existing Cape franchise for Blacks. Despite this entrenched clause, the constitution gave the Union's White minority an almost total monopoly of political power and nearly eliminated effective representation for Africans, Coloureds, and Indians. A second entrenched clause requiring a similar two-thirds majority settled the Dutch and English language issue by giving them equal status throughout the Union.

Regarding the question of electoral divisions, the delegates decided that for seats in Parliament's lower house, each constituency would have the same number of voters. These would be determined by dividing the number of seats allotted to each province by the number of its voters. A judicial commission, however, could vary that number for individual seats by 15 percent in either direction according to a list of factors that included "sparsity or density of population." As it turned out, this weighting of constituencies favored thinly populated rural areas, for the commissions consistently allowed them to have fewer voters than the provincial norms, and the densely populated urban areas needed more. This gave a significant advantage to Afrikaner political parties, which received a much larger share of the rural White vote. (Weighting became a decisive factor in the crucial election of 1948.)

On 31 May 1910, Louis Botha, former general in the Republican military forces, became the first prime minister of the Union of South Africa, eight years to the day after surrendering to the British. Afrikaners now held political power, not just in the former republics but over the entire country. Although South Africa was nominally a British dominion, British influence had been significantly reduced. Black South Africans were left with no political power and were subject to racist discrimination and economic exploitation by a privileged White minority.

7

White Union and Black Segregation: Preparing for Apartheid, 1910–1948

The 1910 Act of Union created a single nation with a population of 1,275,000 Whites, 150,000 Indians, 500,000 Coloureds, and 4 million Africans. Only White South Africans, however, were truly citizens. Asians, Coloureds, and especially Africans might as well have lived in another world. In many ways, they did. Over the next forty years successive white governments passed laws creating a segregated society, preparing the way for the harsher apartheid system that followed.

During the same forty years the South African economy prospered, driven by the enormous wealth produced by the gold mining industry. English-speakers initially benefited the most from this prosperity, as they dominated the commercial and financial sectors and the professions. The majority of Afrikaners still farmed, although in the early 1900s many lost their land to commercial agricultural interests. Refusing to do common farm labor, menial "kaffir work" as they termed it, they became impoverished "poor Whites" instead. Forced to the cities, they formed a largely unskilled and poorly educated labor pool that competed with Blacks for jobs. The government could not ignore Afrikaner votes, however, for they made up more than 55 percent of the electorate. Job reservations, artificial wage levels, government subsidies and loans, and economic growth caused White poverty to diminish over the next four decades, but always at Black expense.

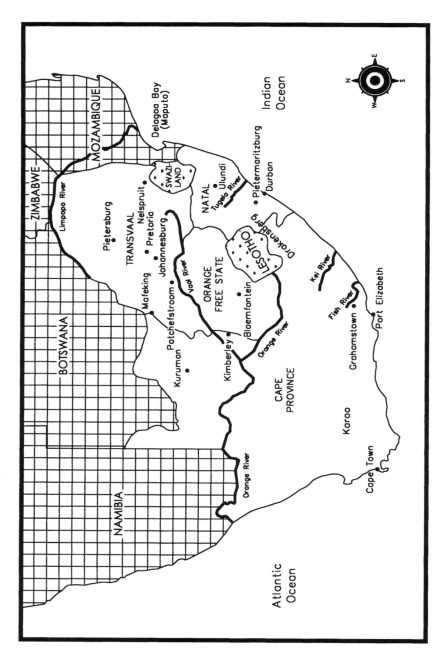

South African Provinces, 1910–1994

THE NEW UNION, 1910–1939

The South African Party led by former Republican generals Louis Botha and Jan Smuts won the 1910 general elections. On 31 May Botha, a prosperous farmer, became prime minister, with the Cambridge-educated Smuts as his deputy. The South African Party was a coalition of the Het Volk and Nationalist parties of the Transvaal, the Orangia Unie Party of the Orange Free State, and the South African Party in the Cape. It represented a wide range of English and Afrikaner interests. The Unionist Party, dominated by wealthy mining magnates and capitalists, generally supported South African Party policies. A small Labour Party represented White workers.

The new Union government faced four major challenges. First, it had to decide whether to remain a British dominion or become a republic. Second, it had to placate White laborers—who constantly demanded greater job security, higher wages, and privileged positions—without alienating White mine and land owners and impeding their access to cheap Black labor. Third, it had to settle the "race question," which for South African politicians meant resolving the differences between Afrikaners and English-speakers. Fourth, it had to address the "native problem," which meant determining what role Blacks had in a White South Africa. South Africa's leaders did not resolve the first of these issues until 1961, when then–prime minister Verwoerd declared the country a republic. The leaders' responses to the other three issues nearly destroyed the nation and made it a pariah state for much of the twentieth century.

Dominion or Republic?

Botha and Smuts supported South Africa's dominion status within the British Empire; although like the Australians, New Zealanders, and Canadians, they sought greater autonomy. Their efforts were frustrated, however, by opposition from a republican element within their own party and by the events of World War I. The Orange Free State leader, J.B.M. Hertzog, joined Botha's cabinet in 1910 as minister of justice and represented Afrikaners who wanted a South African republic. In a 1912 speech, Hertzog demanded complete South African independence and declared that South Africa should be ruled by "true Afrikaners." Despite later assurances that "true Afrikaners" included English-speakers loyal to South Africa, his words disturbed the English community and caused Botha great embarrassment. Botha called for Hertzog's resignation from the cabinet, but he refused. Botha himself then resigned and, when asked, formed a new government without Hertzog.

Hertzog and his followers responded by organizing the National Party in 1914. Their support came from lower-class Afrikaners, especially the poorer farmers who were losing their land to commercial agriculture and being forced into the cities. The National Party also had the backing of the small class of Afrikaner intellectuals and professionals who resented English dominance in business, government, and the professions. Hertzog's appeal to Afrikaner nationalists, however, was damaged when he included loyal English-speakers in his description of true South Africans. And Hertzog's National Party and Botha's South African Party still agreed on the critical issue of White dominance over the Black population. They might have found common ground again, but World War I intervened.

South Africa's dominion status within the British Empire gave it autonomy over internal affairs, but the British still managed external matters, and the King made decisions about war and peace. In 1911 Botha attended an Imperial Conference in London to discuss this arrangement. He returned with the signed Union Defence Act of 1912, which allowed South Africa an entirely autonomous defense force. Dominion governments could also send representatives to the Imperial War Cabinet. Nonetheless, they had no say in the king's decision to declare war on Germany in August 1914.

Many Afrikaner nationalists welcomed the war because they hoped to restore their independence while the British were distracted in Europe. They were upset when South Africa entered the war as a British ally. They rebelled when Botha ordered South African forces to attack the German protectorate of South West Africa (modern Namibia). Several former republican military leaders, many of whom now served as officers in the South African forces, formed commandos against the government. Some went over to the German side with the troops under their command. When Botha's former comrades-in-arms refused to surrender, he turned against them with force and quickly put down the rebellion. More seeds were sown for Afrikaner nationalism, however, as Afrikaners who died were linked as martyrs with those heroes of the South African War of only a few years earlier. A voluntary organization, Helpmekaar (Help One Another), was also born during the rebellion to cover the rebels' legal expenses. Surplus monies helped fund the first Afrikaner finance company, the South African National Trust and Assurance Company (SANTAM). The first Nationalist newspaper, *De Burger*, went to press in 1916.

Having suppressed the rebellion, Botha completed the conquest of South West Africa by 15 July, 1915. South African troops then played an important role in the East African campaign, where Smuts commanded all the British imperial forces. South African forces, including Coloureds and Africans, eventually served in Egypt and then went to Europe in 1916. The South African brigade lost large numbers of men at the Battle of the Somme and Delville Wood. The brigade was nearly wiped out and forced to surrender in the German offensive of March 1918. Although they were not allowed to carry firearms and were limited to noncombatant roles, Coloured and African troops also played a vital role in the war, often under very dangerous conditions.

After his East Africa successes, Smuts served in the Imperial War Cabinet and then in the British War Cabinet. At the Versailles Peace Conference he proposed a mandate system to administer colonies taken from Germany and its allies. In an odd twist, he asked that African territories not be included under this system and that South Africa be allowed to annex South West Africa outright. The peace conference delegates denied his request but did mandate German South West Africa to South Africa. Smuts returned home an important figure on the international scene, but Afrikaner nationalists viewed him as a traitor.

When Botha died in 1919, Smuts inherited leadership of the South African Party. He retained control of the government following the 1920 general election with the support of Unionists and Independents. Hertzog's National Party made significant gains, picking up three more seats than the South African Party did. Smuts's harsh suppression of White labor unrest in the early 1920s lost him more support. Hertzog's Nationalists joined with the Labour Party to win the 1924 general election.

As prime minister, Hertzog worked to obtain political independence for South Africa. A step in this direction occurred in 1926 when an imperial conference of prime ministers from Great Britain and the self-governing British dominions drafted the Balfour Declaration. This document stated that Great Britain and the dominions were each "autonomous communities within the empire, equal in status . . . though united by a common allegiance to the Crown." The British Parliament gave approval to this declaration in 1931 by passing the Statute of Westminster. South Africa, Australia, and Canada had already appointed diplomats to major foreign countries by that time, however, and were acting independently in international matters. Following his return from the imperial conference in 1926, Hertzog pressed for the Union Jack to be replaced by a flag symbolizing South Africa's new independence. After two years of long and bitter debate, the Parliament adopted a new national flag incorporating a miniature Union Jack and the flags of the former Afrikaner republics in the center.

Despite these significant gains in autonomy, Afrikaner nationalists wanted nothing less than withdrawal from the empire and total independence as a republic. They viewed Hertzog's support for the Balfour Declaration and the Statute of Westminster as a betrayal. Successive governments after 1931 continued to push for greater national autonomy. The Status of Union Act (1934) stated that the South African Parliament had to approve any acts of the British Parliament before they became valid in South Africa. This act generally resolved the issue of South Africa's autonomy within the empire until 1939. The outbreak of World War II again raised the question of South African independence and allegiance to the British Crown.

White Labor and Black Labor, 1910–1939

Botha and Smuts realized that South Africa's economic prosperity lay in the wealth produced by the gold mines. The mine owners argued that successful mining operations depended on cheap labor—and that meant Black workers. Botha had suppressed a strike in the Transvaal in 1907 by White gold mine workers who were protesting plans to reduce wages and increase the number of Chinese and African laborers. The Whites' anger continued to simmer and then boiled over again soon after Union. In May 1913 White workers, unhappy with working conditions on the mines and fearing Black competition, struck for the right to establish trade unions and to enhance their privileged positions in the mines. As South Africa had no national security force at the time, British imperial troops were sent to Johannesburg to maintain the peace. Botha and Smuts arrived there in July and promised improved conditions for White miners, but later that year the Parliament voted down legislation to make these improvements and recognize trade unions.

When White railway and harbor employees learned of a threatened layoff in early January 1914, they touched off another strike that spread to the gold mines and soon became a national strike. This time Smuts was prepared: He deployed 10,000 troops of the year-old Active Citizen Force to suppress the strike. He proclaimed martial law and aimed cannons at the Trades Hall in Johannesburg, the strike's command center. The strike collapsed, and many strikers and their leaders were arrested. Smuts had nine strike leaders deported. On Smuts's recommendation, Parliament passed a Riotous Assemblies Bill that significantly increased police powers and the government's ability to prohibit public meetings. The 1913 and 1914 strike actions might have led to further confrontations and political and economic repercussions had World War I not overtaken these events.

The war years from 1914 to 1918 witnessed a soaring rate of inflation while gold prices remained low and production costs rose. The mine owners responded by calling for an end to the color bar, which would allow them to replace highly paid, semi-skilled White workers with Blacks. They wanted the wage bar to remain, however, to guarantee Blacks would receive a lower wage than Whites for the same job. The wage gap between Whites and Blacks grew during the war, mostly as a result of a 40 percent increase in White wages. Blacks made only a penny more in 1919 than in 1912. By the end of the war, Black and White workers alike were ready to take action.

Black municipal workers went on strike in May 1918 for a wage increase, an action that soon led to a general strike. Intermittent Black work actions continued over the next two years, with government and employers making many promises but few significant changes. Growing increasingly bitter and unable to survive on their meager wages, 71,000 African mine workers struck in February 1920 for an across-the-board wage increase. The strike affected twenty-one of thirty-five mines. When the Chamber of Mines argued that such a large increase in wages paid would destroy the gold mining industry, the government sent in troops. Strike leaders were arrested, mine compounds were sealed off, and miners were threatened with arrest if they did not return to work. The government soon put down the strike.

Although White miners had enjoyed a substantial wage increase during the war years, they still feared competition from Black miners. While many White miners were performing military duty, Afrikaner migrants came in from rural areas to take over semi-skilled and supervisory positions. Substantial numbers of African and Coloured laborers also filled some semi-skilled jobs normally held by Whites and many newly created positions not falling under the job reservations legislation. At war's end, White miners pressed for a return to the prewar arrangement. Mine owners insisted, however, on a status quo agreement whereby Blacks holding semi-skilled jobs would retain their positions but no more "White" jobs would go to Africans or Coloureds. White workers agreed to the mine owners' proposal in September 1918.

A precipitous drop in gold prices, a rise in costs for goods and materials, and increasingly higher White wages brought mine owners and White workers into conflict once again in January 1922. Mine owners wanted to use more cheap Black labor in semi-skilled positions and cut back on expensive White supervisory positions. When the Chamber of Mines announced its intent to renege on the September 1918 agreement, White workers launched a strike that soon became a revolution. The National and Labor parties urged the strikers on. Some strikers marched under a communist banner carrying a uniquely South African twist: "Workers of the World Fight and Unite for a White South Africa." Many Afrikaner workers viewed this as a fight for Afrikaner independence. The more militant among them formed commandos and led the revolt. By early February workers had seized control of much of the Rand and called for the overthrow of the state. Smuts tried to maintain an air of neutrality, recognizing that the nation's economic health depended on mining profits, but also not wanting to alienate the White workers. When faced with armed resurrection, however, Smuts had to protect the nation. He declared martial law; took personal command of more than 20,000 troops along with tanks, airplanes, field artillery, and machine guns; and put an end to the strike after a few days of bitter fighting in mid-March.

In the peace that followed, White miners were forced to accept the mine owners' terms, including a partial lifting of the color bar (but not the wage bar) for Black workers and the retrenchment of 2,000 White jobs. The 1922 strike was the high point of militant White action against the mines. White workers now turned to the political arena to press their demands. Smuts and his South African Party lost the confidence of White miners and Afrikaner workers and farmers. An alliance of Hertzog's National Party and the Labour Party won the 1924 general election. Hertzog also won the infamous "Black Peril" election of 1929 when he made race and the preservation of a White South Africa the main campaign issues.

Following his 1924 election victory, Hertzog set about to improve the economic and political power of the White population, particularly that of Afrikaners. To assist his Afrikaner farmer constituency Hertzog made more credit available through the Land Bank, instituted market controls, and established price supports for farm produce. To advance industrial development he established a government-owned Iron and Steel Corporation (ISCOR) in 1928 to manufacture steel, and he implemented protective tariffs for secondary industries. He also expanded White job opportunities by encouraging a state-supported "civilized labor" policy that would guarantee work for poor white workers at the expense of African laborers. Railroads and other state-controlled enterprises replaced Black workers with Whites, and private industry was also encouraged to hire more Whites. A Mine and Works Amendment Act (1926) guaranteed the reservation of skilled jobs for White miners.

The worldwide Great Depression that began in October 1929 caused a dramatic downturn in the South African economy. Exports plummeted and import prices fell as Hertzog tried to maintain the gold standard while other countries abandoned it. Prices for South African goods rose as Britain, Australia, and others devalued their currencies. When South Africa finally abandoned the gold standard in December 1932 serious damage had already been done. Profits for South Africa's two major exports, minerals and wool, had been slashed. Farmers were especially hard hit, and many left the land.

The economic state of both rural and urban Afrikaners had been deteriorating since the late 1800s, but the Depression worsened their plight. The Carnegie Commission Report, issued in 1932, documented the desperate lives of thousands of "poor Whites," most of them Afrikaners. The report identified over 300,000 Whites, out of a total White population of roughly 1.8 million, as "paupers." Part of Hertzog's economic agenda focused on improving the lives of poor Whites. Neither the Commission nor the government took much notice of the Black population, most of whom were just as poverty stricken and desperate as poor Whites, if not more so. Indeed, government policies such as job reservations, wage bars, social welfare programs, and credit loans that gave preferences to Whites only made Black South Africans' lives more wretched.

When the government abandoned the gold standard in December 1932, gold prices rose and gold mines returned to profitability. The country began a phase of tremendous economic growth that left it nearly self-sufficient by 1948. Yet the Depression and the government's unwillingness to abandon the gold standard undermined Hertzog's support, and his government fell from favor. Hertzog and Smuts formed a coalition government that won a landslide victory in the 1933 general election. In December 1934 the National Party and South African Party merged to form the United Party. Other political realignments also occurred. The most important was the formation of the Purified National Party by a breakaway nationalist faction of Hertzog's National Party led by a Dutch Reformed minister and newspaper editor, D.F. Malan.

The "Race Question" English-Afrikaner Relations, 1910–1939

One might logically think that a "race question" in South Africa would refer to relations between Blacks and Whites. Logic has seldom applied to questions about race in South Africa, however; here the term referred to the English and the Afrikaners. These two peoples had been at odds since the early 1800s. At the time of Union moderate Afrikaners must have believed their prayers had finally been answered. Yet many nationalist Afrikaners wanted independence. Soon after World War I a group of young Afrikaners, mostly white-collar workers, teachers, and clergy, formed a new Afrikaner nationalist organization initially called Jong Suid-Afrika (Young South Africa), later changed to Afrikaner Broederbond (Afrikaner Brotherhood). Dismayed at English dominance of the South African economy and society, the organization began with the simple goal of preserving the Afrikaner language and culture. Soon, however, this modest group became a secret society using the Federasie van Afrikaanse Kultuurverenigings (FAK, or Federation of Afrikaner Cultural Organizations), formed in 1929, as its public front organization.

The Broederbond, together with the Helpmekaar movement, the Afrikaans language newspaper *De Burger*, the insurance and investments firms SANTAM and SANLAM (South African National Life Assurance Company) and a Volksbank (People's Bank), were all established during the war years or immediately thereafter. They prepared the way for an Afrikaner revival. An important step in this revival occurred in 1925 when Hertzog pushed through a constitutional amendment making Afrikaans the official language in place of Dutch. In the Act of Union both English and Dutch had equal status as official languages. By the mid-1920s, however, Afrikaners not only spoke Afrikaans, a language developed from Dutch, but they had a dictionary, a significant body of literature, and a Bible in Afrikaans.

Afrikaner nationalism reached a fever pitch in the 1930s, much of it under Broederbond direction. The efforts of this secret group of Afrikaner elite to foster Afrikaner society, under cover of the FAK, often resulted in further isolation and separation from the English community. As an alternative to Lord Baden-Powell's Boy Scouts, the Broederbond established the Voortrekkers for Afrikaner youth. In 1933 Afrikaner students broke away from the National Union of South African Students over the issue of African membership and formed the Afrikaanse Nasionale Studentebond (Afrikaner National Student Union). A "Buy Afrikaans" movement began as Afrikaner-owned chain stores spread across the country. By 1937 the FAK included around three hundred Afrikaner cultural groups. It coordinated radio programs, Afrikaans art and book exhibits, and "Culture Days" promoting Afrikaner culture and the Afrikaans language. Large-scale *volkskongresse*, or folk congresses, were held to discuss such issues as poor whiteism.

When Hertzog and Smuts merged their two parties in 1934, Afrikaner nationalists felt betrayed and joined D.F. Malan's new Purified National Party. Malan's support came mostly from the Cape, where there existed a strong Afrikaner nationalist press and where he could count on financial aid from wealthy wine farmers and the SANTAM and SANLAM finance and insurance companies. He enjoyed little support in the Orange Free State or Transvaal, except from the Broederbond.

The Broederbond leadership consisted primarily of Afrikaner theologians, academics, and businessmen. They introduced a strongly religious element into the organization's ideology, based on the Calvinist doctrines of the Dutch Reformed Church. They created what is sometimes referred to as an Afrikaner "civil religion," which claimed that God intended for each nation to develop separately. According to this view the nation, not the individual or family, would develop its own unique moral and cultural values; moreover, God had specifically created the Afrikaner nation as His chosen people to fulfill a divine destiny in southern Africa. To validate their claim to this divine role, the Broederbond leadership enhanced Afrikaner history to mythological proportions. It became the saga of a people who had established a civilization where only barbarism and paganism existed before, then fled from English oppression on the Great Trek and began life again in a new wilderness of heathenism. The Great Trek became the defining moment in Afrikaner history, an exodus rivaling that of the Israelites under Moses leaving Egypt. Afrikaner writers and scholars recounted *voortrekker* lives like the worshipful biographies of saints and offered them as models for emulation. The *voortrekker* victory at Blood River was a sign of God's divine favor; the Day of the Convenant became the Afrikaner holy day. Victims of British imperialism and African savagery—such as the men hanged at Slagtersnek and Piet Retief, and the dead in British concentration camps—became martyrs in the Afrikaner pantheon. Ironically, those Cape Afrikaners who made up Malan's power base were not *voortrekker* descendants. But nationalist fervor swept such minor details aside. This ideology, developed in the 1930s, of Afrikaner nationalism and separate development formed the theoretical basis for apartheid.

Although religion and the idea of a unique *volk,* or people, were key elements in Afrikaner nationalism, economic considerations were also important. Afrikaners always resented the English monopoly of finance and capitalist enterprises in South Africa. Initial ventures, such as SAN-TAM and SANLAM, which had drawn start-up capital from voluntary contributions, now served as models for other capitalist undertakings, such as banks and financial houses. By promoting Afrikaans, by recalling Afrikaner history, by resurrecting Afrikaner art, literature, songs, and culture, Afrikaner leaders made a highly charged appeal to the *volk.* It was hoped that a unified Afrikaner community would put the *volk* first and save, buy, and invest in Afrikanerdom, thereby creating jobs and breaking the English business monopoly. In what must have seemed sheer pipedreams at the time, Afrikaners believed they would eventually take control of the state and channel the nation's resources through these Afrikaner enterprises, thereby solidifying their hold on both economic and political power. When Malan and his Purified National Party won the 1948 election, these dreams became reality.

The most visible expression of all these efforts was the ox-wagon trek in 1938, the centenary of the *voortrekkers'* victory over the Zulu at Blood River. Organized by the Broederbond, the FAK, and Malan's Purified National Party, this symbolic re-creation of the Great Trek produced an outpouring of Afrikaner nationalism. A carefully orchestrated procession of covered ox-wagons, accompanied by men and women in period cos- tumes, traveled from all parts of the country to either a memorial site near Pretoria or to the Blood River battlefield. In a torchlit ceremony on a hill outside Pretoria, the celebrants dedicated a huge monument with accompanying speeches glorifying the earlier pioneers' heroism and reli- gious conviction. At Blood River, Malan invoked the memory of the *voor- trekkers'* fight against the African, summoning modern-day Afrikaners to "make South Africa a White man's land."

The centennial events raised Afrikaner nationalist spirit to a fever pitch. Certain extreme elements in the Afrikaner community took advan- tage of these emotions to form a paramilitary organization called the Ossewabrandwag, (Ox-Wagon Sentinel). Founded initially to promote Afrikaner nationalism and culture, it assumed a pro-Nazi, paramilitary character when World War II began. On a more constructive note, the FAK organized an Ekonomiese Volkskongres (Economic Peoples' Con- gress) in 1939, which led to the establishment of an Ekonomiese Instituut (Economic Institute). This institute initiated various projects, such as trade schools, worker insurance plans, and a *reddingsdaadbond* (salvation-deed fund, or Rescue League), that made use of voluntary contributions to provide relief for poor Afrikaners and investment capital for Afrikaner businesses.

In 1910 it seemed that English-speakers and Afrikaners might put aside their differences and come together in a spirit of mutual White cooperation. In succeeding decades, however, ever more extreme Afrikaner nationalists assumed leadership over the Afrikaner community. These "bitter-enders" sought to regain the independence Afrikaners had lost in the South African War, and they had no desire to share economic and political power with English-speakers.

White Rule and Black Response, 1910–1939

Between 1910 and 1924, Botha and Smuts instituted racial segregation through a series of laws known as the "bedrock legislation." The Mines and Works Act (1911) established a nationwide system of White job reservations in mines and on the railroads. The Defense Act (1911) established a White Active Citizen Force. The Native Affairs Act (1920) created a separate and segregated administrative and legal system for the reserves. One of the most important pieces of South African legislation of the twentieth century was the Natives' Land Act (1913). It limited African landownership rights to African reserves constituting around 22 million acres, or about 7 percent of the Union's total land area. A later law, the Natives' Trust and Land Act (1936), extended that total to 13.5 percent of the land for use as African reserves, located primarily in the country's eastern half. White farmers or the mines had already occupied much of the best land in these reserves, however. The Transkei was the only substantial land area set aside for Africans. The carrying capacity of these small bits of land came under increasing stress as local African and livestock populations multiplied and thousands more were relocated from so-called White areas. A controversial point in the passage of the 1913 Natives' Land Act was the question of how Africans could maintain their entrenched franchise right in the Cape province if they could not own land. It took court action to prevent the act from being applied to the Cape.

Just as the 1913 Land Act limited Black access to land in the nation as a whole, the 1923 Natives (Urban Areas) Act limited Black access to White urban areas. It set forth the principle that urban areas were solely the White man's preserve and that the Black man was there only as a unit of labor. Local authorities were to situate African locations (or townships) separate from, but near to, White urban areas. Any African not living in a location had to be provided with housing by his or her employer. When an African's labor was no longer needed in the urban area, he or she could be deported to the reserves. This so-called influx control—that is, control over the entering and leaving of urban areas by Blacks—was to be managed through tougher, and stricter enforcement of, pass laws.

Two other major pieces of segregationist legislation passed by later governments were the Native Administration Act (1927) and the Native Representation Act (1936). The Native Administration Act gave the government unlimited authority over all Africans outside the Cape province without its having to consult with Parliament. The British governor-general in South Africa became in effect the Paramount Chief of All Africans, thereby gaining, among other powers, the right to appoint chiefs and headmen, relocate "tribes," and set "tribal" boundaries. The Native Representation Act removed Cape province Africans from the ordinary voters' rolls, a right they had held in the Cape since 1854. Instead, they could now elect Whites to represent them in the House of Assembly and the Senate. This act also established a purely advisory Natives Representative Council.

Black populations were bitterly disappointed by these laws and governmental actions. Mohandas Gandhi organized the small Indian community of roughly 200,000 in responding to the legislation. In 1910 most Indians were the free descendants of indentured laborers; they practiced the Hindu religion and lived in Natal and the southern Transvaal. There was also a significant class of mostly Muslim merchants, some quite wealthy. Gandhi had led a protest over Indian voting rights in Natal a year after his arrival in South Africa in 1893. He remained a major voice in South African Indian politics for the next twenty-one years, sometimes in cooperation with the Natal Indian Congress that was formed in 1894. In the Transvaal in 1907, Gandhi had his first confrontation with Smuts over the institution of pass laws and fingerprinting of Indians. The outcome was inconclusive, but it did test Gandhi's famous *Satyagraha* ("truth force") campaign of active, nonviolent resistance. In 1913 Gandhi again challenged Smuts, who also served as government interior minister, over a tax on formerly indentured men, women, and children. Gandhi's protest quickly spread across Natal and into the Transvaal. Smuts finally scrapped the tax and Gandhi returned to India in 1914 to challenge the British Empire there. Gandhi's movement, limited to the improvement of Indian rights and lives, won only minor victories for the South African

Indian community, however. The South African Indian Congress (SAIC, founded in 1923) carried on after Gandhi's departure, trying to advance Indian civil and human rights, but it had little contact with African or Coloured communities.

The Coloured community in 1910 was an ethnically, culturally, and economically diverse population of about 500,000, mainly living in the Cape province. Most Coloureds were desperately poor and illiterate. Because much of the nation's industry was in the north, Coloured labor remained concentrated on farms or at menial urban jobs. Abdullah Abdurahman, a Scottish-trained medical doctor, and his African Political Organization (later the African People's Organization, or APO) represented the Coloured community. Abdurahman became president of the fledgling APO in 1905 and soon fashioned it into the most powerful Black political force in the country, with about 20,000 members. Coloureds were most concerned about the civil and franchise rights they enjoyed in the Cape. Legal discrimination was forbidden there before Union, but after Union the discrimination against Coloureds and Africans increased in the Transvaal and Orange Free State and Cape Coloureds worried it would spread to the Cape. As APO president until his death in 1940, Abdurahman made great strides in bringing Coloureds and Africans together to fight for equal rights. Many Coloureds felt a closer affinity to Whites than to Africans, however, and continued into the late 1990s to hold prejudices against Africans and to remain fearful of majority African rule.

Africans numbered about four million in 1910, most still living a rural existence but with increasingly large numbers migrating to urban areas for jobs. John Tengo Jabavu and John L. Dube first gave voice to African political concerns in the late 1800s by publishing African newspapers in the Cape and Natal, respectively. Jabavu, Abdurahman, and other Black leaders led a futile mission to London in 1909 to protest the racist provisions of the South Africa Act. In 1912 a group of politically conscious, Western-educated Africans formed the first nationwide African nationalist movement, the South African Native National Congress (later the African National Congress, or ANC). Most of the founders received their early educations at mission schools, with some going to college in Europe or the United States or, after 1915, to the South African Native College at Fort Hare in the eastern Cape. The ideas of African American leaders such as Booker T. Washington and W.E.B. Du Bois significantly influenced their thinking. Their political base was in the Cape, where, as "civilized Africans," they had a limited franchise.

Pixley ka Izaka Seme, a Zulu lawyer, was the initial force behind the ANC's formation. Seme attended a Natal mission school, received a B.A. degree at Columbia University in the United States, then studied law at Oxford and was called to the Bar in London in 1910. In January 1912, Seme organized a conference at Bloemfontein to found a Native Congress to defend African rights. In his address to the assembled African elite, dressed in their suits, frock coats, and top hats, Seme charged that the new Union government intended to make Africans hewers of wood and drawers of water. The Union of South Africa was a White creation, he noted, in which Africans had no political voice.

The Congress elected John Dube, a Natal minister and schoolmaster, as its first president. Dube had studied in the United States and was strongly influenced by the African American educator Booker T. Washington, particularly Washington's concept of individual advancement through education. The Congress's Constitution called for the removal of the color bar and the establishment of African representation on public legislative bodies. Mutual help and the discouragement of tribalism and tribal feuds were also cited. The delegates were products of their Western educations and, like Abdurahman, believed White South African Christians would respond humanely and positively to their attempts to bring about change "by constitutional means." They agreed with Rhodes's dictum of "Equal rights for all civilized men" and therefore proposed modest objectives and stressed their support of Christian principles, Western models of "civilization," and civic and moral responsibility. Their fellow Christians in the White government, however, ignored their peaceful appeals and crafted an ever more segregated and unequal nation. Perhaps they should have seen the writing on the wall from the beginning, for not a single White newspaper reported on their meeting.

Only a year after the ANC's formation the Union government passed the 1913 Natives' Land Act. Politically astute Africans immediately recognized the tragic implications of this law: Africans lost their rights to 90 percent of South Africa's land, and South Africa would forever be a racially divided country. The ANC sent a petition to the English governor-general and deputations to the Parliament in Cape Town and to London in 1914, calling for the act's repeal. They were ignored.

Soon after arriving in South Africa, the Western-educated, Western-attired, English-speaking Indian lawyer Mohandas K. Gandhi was thrown off a train for riding in a first-class, "Whites only" car. This was a defining moment in Gandhi's life. It was a moment shared by many other Westernized Africans and Asians who usually found, like Gandhi, that in the end only their skin color mattered. Thus, South African Blacks went off to the White man's World War I and displayed their loyalty to their native land and to democracy. Speeches by U.S. president Woodrow Wilson and British prime minister Lloyd George about democracy and the rights of free people raised their hopes that when the war ended Britain would see to it that Africans took their rightful place in a democratic South Africa. In 1919 when they were not allowed representatives on the official South African peace delegation to the peace treaty talks at Versailles, they sent their own delegation. Their requests for the vote, equal representation, and equal land distribution were sympathetically received and politely ignored.

In 1919 the Transvaal ANC branch called on African workers on the Rand to strike for higher wages and against the pass system. When the strike was brutally repressed by government troops, the ANC stopped sanctioning such potentially violent activity and returned to making petitions. The ANC's failures at Versailles and on the Rand caused it to lose its following among the African masses. During the 1920s and 1930s the ANC, SAIC, and APO, along with some White liberals such as Edgar Brookes, formed Joint Councils to discuss the racial situation in the country. In 1929 they established the South African Institute of Race Relations to research and disseminate information about racial discrimination and segregation. Their efforts were all but ignored by the White population, however, and they had little support in Black communities. By the 1930s these African, Indian, and Coloured elites, together with a few White liberals, were generally only communicating with each other.

When the Natives' Trust and Land Act and the Representation of Natives Bill were proposed in 1936, they provoked a brief resurgence of African political activity. An All Africa Convention (AAC) met in Bloemfontein in December 1935 to condemn the government's plans. Under the leadership of Professor Davidson Jabavu and Dr. Alfred Xuma, the AAC adopted a series of moderate objectives. Delegates rejected calls by Communists and other radicals for militant action, and they advocated the use of constitutional methods of protest. The AAC received little notice from Hertzog, who, following his party's merger with Smuts's South African Party in 1934, now had more than enough votes to easily pass the measures, which Parliament did on 6 April 1936. Though angry and bitter, the AAC tried to work within the new political framework rather than boycott it. Elections for Senate, House of Assembly, and Natives' Representative Council representatives were held in 1937. Although some elected White representatives, such as Margaret Ballinger, were strong advocates for African rights and harsh critics of the government, they could not stop the White racist juggernaut.

African living standards continued to deteriorate as the twentieth century progressed. The majority of Africans, whether rural or urban, were concerned simply with daily survival. In the countryside, drought, crop failure, cattle fever, and locust plagues added to the overcrowded conditions and low carrying capacity of the land to produce an increasingly desperate situation. As American commissions studied the plight of "poor Whites," South African commissions, such as Sir William Beaumont's Commission in 1913, visited African reserves ostensibly to consider their condition and possible expansion. Members often came away shocked by the misery and poverty they found. Urbanization and industrialization put severe strains on traditional African values and support systems. Families fell apart as husbands labored in the mines, wives served as maids, and children lived with grandparents.

Besides the ANC, APO, and SAIC, various other organizations gave national expression to Black concerns in the interwar years. One of the most important was the Industrial and Commercial Workers' Union (ICU), founded among Coloured Cape Town dock workers in 1919 by a young Black man from Nyasaland (modern Malawi) named Clements Kadalie. His trade union movement spread to other urban areas and to Natal, where it found an effective provisional secretary in George Champion, a Zulu. By the mid-1920s, however, the ICU was torn by dissension between its moderate and radical wings, the latter consisting largely of Communist Party members. Questions also arose about the misappropriation of funds and the autocratic powers assumed by Kadalie and other ICU officials. In 1926 Kadalie expelled Communist Party members from ICU membership. A new membership drive into rural areas of Natal, the Transvaal, and the Orange Free State later in the same year met with considerable success, as the ICU switched its focus from trade unionism to militant nationalism. At its peak in 1927–1928 the ICU claimed more than 100,000 African members, a few thousand Coloureds, and some Whites nationwide.

However, the ICU leaders were unable to hold all their various constituents together. Rural members, isolated and poor, could only participate in local actions. Christian converts, Marxists, and followers of black nationalist leader Marcus Garvey's Back-to-Africa movement popular in the United States had little in common, either in methods or goals. Vague promises of land repossession and national liberation came and went. The ICU leadership could not mobilize its members for large-scale action. Isolated incidents such as livestock thefts, property destruction, and random work stoppages, were ineffectual and only served to foment White anger. After Kadalie resigned in January 1929 and Natal banished Champion for three years in 1930, the ICU disintegrated and died out in the early 1930s.

During the 1920s the Communist Party of South Africa (CPSA) also gained a following, but it had limited appeal because it had to follow directives from the Communist International in Moscow. The directive given to CPSA members was to form an "independent South African Native Republic" based on African majority rule. Because the CPSA recruited members from all racial groups, its White members, and many Africans, opposed this proposal on the grounds it would destroy White and Black unity and push White workers into White nationalist parties. Nevertheless the Party contested two seats in the 1929 parliamentary election on the "native republic" platform. It lost badly. CPSA membership dropped off after this election but enjoyed a slight resurgence a decade later among younger members of the ANC, APO, and SAIC.

The lesson learned by Black activists from events in the 1910s, 1920s, and 1930s was that no matter how divided Whites seemed among themselves, they were united in their determination to preserve a White South Africa. Even relatively minor attempts to challenge White authority were met by harsh repression. In 1920 an independent African religious sect, calling themselves the Israelites and led by a "prophet," Enoch Mgijima, gathered at Bulhoek Common near Queenstown for a Passover celebration. They combined demands for land, tax relief, and self-rule with elements of Judaism, Christianity, Western morality, and millenarianism. After the celebration they remained encamped to await the "judgment day," and their numbers began to grow. After a year they were given an ultimatum but refused to leave. In the ensuing confrontation a large police force opened fire with machines guns and rifles, killing 163 Africans and wounding 129 more in what became known as the Bulhoek Massacre.

As World War II began in Europe in 1939, racial domination and political and economic power were firmly secured in White hands. Most Blacks must have believed the situation in their native land could not become much worse. But it did.

A WAR FOR DEMOCRACY AND A VICTORY FOR APARTHEID, 1939–1948

Britain's declaration of war against Germany in September 1939 brought an end to the United Party coalition. Smuts wanted to side with

Britain, whereas Hertzog wanted to declare South African neutrality. When Smuts won a parliamentary vote for a declaration of war on Germany, Hertzog resigned as prime minister. A deeply divided South Africa once again went to war as a British ally, with Smuts as prime minister.

South Africa in World War II

South Africa played an important role in the allied war effort, both militarily and strategically. In June 1940, South African bombers attacked Italian troops in Abyssinia (modern Ethiopia) and Italian Somalialand, forcing Italy to abandon its East African colonies. A South African expeditionary force seized Madagascar in May 1942 to prevent it from falling into Japanese hands. Following a major setback at Tobruk, North Africa, in June 1942, where the Germans took more than 10,000 South African prisoners, a South African division joined with Commander Bernard Montgomery's Eighth Army to drive the German and Italian forces out of North Africa. The Sixth South African Armored Division then fought alongside the American Fifth Army as it swept through Italy, defeating Mussolini and pushing out the Germans. By war's end, 135,000 White men, 12,878 White women, 27,583 Coloured men, and 42,627 African men had served in uniform, all as volunteers. Only White men were allowed to carry arms. African and Coloured soldiers were restricted to noncombatant roles such as transport drivers and trench diggers, but still they served with distinction, often in very dangerous circumstances. Nearly half the total number of South Africans killed in World War II were Black.

Strategically, South Africa provided safe harbors at Durban and Cape Town as Allied ships plied the sea route around the Cape of Good Hope to supply their forces in North Africa and Asia. South Africa's industries expanded their production capacity to supply munitions and other provisions to their own troops, as well as those British, Australian, and other forces passing through South African ports. South Africa also furnished the Allies with the strategic minerals that were critical for success in the war effort.

Although more than half the White South Africans in uniform were Afrikaners, a large segment of the Afrikaner community fiercely opposed the war. In fact, Afrikaner nationalist sentiment was at its peak in 1939 when war broke out. The call to arms revived bitter memories of the South African War and World War I. Some Afrikaners supported Germany simply because they accepted the dictum that "the enemy of my enemy is my friend." For other, more extreme elements in Afrikanerdom, the racial, social, and political ideals of Adolf Hitler's National Socialism were very appealing. These Afrikaners believed they too were part of the Aryan master race, that the community came before the individual, and that strong leaders were preferable to British-style democracy. Nazi anti-Semitism also found support among some Afrikaners.

In the first three years of the war, when the Axis powers Germany and Italy together with Japan, appeared invincible, many Afrikaners believed Smuts had bet on the wrong horse. Hitler's invasion of the Soviet Union in June 1941, and the subsequent military alliance between the Soviet Union and the Allies, only strengthened the Afrikaners' resolve in opposing the war. They were incensed that the atheistic Russian communists were now South Africa's allies. Some Afrikaner nationalists resorted to armed rebellion. The pro-Nazi Ossewabrandwag (OB) and its military wing, the Stormjaers (Stormtroopers), carried out numerous acts of sabotage and random violence. By 1942 they claimed a membership of 400,000 and were busy blowing up railroad lines, power lines, post offices, and banks and attacking soldiers and Jews. Some 370 OB members were suspended from the country's police force and arrested. Other OB members arrested during this period included future prime minister John Vorster and his brother Koot, future government minister Ben Schoeman, and future speaker of the Parliament Henning Klopper. In the 1960s and 1970s, anti-apartheid activists in the United States and Great Britain recalled Prime Minister Vorster's pro-Nazi sympathies when conservative politicians said the West should support the apartheid regime because South Africa was a Western ally in World War II. The OB quickly lost its appeal, however, after the United States entered the war and the likelihood of German and Japanese victories receded. Most OB members returned to the National Party.

The National Party they returned to had changed significantly since 1939. Soon after Hertzog resigned the prime ministership, he began negotiations with D.F. Malan to unite their two parties. Despite their differences they agreed to work together in Parliament in a reunited party under Hertzog's lead. When Hertzog came under pressure, however, from Republican elements within the party to more actively pursue the goal of an independent republic, he resigned from Parliament. After he died in 1942, Malan replaced Hertzog as leader. He attacked extraparliamentary groups such as the Stormjaers and the OB, and eventually he expelled former OB members from the National Party. In the 1943 wartime election Smuts's United Party won eighty-nine seats and the Nationalists won forty-three. Pleased at their strong showing in a first election, the Nationalists prepared for the next election round.

Various pro-democracy declarations by world leaders, the rise of Pan-Africanist movements, and the establishment of the United Nations prompted a revival of South African organizations calling for an end to racial discrimination. The Atlantic Charter of 1941, emphasizing human rights and self-determination, emboldened Black South African nationalists to adopt a manifesto, "Africans' Claims in South Africa," that called on South Africa's White leaders to abide by these principles. Three young African professionals, Nelson Mandela, Oliver Tambo, and Walter Sisulu, founded a Youth League within the ANC in 1943. They generally shared the traditional ANC goal of a democratic, nonracial society but also endorsed more militant tactics to attain it, such as mass action campaigns. They were encouraged by anticolonial movements around the world, particularly in the former Dutch and French colonies in Asia, and by Gandhi's *Satyagraha* campaign for independence in British India.

The few minor concessions made to Black workers during the war years, however, did little to improve Black rights or standards of living. In 1946, Black workers' wages remained below the poverty line. The government spent up to twenty times more on White education than on Black. African populations in urban areas grew rapidly during the war years. More Africans than ever now lived in squalid, violent squatters' camps on urban peripheries, and by 1946 they outnumbered urban Whites. The main causes of this urbanization were economic factors such as the mechanization of White farms, expanding opportunities for service jobs and work in industry, and a desire to escape the increasingly harsh impoverishment of the reserves.

Africans made few advancements in the political arena during the war years. Black trade union membership did increase significantly (although Black unions were officially illegal), and this was the one bright spot. But when the African Mineworkers' Union launched a strike on the Rand gold mining industry in 1946, the Smuts government crushed the action with savage brutality. The government also ignored the advice of the Natives' Representative Council. The Council's White chairman refused even to raise the issue of the mine workers' strike in 1946. Black members protested by unanimously adjourning the session after passing a series of resolutions calling for the end of discriminatory practices and laws. Despite the formation of the ANC Youth League in 1943, the ANC still remained fairly ineffectual, claiming fewer than 6,000 members in 1948. These strikes, resolutions, and other activities did little to advance Black rights and political power, but they did arouse White anxieties and reduce White confidence in Smuts's government.

The General Election of 1948

At war's end, Smuts was a major figure on the world scene. He played a prominent role in shaping the postwar settlement and in the formation of the United Nations. In one of the supreme ironies of the twentieth century, Smuts was asked to draft the Preamble to the United Nations Charter. This document called on the world community to guarantee fundamental human rights, individual dignity, and nondiscrimination between the sexes, none of which Smuts guaranteed in South Africa.

But Smuts was viewed increasingly as an old man who could not protect White power in South Africa against its enemies both from within and without the country. He still endorsed White superiority and racial segregation, but various foreign and domestic issues eroded White confidence in his government. For example, legislation passed between 1943 and 1946 restricting Indian rights angered India's leaders and resulted in the recall of the Indian high commissioner and an economic boycott. India led United Nations opposition to South Africa's request for the incorporation of South West Africa. Many Whites resented this public censure by a non-European nation. They were also troubled by the influx of Coloureds, Indians, and Africans into urban areas, the growth of their shantytowns, and the subsequent increase in violence and crime. When the United Party suggested that permanent Black residence in urban areas was necessary to meet industry's labor requirements, White workers were furious, White farmers feared the loss of laborers, and White town dwellers worried about a Black threat to their lives and property. The thought of Smuts's deputy, Jan Hofmeyer, becoming prime minister raised even more concerns among the White electorate, as he was viewed as an extreme liberal and a friend of the Blacks.

Meanwhile Malan's National Party continued to grow. It garnered the full support of the Broederbond, the Dutch Reformed Church, other cultural and social groups, and newly formed Afrikaner trade unions such as the Afrikaner nationalist-led railway union, the Spoorbond. The National Party's emphatically segregationist position on economic and political issues earned it the White voter confidence that the seemingly ambiguous position of the United Party did not. As the 1948 election approached, the National Party concentrated its message to White voters on a single theme: racial purity and continued White dominance.

The National Party framed its political agenda around the Sauer Committee Report of 1946, which turned the apartheid concept into a working blueprint for action. It declared Indians to be permanent aliens and called for the repatriation of as many of them as possible. It stated that Africans were temporary visitors to White areas and should otherwise be restricted to their reserves. Severe quotas were to be placed on African migration to towns, with no possibility of Africans gaining political or social rights equal to those of Whites. Missionary education for Africans was to be ended and a separate educational curriculum adopted for them. The Natives Representative Council was to be abolished, along with African representation in Parliament. Strict segregation of the Coloured population was recommended, as well as their removal from the common voter roll in the Cape. The inherent contradiction of the apartheid system was also evident in the Sauer Report, however. While calling for the increased segregation of Africans on reserves, the Report allowed that African labor had to be available to White industry and farming.

On this apartheid platform the National Party fought the 1948 election against a badly prepared, overly confident United Party led by a tired and out-of-touch Jan Smuts. The poorly timed issuance of the government-sponsored Fagan Commission Report in February 1948 frightened the White electorate more. The report concluded that African migration to urban areas was irreversible and called for an end to pass laws and influx control. The National Party won the propaganda war by linking the United Party to communists and rich capitalists.

Nevertheless the United Party had a large following and a seemingly huge lead going into the 26 May election, and it did actually receive more votes than the National Party and the Afrikaner Party combined. But that clause in the 1910 Act of Union apportioning extra electoral weight to rural areas gave the advantage to the National Party, which had White farmer and worker support. It won seventy seats as opposed to the United Party's sixty-five. Malan made an alliance with the Afrikaner Party and formed a government dominated by Afrikaners, who made up less than 12 percent of the population. The bitter-enders had won, and apartheid became the law of the land.

8

The Apartheid Years, 1948–1973

Apartheid in Afrikaans means "apart-ness" or "separate-ness." It refers to the system of racial discrimination and white political domination adopted by the National Party while it was in power from 1948 to 1994. Apartheid officials legislated the quality and nature of life for every White, African, Coloured, and Indian South African from cradle to grave. A distinction is often made between "petty" apartheid and "grand" apartheid. Petty apartheid refers to the racist laws affecting one's daily routine, beginning with birth in a racially segregated hospital and ending with burial in a racially segregated cemetery. In between, South Africans lived, worked, and played out their lives at racially segregated offices, businesses, schools, colleges, beaches, restrooms, park benches, restaurants, theaters, and sports fields. Grand apartheid relates to land and political rights. The apartheid government extended the 1913 and 1936 Land Acts to create ten African homelands as "independent," or at least semi-autonomous, nations. The goal was for all South African Africans ultimately to be citizens of these "independent" nations, and South Africa a nation with a White majority. Grand apartheid also defined where Whites, Africans, Coloureds, and Indians could live by race, which required the uprooting and relocation of millions of South Africans. Politically, the rights to vote and to hold public office were reserved for

Whites only. Under this system around 13 percent of the population controlled the entire political structure.

The apartheid system rested on four basic principles. First, there were four official "racial groups" identified as White, African, Coloured, and Indian. Second, Whites were regarded as the only "civilized" race and therefore exercised absolute political power over the other racial groups. Third, White interests always came before Black interests. Fourth, all Whites, no matter what their European origins, were simply considered White. However, the government refused to recognize the common Bantu-speaking origins of most Africans and classified them into nine separate African subgroups: Xhosa, Tswana, Zulu, North Sotho, South Sotho, Venda, Swazi, Tsonga, and Ndebele. Indians were considered aliens in South Africa.

The apartheid era can be divided roughly into three phases. The first phase began in 1948 with the National Party election victory and ended in 1959 when the government introduced separate development and self-government for the African reserves. This period is the classical, or *baasskap* (White supremacy) phase, during which apartheid ideology became law. The second phase, which lasted into the early 1970s, witnessed the implementation of separate development. This period was the high point of the apartheid state and Afrikaner nationalism. During this phase as well, anti-apartheid organizations adopted violent means for affecting change. The third phase witnessed a shift away from complete racial segregation, the granting of limited political rights to Asians and Coloureds, and a relaxation of the color bar in business and industry. After the mid-1970s, anti-apartheid groups both inside and outside the country put increasing economic and political pressure on the government to change. Apartheid came to an official end with Nelson Mandela's election as South African president in 1994.

BAASSKAAP APARTHEID, 1948–1959

Baasskaap literally means "boss-ship" in Afrikaans; it refers to White domination or supremacy. During this phase the National Party built on the segregationist policies of Union governments and turned *baasskaap* apartheid theory into law, creating a system of White political and economic dominance. The National Party also constructed a vast governmental bureaucracy. To ensure that this bureaucracy did its bidding, the government issued a simple directive shortly after taking power requiring that all civil servants be bilingual in Afrikaans and English. Because few English-speakers bothered to learn Afrikaans, the civil service quickly became a citadel of Afrikanerdom, loyal to the party and loyal to the *volk*.

The apartheid government's initial legislation sought to define racial classifications and guarantee racial "purity." The Prohibition of Mixed Marriages Act (1949) and the Immorality Act (1950) prohibited Whites from marrying or having sexual relations with people of other racial groups. The Population Registration Act (1950) provided a framework by which to classify and register every human being in South Africa by race. The government created a Race Classification Board as well to rule in questionable cases (e.g., Is this person White or Coloured, Zulu or Xhosa). One of the cruelest apartheid laws, it caused enormous suffering. For example, in the 1960s in a small, predominantly Afrikaner town in the eastern Transvaal, students complained that one of their classmates, Sandra Laing, "looked colored." Although her parents and siblings were all classified as White Afrikaners, Sandra was reclassified as Coloured, forced out of the school, and shunned by Whites. Each year the Race Classification Board reclassified hundreds of South Africans from one racial category to another.

The government next passed the Group Areas Act (1950), under which residential and trading zones were segregated by race. The Native Re-settlement Act (1956) nullified existing property rights. Black areas that had been inhabited for decades and even centuries were now zoned for Whites only. The government relocated few Whites but forced millions of Blacks from their homes. Indians, who often operated businesses in city centers and lived above their shops, had to sell their property and move to areas designated for Indians only. These were often outside the city, leaving the lucrative city center trade to White businesses. Two notorious examples of mass removals occurred in the African township of Sophiatown, near Johannesburg, and the Coloured District Six, near the center of Cape Town. Sophiatown's long-time African residents, many of whom owned their land, were removed to the newly created but more distant (from Johannesburg) township of Meadowlands. Mead-owlands itself eventually merged into the sprawling complex southwest of Johannesburg known today as Soweto (South Western Townships). Sophiatown became the White town of Triomf (Triumph). Coloureds had lived in District Six since the early nineteenth century. In 1966 the government declared it a White area under the Group Areas Act, razed all its buildings save for churches and mosques, and relocated its residents to new townships miles away from Cape Town in the sandy, windy Cape

Flats. Such mass removals had a devastating impact on family and community networks. They burdened workers with high transportation costs and long commutes. Poverty increased, and crime rates—especially juvenile crime—skyrocketed. Whites were hesitant to develop the vacant plots in District Six, now renamed Zonnebloem (Sunflower). The area remained an empty, barren patch for decades, bearing silent witness to the sterility of the apartheid system. (In September 1998 the government presented a plan to return 45,000 dispossessed people to the former District Six.)

The Nationalists responded to court challenges over separate and unequal public facilities by passing the Reservation of Separate Amenities Act (1953). This law permitted segregated, but not necessarily equal, public facilities. "Whites only" and "Non-Whites only" signs appeared on facilities ranging from train cars to park benches. This petty apartheid legislation was most onerous in denying equal facilities to all. Although South Africa's White rulers promoted the country as a bastion of Western civilization at the tip of Africa, apartheid policies deviated sharply from the anti-racist, pro–human rights trends that were current in Europe and the United States. In 1954 the United States Supreme Court in *Brown v. Board of Education of Topeka, Kansas* took the opposite position from the Separate Amenities Act, ruling against school segregation and, subsequently, segregation in general.

The National Party constructed grand apartheid on a foundation of legislation passed by previous Union governments, such as the 1913 and 1936 Land Acts, various pass laws, and the Natives (Urban Areas) Act of 1923 (with subsequent amendments). D.F. Malan's government conceived of "White" South Africa as divided in two: rural and urban. Under the initiative of Minister of Native Affairs Hendrik Verwoerd, a Native Laws Amendment Act (1952) controlled African movement to all urban areas and included a vagrancy clause allowing local officials to remove "idle or undesirable natives." The infamous "Section Ten" of the Urban Areas Act prohibited Africans from remaining in any urban area longer than seventy-two hours without appropriate permission stamped in their passbook. Under Section Ten only those Africans, male or female, who were born in the particular urban area or had lived there continuously for fifteen years or had served the same employer for ten years, had the right to be there. Although these acts essentially delimited all of South Africa by racial groups, the apartheid government remained concerned about a few so-called Black spots. These included African squatter camps on city peripheries, Black landowners in Whites-only areas, and

African squatters on White farms. The Prevention of Illegal Squatting Act (1951) and subsequent legislation effectively took away the last land rights Africans possessed, expelled these "surplus" Africans to the African reserves, and literally eliminated the squatter camps.

In apartheid language, the Abolition of Passes and Consolidation of Documents Act (1952) actually replaced passbooks with 96-page reference books and for the first time required that African women as well as men possess them. These reference books contained a photograph, fingerprints, personal history, employment record, and documentation of residency. All Africans had to carry them and produce them for any policeman who asked; otherwise they faced criminal punishment. Police arrested more than 100,000 Africans each year (more than 350,000 yearly in the riotous mid-1970s) under these oppressive pass laws. The laws failed to prevent Africans from migrating to urban areas, but they exacted an enormous toll on the South African economy to cover the cost of maintaining police, courts, and jails.

Africans, Asians, Coloureds, and some Whites vehemently protested these laws, but the government made such opposition a criminal act in itself. The National Party government inherited a considerable code of coercive legislation that it expanded to secure its control. In these early Cold War years, Malan's government used its fiercely anti-communist convictions to ally itself with the West. The Suppression of Communism Act (1950) outlawed the Communist Party of South Africa (CPSA) and defined nearly all opposition as promoting "communism." Ironically, this act gave the minister of justice almost unlimited totalitarian authority, just as in communist states. The minister could arbitrarily "ban" a person—which meant he was restricted to a magisterial area where he had to report regularly to police. A banned person also could not meet with more than one other person at a time, attend meetings, publish anything, or make speeches. Banned organizations could not hold meetings, promote their cause, publish literature, or exist in any meaningful way. Members of banned organizations could be arrested. This anti-communist measure gave the apartheid regime a strong propaganda tool in the West. Many European and American political leaders excused South Africa's horrible abuse of fundamental human and civil rights, as they did right-wing dictatorships in Central and South America, because it was allegedly fighting communism.

The Suppression of Communism Act was only one of many oppressive laws that enabled the racist regime to act with impunity. Two others were the Public Safety Act and the Criminal Law Amendment Act, both passed in 1953. The first gave the government broad emergency powers. Under the second, any protest against a law, incitement of others against a law, or breaches of the peace were considered punishable crimes. The Natives (Prohibition of Interdicts) Act (1956) prevented Africans evicted from residential areas from turning to the courts for legal relief, and the amended Riotous Assemblies Act (1926, 1956) expanded the anti-labor, anti-strike legislation of the 1920s. The Terrorism Act (1967) gave authorities the right to detain indefinitely for interrogation any person thought to be a "terrorist" or who might have knowledge of "terrorists."

To enforce these various draconian measures, the apartheid regime created the best equipped and best trained police force in Africa. By the mid-1970s the fulltime police and reserves numbered about 75,000. By 1984 nearly half the force was Black, and there were sixty Black officers. In 1969, then–prime minister B.J. Vorster created a Bureau of State Security (BOSS), later called the Department of National Security, and in 1978 the National Intelligence Service. Despite its name the security force operated secretly and with no parliamentary oversight. It interrogated political suspects and carried out clandestine military operations against anti-apartheid opponents and organizations. It also destabilized neighboring independent governments (e.g., those of Angola and Mozambique) by giving anti-government movements in those countries financial and military aid. It was notorious for its brutal treatment of detainees, including torture, and its assassination of opponents. Like most authoritarian regimes, the South African government used most of its manpower and resources not to fight crime but to crush its opposition. Crimes against Whites were investigated and punished severely. South Africa had one of the highest capital punishment rates in the world, but its death row was nearly entirely Black. Meanwhile crime, violence, and drugs ran rampant in Black townships, receiving little attention from White authorities or from average White South Africans. The extent of the apartheid regime's inhumanity only truly became evident in the 1990s when files were opened and testimony was given before the government appointed Truth and Reconciliation Commission.

The government also significantly expanded the South African Defence Force (SADF). A booming economy in the 1960s and early 1970s enabled the government to raise the level of defense spending from an estimated U.S. $63 million in 1960 to over U.S. $1 billion by 1975, or nearly 20 percent of the national budget. There were over 16,000 regular troops, of whom about 5,000 were Black, more than 38,000 White conscripts, and another 255,000 White reservists in the mid-1970s.

To provide a modern arsenal for the military and police and to reduce dependence on foreign imports, South Africa established the Armaments Corporation of South Africa (ARMSCOR) in 1964. This state-run venture eventually manufactured a significant proportion of the nation's military hardware, including military vehicles, fighter aircraft, and missiles. By the late 1970s South Africa was exporting ARMSCOR munitions and equipment. South Africa also purchased military hardware from the United States, Europe, Israel, and Taiwan. France provided the SADF with helicopters, submarines, and important military technology and equipment. France also sold over sixty Mirage fighter-bombers to the apartheid regime but, more important, gave South Africa's Atlas Corporation the license to manufacture the Mirages. With French and Israeli help, South Africa secretly developed a nuclear capability and had an arsenal of seven nuclear bombs by 1993. The United Nations imposed an international arms embargo on South Africa in 1977, but it was routinely broken, particularly by Taiwan and Israel. By then South Africa already possessed the best trained, best equipped, most powerful military force in sub-Saharan Africa anyway.

Another critical element in the apartheid system was control over education. Following apartheid theory, the different racial groups required different forms of education to develop their separate cultural identities. For Whites, this meant compulsory attendance at public schools in which either Afrikaans or English was the language of instruction, or medium. Coloureds and Indians were provided their own public schools, but attendance was not compulsory.

Until 1953 African schools had been under the Department of Education but operated primarily by church missions. This arrangement troubled the National Party leaders in two ways. First, they worried that mission schools were putting false ideas about equality and human and civil rights in African heads. Second, given the schools' limited funds and manpower, they could not adequately educate enough Africans to satisfy labor demands in an expanding economy. The resulting Bantu Education Act (1953) had some of the most far-reaching and long-term consequences of any apartheid legislation. Dr. Hendrik Verwoerd, minister of native affairs and the "father" of the apartheid system of Bantu education, bluntly explained the government's position regarding African education: Africans should not be educated for jobs they would never be allowed to hold in White-ruled South Africa. Although liberals and missionaries taught Africans that they would someday be "Black Englishmen" and have the same rights as Whites, Verwoerd stated that this was a mistake. Under apartheid, he explained, Africans had no place in White South Africa except to serve as common laborers for Whites; the educational system should therefore prepare them for these roles and for helping their own people.

"Bantu education" now came under the Department of Native Affairs, with the government running the schools, selecting and training teachers, and prescribing a curriculum that emphasized basic skills. African vernacular languages were to be used in the lower grades, with compulsory English and Afrikaans introduced at higher levels. Although attendance was not compulsory for African children, African enrollment did increase significantly when education came under government control, but parents now had to pay more to educate their children. Yet in every area—from the general condition of buildings and classrooms, to the availability of texts, to the caliber of the teaching staff—African schools were far inferior to those for Whites. The government spent as much as ten times more on each White student as on every African student. The quality of Coloured and Indian schools, and the money spent on each student, were somewhere between that for White and African schools. The majority of Africans despised "Bantu education."

The government targeted the university system in 1957, applying educational apartheid to higher education. The South African university system consisted of four English-medium universities; four Afrikaans-medium universities; the University of South Africa, which was a correspondence university; and the South African Native College (for Africans) at Fort Hare. The government set out to put an end to African, Coloured, and Indian students attending "White" universities, mainly the University of Witwatersrand and the University of Cape Town. Under the Extension of University Education Act (1959), separate universities were established for "non-White" students. Faculty at these separate universities were usually Afrikaners who firmly believed in the apartheid ideals of separate development and White superiority. Faculty and staff at South African universities bitterly opposed the new law and managed to delay its passage for two years. White universities received much more funding than did Indian, Coloured, and African universities. Because Black primary and secondary schools provided a generally lower standard of instruction, few Indian, Coloured, or African students graduated from high school and went on to university. Eighty percent or more of all South African university students were White until the late 1980s.

Finally, the apartheid strategists needed to consolidate all political power in White hands. In the years between 1910 and 1948, Coloureds were generally better off than Africans but still were not accepted by Whites as equals. The most important right Coloureds possessed was that of Coloured men to have their names on the common voters' role in the Cape Province. An entrenched clause in the 1910 Constitution protected this right by requiring a two-thirds majority vote of the joint houses of Parliament to change it. The National Party was determined to overturn this clause. Its motives were primarily racist, but it was also afraid a solidly Coloured vote for the United Party could topple the Nationalist government. Malan tried various legal maneuvers in the early 1950s to eliminate the Coloured franchise, but South Africa's highest court, the Appeal Court, struck them down each time.

When Malan retired in 1954, his successor, J.G. Strijdom, instituted a complex strategy to overturn the clause. First, Parliament passed legislation raising Appeal Court membership from five to eleven members and requiring that the full court be present when deliberating on constitutional matters. Second, the Senate Act (1956) expanded the Senate from forty-eight to eighty-nine members. Both actions included safeguards guaranteeing that loyal Nationalists would occupy the Court and Senate seats. With a packed Senate and Appeal Court, the Separate Representation of Voters Bill (1956) easily passed a joint sitting of Parliament by a vote of 173 to 68. When challenged, all but one of the Appeal Court judges upheld the legislation. By means of this legal and political stratagem, Coloureds lost the common franchise rights they had enjoyed for a hundred years. The law removed Coloureds from the common voters' roll in the Cape Province and placed their names on a separate voters' roll. They could now only elect White representatives for the House of Assembly and Cape Provincial Council.

Africans had been removed from the Cape's common voters' roll in 1936, leaving them with the merely advisory, and now moribund, Natives' Representatives Council. Even this was abolished in 1951. In its stead, the Bantu Authorities Act (1951) established a hierarchical system of authority and self-government to the African reserves created by the 1913 and 1936 Land Acts. This legislation linked each reserve to a specific African ethnic group. As "tribal" authorities, chiefs and headmen continued to perform many of their traditional duties and any others required by White officials. The government intended for each reserve to have the appearance of a separate African polity. Because Africans themselves had no say in the establishment of this polity, however, and because the minister of native affairs appointed the chiefs and headmen, the entire exercise was merely a part, albeit a hugely important one, of the grand apartheid facade.

The government also appointed Professor Frederik Tomlinson chair of a commission to study the economic viability of the African reserves. The Tomlinson Report, issued in 1954, began with the premise that there would never be a united, multiracial South Africa because Whites would never relinquish their political power and privileged positions. African reserves, therefore, had to be developed in order to support a growing African population. The Commission concluded that to do this, the South African government needed to make extensive investments—at least £105 million over the following decade. Additional land beyond that called for in the 1936 Land Act had to be purchased to enlarge the present reserves. Also, because even larger reserves could not support all the African farmers, the government had to create an additional 300,000 jobs by locating industries near to, or within, the reserves. Yet the Commission estimated that even if all these measures were carried out to the full, the reserves could only accommodate about two-thirds of the projected African population by century's end. The Tomlinson Report also concluded that the traditional "tribal" systems of authority used to rule these reserves were not suitable for a modern industrial state.

Verwoerd dismissed the Commission's report as extravagant in its cost projections, and he implemented policies completely at odds with it. He rejected the idea of additional land purchases, forbade any private White capitalist investment within the reserves, and declared that traditional "tribal" authorities would rule over them. In the early 1950s Verwoerd did not favor complete independence for the reserves, but his thinking had changed by the time he became prime minister in 1958. The Promotion of Bantu Self-Government Act (1959) limited African political rights to the reserves, thereby taking away their elected White parliamentary representatives. There were eventually ten homelands, or *bantustans*, based on ethnicity: the Ciskei and the Transkei for the Xhosa, and one for each of the other ethnic groups (the Venda, Shangana/Tsonga, South Ndebele, North Sotho, South Sotho, Tswana, Swazi, and Zulu). The *bantustans* were allotted within the limits of the 13.7 percent of land set aside in the 1936 Land Act and varied considerably in size and quality. Furthermore, in an effort to guarantee White access to the best farming land and mineral wealth, only the tiny *bantustan* of Qwaqwa was a single piece. Bophuthatswana consisted of nineteen fragments, some separated by hundreds of miles; and KwaZulu had twenty-nine major and forty-one minor fragments.

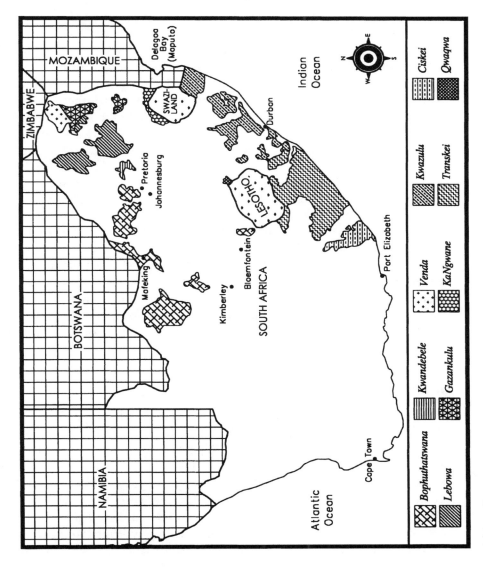

African Bantustans

Verwoerd's decision to grant autonomy to the African homelands represented a significant shift away from his own earlier position and from *baasskaap* apartheid principles generally. This was partly in response to African decolonization. The granting of independence to Ghana (formerly the British Gold Coast colony) in 1957 placed increased international pressure on South Africa to provide its African population with political rights. Verwoerd argued that South Africa was "decolonizing" the *bantustans* and granting them independence; as citizens of their respective *bantustans*, Africans enjoyed full political rights according to their own practices and traditions. According to Verwoerd, there could be no racial discrimination against Africans in South Africa because there were no African citizens; African rights in White South Africa were not restricted because of race but because they were foreigners.

Of course, Africans had no say in the creation of the ethnicity-based *bantustans*. An African's ethnicity was anyway often difficult to determine because the various African ethnic groups had been intermarrying for centuries. And many Africans had never been near their assigned *bantustan*, having lived for generations on distant farms or in urban areas. All this mattered little to Verwoerd, however. To present an acceptable face to the world, he increasingly referred to "separate development" rather than apartheid; "Natives" became Bantu; *bantustans* became "homelands." Verwoerd envisioned a "commonwealth" of southern African nations to include the *bantustans*; the High Commission Territories of Lesotho, Swaziland, and Botswana; and a South African republic completely free of political ties to Great Britain.

OPPOSITION TO APARTHEID, 1948–1959

The National Party won the 1948 election on an apartheid platform by the slimmest of margins, receiving less than 40 percent of the votes. It increased its number of seats in the 1953 general election but still polled less than 50 percent of the vote. Only in the 1958 general election did the National Party win a majority, 55 percent as opposed to 42 percent for the United Party. For much of the 1950s, therefore, the majority of White voters opposed the National Party and its apartheid agenda.

White opposition came from many quarters. Many White South African church leaders took strong stands against apartheid; these included the Anglican priest Trevor Huddleston and the Dutch Reformed Church leader Beyers Naudé, both of whom were banned by the South African government. In addition, the Dutch Reformed Church expelled Naudé for his anti-apartheid activities. A group of liberal, predominantly White, English-speaking women formed the Women's Defence of the Constitution League in 1955, better known as the Black Sash. They opposed the attack on the constitution over the Coloured vote issue and made silent, but highly visible, protests outside Parliament and other public buildings wearing white dresses with black sashes as a symbol of mourning for the constitution. The government banned their demonstrations in 1976, but the Black Sash continued working against the apartheid system by opening counseling offices to help Africans with problems ranging from pass law offenses to issues of housing, pensions, and unemployment.

Opposition to apartheid also came from White academics, staff, and students at English-medium universities, particularly the universities of Cape Town and the Witwatersrand. They held large rallies in the late 1950s opposing the Extension of University Education Act that forbade Black students from attending White universities. The government also faced continual opposition from the National Union of South African Students (NUSAS). Originally formed in 1924 with both English and Afrikaner members, when NUSAS became increasingly liberal in the 1930s and 1940s the Afrikaners dropped out. Black students became members in the 1950s. In 1966 NUSAS invited U.S. senator Robert Kennedy to South Africa, and he gave a series of speeches denouncing apartheid. The government constantly harassed the organization and its members, many of whom were banned. In the late 1960s most Black members left to join black consciousness leader Steve Biko and his South African Students' Organization (SASO), but NUSAS continued to work closely with Black opposition groups and to educate generations of White, mostly English-speaking, students about the evils of apartheid. In 1991 NUSAS disbanded and joined with other student organizations to form a multiracial association called the South African Students' Congress Organization.

Many other Whites used their intellectual and creative powers to speak out individually against apartheid. Authors such as Alan Paton, Breyten Breytenbach, Andre Brink, Nadine Gordimer, and Athol Fugard wrote passionate descriptions of the suffering and pain caused by officially sanctioned racism and brutal government oppression. When editors and journalists of English-language newspapers, such as the *Rand Daily Mail*, became too critical, or when books or journals published forbidden material, they were immediately banned. Publishers constantly had to guess where the government might draw the line. Historians, economists, sociologists, political scientists, lawyers, and others wrote and spoke about the injustices of the apartheid system.

The National Party faced little significant parliamentary opposition throughout almost the entire apartheid era. After the United Party's surprising defeat in the 1948 election, it was thrown into further disarray by the death of Smut's deputy, Jan Hofmeyr, in 1948, and by Smuts's in 1950. It out-polled the National Party in each election for the next ten years but was never again a force in South African politics. As it continued to lose seats, English-speakers increasingly supported the National Party. Its continued endorsement of White supremacy and its refusal to oppose apartheid legislation finally led some of its members to break away in 1959 and form the Progressive Party. The Progressives began with eleven Parliament members but lost all but one in the 1961 general election. From that time until 1974, Helen Suzman was its lone but formidable voice in Parliament, relentlessly attacking the government over human rights issues and apartheid legislation. The Progressive Party initially supported a qualified (not universal) franchise, a bill of rights, the end of racial discrimination, and a multiracial government. Both the Progressive Party and the Liberal Party, founded in 1953, had members of all races until the Prohibition of Political Interference Act (1968) outlawed multiracial political parties and even multiracial political gatherings. The Liberal Party dissolved itself rather than accept this legislation, but the Progressive Party continued with a Whites-only membership. After 1974 it gained more seats in the General Assembly, including some breakaways from the United Party, and became the Progressive Federal Party in the following year. Following the 1977 general election it became the official opposition party and called for universal suffrage, "one person, one vote." In the late 1980s the Conservative Party replaced it as the main opposition party, and in 1989 the Progressives merged with other left-leaning parties to form the Democratic Party.

White voices in mining, business, industry, and agriculture—voices the government might have listened to—seldom expressed real opposition to apartheid until the late 1970s. White, English-speaking capitalists had little affinity with the Afrikaner-controlled National Party or its apartheid agenda. The National Party had always excluded them; indeed, it had been formed partly to help Afrikaner capitalists gain control of the South African economy from them. The White capitalists therefore voiced their concern about the more abhorrent apartheid laws and distanced themselves from the National Party, while continuing to benefit from the supply of cheap Black labor, government subsidies, and tight government control of Black unrest. For White workers the apartheid system was a dream come true, which explains the large number of Europeans and British who immigrated to South Africa well into the 1980s. They established one of the highest living standards in the world, enjoying swimming pools, maids, gardeners, and nannies. Whites possessed a virtual monopoly on skilled jobs and high wages. Farmers, mine owners, and industrialists extracted the number of cheap African workers they needed from *bantustans* and then "dumped" them back when their labor was finished. As the economy expanded and profits rose throughout the 1950s and 1960s, few Whites saw any need for change.

African opposition to the new apartheid government acquired a youthful zeal following the 1949 election of three Youth League members to the ANC national executive: Walter Sisulu, Oliver Tambo, and Nelson Mandela. Sisulu was a trade unionist; Tambo and Mandela shared a Johannesburg law practice. All were in their thirties, and they had all imbibed the spirit of African nationalism sweeping across the continent. Mandela was the dominant personality, though the youngest of the three. The son of a Thembu royal official in the Transkei, Mandela was a large man with a commanding presence, a keen intellect, and an unshakable belief in the justice of the liberation struggle.

With pressure from these younger members, the ANC adopted a Program of Action in 1949 that included new methods of resistance such as strikes, boycotts, and civil disobedience. In 1952 the ANC elected Albert Lutuli as its president-general. Born in 1898, Lutuli was a Zulu chief, a schoolteacher, a devout Christian, and a man of great charm and effective oratory. He played a moderating role between the ANC's older, more conservative members and the younger, more radical generation. In June 1952 the ANC together with the South African Indian Congress launched a Defiance Campaign in which volunteers were asked to actively resist such discriminatory legislation as pass laws, the Groups Areas Act, livestock limitation, the Bantu Authorities Act, the separate representation of voters, and the suppression of communism. The ANC halted the campaign at year's end after many organizers—and 8,326 volunteers—had been arrested and outbreaks of violence had occurred. The campaign's positive outcomes were greater ANC recognition and increased membership from 20,000 to 100,000, but it also had negative consequences. It frightened the White population, helping the National Party gain more votes in the 1953 general election. And it gave the government an excuse to pass new repressive measures.

A defining moment for the South African liberation struggle came in

1955 when the ANC joined with the South African Indian Congress, the South African Coloured People's Organization, the predominantly White Congress of Democrats, and the multiracial South African Congress of Trade Unions to form the Congress Alliance. The Alliance convened a Congress of the People on 26 June 1955 at Kliptown, near Johannesburg; at which 3,000 delegates representing all racial groups approved the Freedom Charter. This document boldly declared that "South Africa belongs to all who live in it, Black and White, and that no government can justly claim authority unless it is based on the will of the people." It contained a list of basic rights and freedoms gleaned from liberal ideals in the United States, Britain, and Europe. It was less clear as to how meaningful social and economic equality might come about. Black activists viewed it as communist inspired because it called for the redistribution of land and the nationalization of banks, mines, and heavy industry. Workers complained that it made no reference to the right to strike or worker control. Africanist groups found fault with its multiracialism and recognition of all "national groups" rather than Black supremacy. For the ANC, however, the Freedom Charter became the platform on which their decades-long struggle would stand. (Even after Nelson Mandela and the ANC came to power in 1994, they still referred to the Freedom Charter as they created a new South Africa.)

The government responded to the Congress Alliance and the Freedom Charter by enacting more repressive legislation, raiding Alliance leaders' homes and offices, and arresting 156 Alliance leaders on 5 December 1956. It labeled the Freedom Charter a communist manifest for the overthrow of the state, and it charged those arrested with treason. The resulting Treason Trial dragged on for years, as cases were thrown out for lack of evidence. The last thirty leaders held in custody, including Nelson Mandela, Walter Sisulu, Helen Joseph, and Lilian Ngoyi, were finally acquitted on 29 March 1961 when the Supreme Court ruled that the government had failed to establish any revolutionary intent or that the ANC or Freedom Charter were communist. Although the Treason Trial detainees' release was a stunning victory for the anti-apartheid movement, it came at a heavy price. The movement's leadership had been tied down with legal concerns for several years, and their highly visible opposition made them targets for future harassment, bannings, and arrests by the government.

Anti-apartheid demonstrations went on despite the Treason Trial. Lilian Ngoyi and other members of the nonracial Federation of South African Women, and the Women's League of the African National

Congress, organized large protests in 1955 and 1956 against extension of the pass laws to women. The government arrested thousands of women for failing to have the new reference books. Other demonstrations were localized and focused on immediate concerns, such as higher bus fares and municipal liquor monopolies. Peaceful boycotts became a popular form of protest for people with few other options against a powerful government. School boycotts in 1955 protesting "Bantu education" continued into the 1980s. A massive bus boycott in Alexandra township near Johannesburg in 1957 involved over 60,000 commuters and lasted for more than three months. In 1959 the ANC organized a boycott of potatoes to protest the mistreatment of farm workers. Some protests turned violent. In January 1960 rioters killed nine policemen in Cato Manor, near Durban, who were carrying out a liquor raid.

Nevertheless, by the late 1950s Gandhian methods of peaceful civil disobedience, as well as active, nonviolent resistance, appeared to have little effect on a government that responded with arrests, bannings, and more oppressive laws. Splits occurred in the anti-apartheid movement. The most important took place in April 1959 when Robert Sobukwe led a group out of the African National Congress to form the Pan Africanist Congress of Azania (PAC). The group traced its roots to the 1940s when Anton Lembede and other ANC members began calling themselves Africanists. Under the slogan "Africa for the Africans," PAC members believed that cooperation with White, Indian, and Coloured organizations weakened the African position. They were particularly leery of White radicals and socialist ideology. But Sobukwe did believe Whites might become "Africans," and some Whites eventually did join the PAC. ANC members rejected the Africanists' opposition to multiracialism and the Freedom Charter. The arrests and turmoil accompanying the Treason Trial in the late 1950s, however, enabled the Africanists to challenge the weakened ANC leadership and gain more followers. In 1959 the PAC offered an alternative under Sobukwe's leadership to the ANC of Mandela and Lutuli. But after decades of peaceful, often Christian-inspired protest, the ANC and PAC soon abandoned the pacifist methods of the old Xhosa prophet Ntsikana and adopted those of Nxele, the war doctor.

VIOLENT RESISTANCE, IMPRISONMENT, AND EXILE, 1960–1964

In February 1960 British prime minister Macmillan warned of a "wind of change" sweeping across Africa. One month later Sobukwe and the

PAC organized a national campaign against the pass laws. The idea originally came from the ANC, which, fearing PAC competition, had planned large, nonviolent demonstrations for 31 March 1960 against the pass laws and in support of a £1 minimum wage. Demonstrators were to assemble at police stations without their passes and, in the Gandhian spirit, invite arrest, fill the jails, and swamp the justice system. The PAC, however, preempted ANC plans and began a similar campaign on 21 March. In response the government arrested Sobukwe and hundreds of PAC members throughout the country. The actions of the demonstrators and the police were generally nonviolent. However, at Sharpeville, an African township near Vereeniging, 50 miles south of Johannesburg, about 5,000 people gathered outside the police station. The police were overwhelmed by the crowd and had neither the manpower nor the facilities to arrest and house them all. Nor could they get them to disperse. Police reinforcements were brought in. Early in the afternoon scuffles broke out and the police opened fire on the demonstrators, killing 69 and wounding 180 more, most of them in the back. Police also fired on a crowd at Langa, a township near Cape Town, and killed two Africans there.

The world reacted in horror and outrage to these killings. The United Nations Security Council, the British Labor Party, and governments in Canada, India, Denmark, Holland, and the United States all condemned the police actions. Thousands marched on the South African embassy in London. International investor confidence weakened, exports declined, gold and foreign currency reserves dropped by more than half within a year, and capital flowed out of the country. Sharpeville became a rallying cry for anti-apartheid movements. Within South Africa, Albert Lutuli burned his own pass on 27 March to demonstrate ANC support of the PAC protest. He called for a nationwide stay-at-home on the following day to mourn the victims. Vast crowds attended the funerals. Many Africans continued the mass stay-at-home beyond the day of mourning, to such an extent that it threatened the normal workings of industry. Police and soldiers forced people from their homes and back to work.

Verwoerd responded with further repression. The government declared both the ANC and the PAC illegal organizations under the Unlawful Organizations Act, which Parliament passed on 8 April. It mobilized the Active Citizens Force (the White military reserves), declared a state of emergency throughout the country, banned public meetings, and detained more than 18,000 people of all races. Of these, more than 6,500 were charged with crimes, including many ANC and PAC leaders. Sobukwe received a three-year jail sentence on Robben Island that was eventually extended to nine years under special legislation. The government released Sobukwe in 1969 but immediately placed him under a banning order that kept him off the political scene and prevented him from leaving the country. He died in Kimberley in 1978. Lutuli and other ANC members received one-year sentences or £100 fines for destroying their reference books. Police raids and arrests on the morning of 30 March sparked a seemingly spontaneous march of about 30,000 Africans from Langa to the center of Cape Town, where Parliament was in session. A PAC student leader, Philip Kgosana, got the crowd to return home before they reached Parliament in exchange for a promised meeting with the minister of justice to present their grievances. At the supposed meeting that evening, the police arrested Kgosana.

Many government and business leaders were badly shaken by these events and became even more so when a deranged White farmer shot Verwoerd in the head at the Rand Easter Show on 9 April. Verwoerd himself, however, appeared untouched by events at Sharpeville and by the assassination attempt. He made a remarkable recovery, returning to his office five weeks later. Born in the Netherlands in 1901, Verwoerd had come to South Africa when he was two years old. He studied at the University of Stellenbosch and in Europe, then taught some years at Stellenbosch before becoming editor of the Afrikaans newspaper *Die Transvaler*. After serving as minister of native affairs under Malan and Strijdom, he became prime minister in 1958. He had a brilliant mind and unwavering confidence in the correctness of his beliefs. A statement he had read to Parliament in May left no doubt as to his intentions: "The government sees no reason to depart from the policy of separate development." On the contrary, he said, recent events only reaffirmed his belief that separate development alone could achieve "peace, good order, and friendly relations between the races." In his view those persons, some of them White, and organizations who had caused all the recent turmoil were "imbued with communistic aims." With good reason, Verwoerd is called the chief architect of apartheid.

For the ANC and PAC, the failure of the anti-pass law campaign, the Sharpeville massacre, the subsequent detentions and arrests, and the banning of their organizations were sobering experiences. Forced underground, they considered their next moves. ANC leaders had to admit nothing had been achieved by fifty years of nonviolent protest. After his 1964 arrest for sabotage, Nelson Mandela told the court how difficult it was for the ANC leadership to abandon nonviolence. The ANC "had always stood for nonracial democracy, and we shrank from any policy which might drive the races further apart than they already were." Yet they could not "continue preaching nonviolence at a time when the Government met our peaceful demands with force." In 1961 Mandela, Sisulu, and others founded Umkhonto we Sizwe (Spear of the Nation) as an underground guerrilla army.

Although Albert Luthuli, the aging ANC president, opposed violence, he recognized the organization was at a turning point in its history. When the Treason Trial ended in March 1961, Luthuli sent Oliver Tambo abroad. Tambo established ANC offices in London and Dar es Salaam, and ANC headquarters in exile in Lusaka, Zambia. Tambo became ANC president-general after Luthuli's death in 1967. Before Mandela could be re-arrested after the trial, he vanished into hiding. Mandela became known as the Black Pimpernel for skillfully avoiding police capture. He traveled overseas to raise funds for Umkhonto and trained for guerrilla warfare in Algeria and Ethiopia. In December 1961, Luthuli received the Nobel Peace Prize for his lifelong peaceful struggle against racism and apartheid. Six days later, on 16 December 1961, the anniversary of the Afrikaners' Day of the Covenant, Umkhonto executed its first violent act. Over the next three years Umkhonto carried out a sabotage campaign to destroy the state's infrastructure while trying to avoid any injuries or deaths. It planted more than two hundred bombs, primarily at electrical pylons near industrial centers, post offices, jails, Bantu Administration offices, and other government installations. Meanwhile, some PAC members formed a military wing, Poqo (Xhosa for "Pure," or "Standing Alone"), and a group of mostly White radical liberals and Trotskyites formed the African Resistance Movement (ARM). Poqo, less organized and more violent than Umkhonto, was blamed for some deaths in the western Cape as well as the attempted assassination of Kaiser Matanzima, the future Transkei homeland leader. ARM bombed the Johannesburg railroad station in 1964, killing a woman and injuring dozens of others.

Soon after the Treason Trial verdict was handed down, Verwoerd decided to target the anti-apartheid groups. He was particularly upset that the courts, even with Afrikaner judges, continued to rule against the government. In August 1961 he appointed John Vorster as minister of justice and told him to do whatever was necessary to crush the government's opponents. Vorster, the former paramilitary Ossewabrandwag member, had first hand experience of these matters. He himself had been detained during World War II for terrorism against the state and pro-

Nazi sympathies. He now set about to reorganize the police force, while Parliament passed tough new security legislation. The Sabotage Act (1962) increased Vorster's power to restrict political activism and to place "communist agitators" under house arrest. Penalties for participating in activities considered dangerous to public safety, health, and law and order ranged from five years' imprisonment to death. If found guilty, the defendant had to prove he or she had no political motivation. Under the General Law Amendment Act (1963) the police could arrest any people suspected of political activities without charging them and hold them initially for up to 12 days for questioning without access to family or lawyers. Subsequent amendments extended the 12 days to 90 days, then to 180 days; eventually indefinite periods of detention were allowed. By placing detentions outside the judicial process, the act cleared the way for widespread abuses, including the torture and death of many suspects held in police custody.

Armed with these vast new powers and aided by paid informants and infiltrators, the police began their assault. Near Pietermaritzburg on 5 August 1962 they captured Nelson Mandela. He was sentenced to five years in prison for incitement and leaving the country without a passport. He had served only a few months of his sentence, however, when the police raided Lilliesleaf, a farm near Rivonia north of Johannesburg, on 11 July 1963. They captured most of Umkhonto's high command, including Walter Sisulu and Govan Mbeki. They also collected hundreds of documents incriminating many others, including Mandela, and plans for a guerrilla war, Operation Mayibuye. Brought from his prison cell and charged with the others, Mandela made an eloquent and impassioned statement during the subsequent Rivonia Trial, while believing he might receive the death sentence. He denied the ANC was a communist organization. His relationship to communists, he argued, was no different than that between Churchill and Stalin during World War II. He and the other ANC defendants were African patriots, he claimed, whom the communists treated as human beings and equals. He declared, "I have fought against White domination, and I have fought against Black domination. I have cherished the ideal of a democratic and free society in which all persons live together in harmony with equal opportunities. It is an ideal I hope to live for and achieve. But if needs be, it is an ideal for which I am prepared to die." On 12 June 1964 the judge found eight of Umkhonto's leaders guilty of sabotage and sentenced them to life imprisonment. These men were Nelson Mandela, Waler Sisulu, Govan Mbeki, Raymond Mhlaba, Elias Motsoaledi, Andrew Mlangeni, Ahmed Kathrada, and Dennis Goldberg. All but Goldberg went to Robben Island, the prison for Black male political prisoners located five miles off the coast from Cape Town. The men's defense lawyer, Bram Fischer, was later sentenced to life imprisonment for belonging to the South African Communist Party.

Vorster's police units were just as effective against Poqo and ARM. By 1964 most of Poqo's principal leaders had also been tracked down and imprisoned. Although Poqo members continued to carry out random acts of terror, they never threatened the state. Like the ANC, the PAC went into exile after being banned in 1960 and established its main head-quarters in Dar es Salaam under the acting presidency of Potlako Leballo. It never received the recognition abroad that the ANC enjoyed, but it did obtain weapons and training from China. Internal disputes and rivalries kept the PAC weak and ineffectual into the 1990s. ARM member John Harris was captured and executed after setting a bomb at the Johannesburg train station on 24 July 1964. Other members went into hiding or fled into exile. The government had effectively crushed the anti-apartheid movement with its brutal laws, harsh sentences, and increasing use of torture and intimidation. Another decade would pass before the masses confronted the apartheid regime again.

THE HIGH TIDE OF APARTHEID, 1959–1973

The second phase of the apartheid era began when Parliament passed the Promotion of Bantu Self-Government Act (1959), giving Verwoerd a green light to proceed with separate development. In January 1960 he proposed to Parliament that South Africa break all political ties with Britain and become a republic. On 3 February 1960, British prime minister Harold Macmillan, following a tour across the continent, delivered a speech before both houses of South Africa's Parliament in which he described the "wind of change" sweeping across Africa. African nationalism was on the march, he said, and soon most of sub-Saharan Africa would be independent. Macmillan left no doubt that Britain would not support South Africa's apartheid policy and that political rights in South Africa should be based on individual merit, not on race. Verwoerd rejected Macmillan's remarks and replied that South Africa was a White state in southern Africa and that Africans could exercise their ethnic nationalism in the *bantustans*.

In the following year Parliament approved Verwoerd's proposal for a referendum on the establishment of a republic. Several factors worked in Verwoerd's favor in the build-up to the referendum, set for 5 October. By the late 1950s the Union already had its own flag, a single citizenship, a national anthem—"Die Stem van Suid-Afrika" (The Call of South Africa)—and a currency of rands and cents that replaced the British pound sterling. Furthermore, an independent republic, free from the British Crown, had been a lifelong dream for many Afrikaners. Macmillan's "wind of change" speech had left many English-speakers feeling isolated, believing Britain would no longer help with South Africa's problems. They were also troubled by Britain's decolonization in Africa, which gave legitimacy to African nationalist movements in South Africa. In June 1960 the Belgian Congo gained independence and immediately erupted into a bloody civil war. Verwoerd appealed for White unity and warned Whites that such chaos might occur in South Africa if it did not become a republic and if they did not support his plans for separate development.

More than 90 percent of Whites voted in the referendum, with 850,458 voting for the republic and 775,878 voting against it; the numbers indicate 52 percent in favor. In the end, enough English-speakers voted for the republic for the referendum to pass, and Verwoerd later recognized this support by appointing two English-speaking members to his cabinet. In March 1961 he attended the Commonwealth Prime Ministers' conference in London and presented South Africa's application to remain in the Commonwealth as a republic. But he withdrew the application following harsh criticism of apartheid from African and Asian leaders and the Canadian prime minister, and he returned to South Africa. On 31 May 1961 the Union became the Republic of South Africa, and all links with Britain and the Commonwealth officially ceased.

In constructing the new republican government's constitution, Verwoerd retained much of the old South Africa Act. A new office of state president replaced, in effect, both the British monarch and the governor-general, but the office was largely ceremonial. The prime minister still ran the government. The national languages remained English and Afrikaans. Most important, all political power remained in White hands.

Verwoerd's efforts to restore confidence in the economy were just as successful. Many Whites worried that South Africa's withdrawal from the Commonwealth would hurt its economic ties with Great Britain. British prime minister Macmillan assured Verwoerd, however, that the preferential trade agreements were bilateral arrangements going back to 1932 and would remain in effect. Verwoerd blocked the flow of capital out of the country, including the repatriation of profits by foreign investors, and tightened controls on imports. By 1962 the economy was on the upswing again. As apartheid's opponents were either locked away or forced into exile, and as confidence in Verwoerd's leadership grew, South Africa again became an attractive place for investors. Indeed, the 1960s became a period of unprecedented growth and prosperity.

Verwoerd now turned to his grand plan for separate development. In 1959 Parliament had passed the Promotion of Bantu Self-Government Bill, paving the way for the homelands to become fully independent states. The first to do so was the so-called Xhosa homeland of the Transkei. The Transkei Constitution Act (1963) gave the Transkei considerable autonomy and its own legislative assembly at Umtata. The Transkei's first prime minister, Kaiser Matanzima, managed to win office only with the support of chiefs appointed by the South African government. He was an opportunist who recognized that separate development allowed him to fulfill his own political ambitions, even if it meant oppressing his own people. The Transkei's constitution, which became a model for future "self-governing" homelands, provided for most of the trappings of an independent state. Besides a prime minister and a legislative assembly, the Transkei had a flag, a national anthem, and a separate (from South Africa) citizenship. There were cabinet posts for finance, roads, education, forestry, and justice; but banking, postal services, railways, immigration, defense, internal security, and foreign policy remained under South African control. The true extent of the Transkei's autonomy can be measured by the stipulation that the South African government had to sanction any laws passed by the Transkei legislative assembly. Matanzima, Mandela's nephew, was a dictator hated by the majority of Transkei Xhosa, and several attempts were made on his life. He depended on South African security forces to maintain his tenuous hold on power for more than twenty years.

By 1966 Verwoerd was at the height of his power. He had taken the various building blocks of apartheid theory and constructed a massive edifice of racist social engineering, tightly controlled from Pretoria and managed by thousands of Afrikaner bureaucrats. The republic's economy was growing, anti-apartheid opposition was broken, and Verwoerd's dream of self-governing homelands was becoming a reality. On 6 September 1966, while Verwoerd prepared to address the House of Assembly, a White parliamentary messenger stabbed him to death. The assassin apparently had no political motive and was later declared insane. Subsequently National Party members unanimously selected B.J. Vorster, Verwoerd's minister of justice, as the new prime minister. Unlike Verwoerd, Vorster was not a great intellect; his colleagues selected him primarily because of his toughness and his ruthless suppression of the anti-apartheid organizations. Once in office, Vorster was more pragmatic and flexible than Verwoerd while remaining committed to White supremacy and separate development.

Vorster's more practical approach to statesmanship became evident when he (1) reversed the isolationist policy adopted by previous National Party prime ministers and (2) sought diplomatic links with other African countries. The world had changed significantly since the 1950s, and nowhere more so than in Africa. Thirty-one African countries became independent between 1957 and 1966, including two of the three neighboring British protectorates, Botswana and Lesotho. More soon followed, including the third protectorate, Swaziland, in 1968. As its Asian and African membership grew, the United Nations General Assembly became increasingly outspoken in condemning apartheid. In 1962–1963 it passed nonmandatory resolutions calling for the breaking of all ties with South Africa and for instituting an arms embargo. It formed a Special Committee on Apartheid and a Unit on Apartheid to denounce the racist regime. It removed South Africa from various UN agencies, such as UNESCO in 1956, the International Labor Organization in 1961, and the World Health Organization in 1965. The General Assembly terminated South Africa's mandate over South West Africa (Namibia) in October 1966. In 1974 it rejected the South African delegation's credentials so that South Africans could no longer speak in the General Assembly, but they retained their membership and could confer with the Security Council and the secretary-general. Within Africa, the Organization of African Unity, founded in 1963, called on all countries to isolate and destroy the apartheid state. Many African countries denied South African Airways landing rights and air space, and most refused to give the country diplomatic recognition.

Verwoerd had ignored this worldwide criticism, seemingly believing South Africa could survive without being a member of the world community. Vorster recognized the shortsightedness of this approach and instead adopted what he called an outward-looking policy. Despite their rhetoric, many African nations were willing to talk and trade. South Africa had much to offer as the wealthiest and most technologically and industrially advanced nation on the continent. All its neighbors were economically dependent on South Africa in one way or another. Many sent migrant laborers to its mines, factories, and farms. Even Zambia, one of South Africa's loudest critics, used South African railroads and ports to handle its almost only source of export earnings, copper. For his part, Vorster knew South Africa needed cooperative, neighboring African states for security and for common economic development.

Vorster first approached Malawi, an impoverished former British protectorate. Its president, Kamuzu Banda, had offered to establish diplomatic relations in 1964, but Verwoerd had rejected him. Vorster now accepted the offer, but Banda raised the price. South Africa had to provide loans and pay for construction of a new Malawian capital at Lilongwe. In return Malawi appointed a White ambassador to Pretoria in 1967, shortly to be replaced by a Black ambassador. Banda insisted the Black ambassador be treated like all others, which meant living in a White suburb and having access to normally Whites-only hotels, restaurants, and entertainments. Soon official "White status" was granted to visiting African and Asian dignitaries and important visitors, and racial segregation was dropped in select, upscale hotels and restaurants. The payoff came in 1971 when Banda made a highly publicized state visit to South Africa. Vorster also met publicly with Chief Jonathan of Lesotho (1966), President Seretse Khama of Botswana (1968), and Prince Dlamini of Swaziland (1971). In the mid-1970s Vorster made less publicized visits to the Ivory Coast, Liberia, and Israel.

Vorster also differed with Verwoerd over the highly visible and controversial politics of sport. Verwoerd had taken an uncompromising position by legislating total segregation in sports. There could be no camaraderie between White and Black, he argued, if the White race was to maintain its dominance. Black victories over White teams threatened the image of White superiority. In 1963, however, segregation in South African sport came under attack by the International Olympic Committee (IOC), which ruled that South Africa had to permit members of all races to compete for spots on its national teams or not attend the 1964 Games. When Verwoerd refused, the IOC denied South Africa an invitation. Verwoerd also forbade the New Zealand rugby team from including Maori players on its national side when it toured South Africa, so New Zealand canceled the tour. Vorster took a more pragmatic approach. Only months after Verwoerd's death, Vorster announced that foreign teams could choose any athletes they wanted to compete against South Africa. He also agreed to send a multiracial team to the 1968 Olympic Games, but threats of an African boycott forced the IOC again to withdraw its invitation. In truth, these were relatively minor concessions as sport in South Africa remained almost totally segregated, particularly at the school and sporting club level (and especially in rugby) into the 1990s.

Vorster's acceptance of Black visitors and multiracial sports teams opened the door to a slow and arbitrary elimination of some aspects of petty apartheid. Laws legislating the segregation of public amenities— such as park benches, beaches, public entertainment, and public buildings—were ignored or removed. Policies were usually decided locally, so petty apartheid in Cape Town and other large cities, and in the Cape province generally, was eliminated to a greater extent and earlier than elsewhere. Inconsistencies could be found everywhere, however; in Cape Town, for example, buses were desegrated but local trains remained segregated.

Vorster's "outward-looking policy" and the relaxation of petty apartheid deeply disturbed the National Party's extreme right wing. These ultra-conservatives were known as *verkramptes* ("the narrow ones"). They longed for the simple and straightforward racism of *baasskaap* apartheid. The more pragmatic and reform-minded members were called *verligtes* ("the enlightened ones"). The presence of a Maori player on the visiting New Zealand rugby team in 1968 precipitated an open split in the National Party. Albert Hertzog, leader of the *verkrampte* faction and son of former prime minister J.B.M. Hertzog, resigned in protest from the Cabinet, and Vorster subsequently expelled him and several others from the party. Hertzog formed a new party, the Herstigte Nasionale Party (the Restored National Party, or HNP), which remained a thorn in the side of the National Party but never won a parliamentary seat.

To counter Hertzog's charges of betrayal, Vorster moved forward with Verwoerd's plan for separate development. He first had to remove all Africans living illegally in White areas and relocate them to their homelands. The Bantu Labour Act (1964) had already tightened controls over African workers in urban areas. This legislation created government-run labor bureaus through which employers had to recruit their African workers, who were always migrants, from the homelands. The act ensured the distribution of labor according to White employer requirements and also resulted in an increased proportion of single, African male migrants in the industrial Black labor force. African spouses were not allowed to bring their partners or children with them from the homelands when they obtained work in South Africa. A 1967 government circular listed various categories of "surplus" Africans who no longer qualified to live in urban areas. These included the elderly, the unfit, children, women, redundant farm laborers, African professionals who could work in the homelands, and those not having Section Ten rights under the Black Urban Areas Act. Vorster promoted men to Cabinet posts and bureaucratic offices who implemented apartheid policies with a cold, ruthless conviction and no concern for the human misery and suffering they inflicted.

An artificial demographic revolution now occurred, as human beings were moved around like pawns on a chessboard. An estimated 1,820,000 Africans; 600,000 Coloureds, Indians, and Chinese; and almost 40,000 Whites were forced from their homes in the 1960s alone. The government removed over one million Africans from so-called Black spots. Verwoerd had ignored the dire conclusions of the 1956 Tomlinson Report on the *bantustans'* economic viability. By the 1960s the *bantustans* had collapsed economically, populations were starving, and the carrying capacity of the soil was rapidly deteriorating. Nevertheless, *bantustan* populations increased by 70 percent during the 1960s. Over a 25-year period more than 3.5 million Africans were eventually relocated to these desolate wastelands. Often they were literally pushed out of trucks onto barren ground, with no provisions other than a water tank and a pile of tents.

These "surplus" people were no longer South African citizens but citizens of sham countries, with little choice but to re-enter the Republic in search of work. Those allowed in were given only one-year contracts so they would have to return to their *bantustan* each year. This prevented them from legally acquiring the necessary terms of residency or continuous employment required for Section Ten rights. South African businesses were never allowed to establish industries within the homelands, as suggested by the Tomlinson Report, but some border industries were permitted. The homelands were generally so remote from roads, railways, and major industrial centers, however, that no matter what tax and labor incentives they received from the government, few border industries succeeded. Of course, White South Africans were most concerned with the availability of cheap African labor for their businesses within the Republic, not with economic development in the homelands. The existence of economically self-sufficient, fully independent homelands, with low unemployment and high wages, was not the separate development Verwoerd envisioned.

Verwoerd had convinced the opportunistic Matanzima to accept semi-autonomy for the Transkei in 1963. Vorster took longer to find leaders in other homelands willing to sell out their people in return for immediate financial and political gains for themselves. In 1971 Parliament passed the Bantu Homelands Constitution Act, which provided a constitutional template for the granting of "self-government" to the *bantustans*. Under this act, Bophuthatswana, Ciskei, Gazankulu, Venda,

Qwaqwa, and KwaZulu all received constitutions identical to the Transkei's and became semi-autonomous homelands between 1972 and 1977. Like the Transkei as well, their leaders were hand picked by the South African government, their general assemblies contained mostly appointed chiefs and few elected members, and South African state security police maintained their leaders in positions of power and quashed the opposition.

By the early 1970s South Africa was coming under increasing attack from its overseas opponents, but Vorster's "outward-looking" policy was also starting to bear fruit. Within the country, most major opposition organizations had been silent for almost a decade, and the pragmatic and reform-minded National Party leaders had rid themselves of their more hard-line members. This was the high point of Afrikaner nationalism as Afrikaners controlled the Parliament, the military, the police, and the civil service. Government money was invested in Afrikaner banks, government contracts were given to Afrikaner businesses, and loyal Afrikaners received government jobs. The government maintained tight control over the communications media. The South African Broadcasting Corporation (SABC) was a government monopoly operated by government appointees. SABC radio—and television, when it was finally allowed at a very late date, in 1976—were government propaganda tools. Afrikaners especially were inundated with government propaganda through the Afrikaans media in their churches, social organizations, Afrikaans-language schools and universities, and businesses. Like most propaganda, however, it was not true. White South Africans would soon be jolted out of their peace and prosperity.

9

The Final Years of White Domination, 1973–1994

NEW CHALLENGES TO APARTHEID, 1973–1978

South Africa's White government entered the third phase of the apartheid era in a strong position. The economy was growing, opposition had been crushed, and separate development was proceeding as planned, albeit slowly. Despite the worldwide anti-apartheid criticism of the early 1960s, international commerce with South Africa increased during the 1960s and 1970s, for the nation's mineral wealth could not be ignored. It produced 60 percent of the world's gold, the price of which rose steadily throughout the 1970s to a peak of $800 per ounce in 1980. The giant South African mining conglomerate, Anglo American Corporation, controlled over 80 percent of the world's diamond production. South Africa also produced considerable amounts of asbestos, coal, copper, iron, nickel, phosphates, silver, uranium, and zinc. Perhaps most important in these Cold War days, South Africa's rich earth yielded substantial quantities of four minerals that are critical to industry and defense: platinum (47% of worldwide production), vanadium (for steel production, 42%), chromium (33%), and manganese (21%). The United States surpassed Britain as South Africa's major trading partner and investor in the late

1970s. South Africa's trade links with continental Europe and Japan also grew significantly during the 1970s.

Although South Africa had no natural oil deposits, soaring gold prices helped to offset increased costs for petroleum and its byproducts after the Arab-controlled Organization of Petroleum Exporting Countries (OPEC) placed an oil embargo on South Africa in 1973. With its gold wealth, South Africa could circumvent the boycott. Iran was its largest supplier until the shah of Iran fell from power in 1979. South Africa also began stockpiling petroleum products, and its enormous coal deposits provided energy to produce electricity. In 1974 a state corporation, the South African Coal, Oil, and Gas Corporation (SASOL), expanded production at two large oil-from-coal plants. By the late 1970s these met 10 percent of South Africa's gasoline needs and by the early 1980s one-third of its oil needs.

Black Labor in a Changing Economy

There had never been enough White workers to meet the country's labor demands. Because the labor required of farm workers, herders, dock workers, and even mine workers had always been low skilled or unskilled, the South African economy could employ millions of low-paid, illiterate, low-skilled Black workers to meet most of its labor needs. Apartheid created an enormous pool of such Black laborers in the homelands, and migrant workers from surrounding countries, to draw on.

Blacks had never been allowed to obtain a good education or to acquire managerial skills and thereby pose a threat to White job security and dominance. In the early 1950s Hendrik Verwoerd declared that "Bantu education" would prepare Blacks for little more than manual labor for the White man. But even in those years of *baasskaap* ("boss-ship," implying White domination) apartheid, Verwoerd knew there was already a greater need for literate Black workers, and the National Party government allowed some Black workers to gain skills and take over jobs previously reserved for Whites. They tolerated these exceptions as long as no White jobs were directly threatened. Over the next two decades, however, technological advances, new industries, and modern machinery required more Black workers for skilled positions. In addition, if an industry was going to run smoothly and efficiently, the work force had to consist of stable, loyal, and long-term employees—not single, male migrant transients. Ideally such long-term, skilled workers would live permanently near their work with their families in comfortable housing and would be paid a reasonable wage. None of these conditions conformed to the basic tenets of separate development, however.

As the economy rapidly expanded in the late 1960s and early 1970s, tensions between the apartheid government and business increased. Blacks arrived illegally in urban areas by the thousands to work in jobs still officially reserved for Whites. Central apartheid principles, such as pass laws, residency requirements, and housing restrictions, were routinely broken. Business managers and workers alike flouted the apartheid system, while police, Bantu Affairs Department officials, and even White trade unions accepted pay-offs and looked the other way. Because the National Party's Afrikaner-first policies had caused large numbers of Afrikaner workers to be promoted out of the unskilled, blue-collar work force, White workers were less concerned about direct competition with Black workers.

Black trade unions eventually forced the government's hand. As demand for skilled and unskilled workers increased, the bargaining power of the still unrecognized trade unions began to grow. Union activity was illegal and strikes by Black workers were prohibited, but they could now bring down the economy with a full-fledged strike. In early 1973 a sharp rise in the inflation rate brought thousands of workers out on strike in Durban and later in East London and the Rand seeking higher wages. Although the government suppressed the strikes, the workers did receive pay increases. Strike action intensified after 1973, as did business demands for a relaxation of the apartheid laws. B.J. Vorster considered new policies to recognize trade unions, acknowledge the presence of a permanent Black labor force in a White South Africa, and improve Black education.

Black labor agitation was not the only factor, however, that threatened the apartheid regime. Despite Vorster's modest successes with his "outward looking" policy, South Africa was becoming ever more isolated. Although most countries in northern, western, and eastern Africa had gained their independence by 1974, there still remained some significant exceptions in central and south Africa. These included the two Portuguese colonies of Mozambique and Angola, South African–controlled Namibia, and White-ruled Rhodesia (modern Zimbabwe). The political situations in these four areas diverted the world's attention somewhat from South Africa. In 1974, however, a revolution toppled the Portuguese dictatorship and the Portuguese pulled out of their African colonies in 1975. Mozambique moved quickly to a Marxist government headed by Samora Machel and the liberation movement Frelimo. A bloody civil war erupted in Angola, but the Marxist Popular Movement for the Liberation of Angola (MPLA) gained control of the government and the capital, Luanda, with Soviet, East German, and Cuban support. South Africa allied itself with the National Union for the Total Independence of Angola (UNITA) movement that the United States endorsed. South African troops supporting UNITA almost reached Luanda before having to withdraw to Namibia in the face of advancing MPLA forces in 1975. South Africa played its Cold War card to retain support from conservative Western politicians and businesses: It pointed to the two Marxist governments and claimed the same would happen in South Africa if the White government were to fall.

Rhodesia's White settler government's unilateral declaration of independence from Britain in 1965 eventually led to a savage civil war beginning in 1972 between the White minority and the Black majority. The White government under Prime Minister Ian Smith made a deal to hand over power to Bishop Abel Muzorewa in 1978. Zimbabwe gained its independence in April 1980 under a popularly elected majority African government led by Robert Mugabe. South Africa received its mandate over South West Africa/Namibia from the League of Nations in 1920. It continued to occupy the country despite attempts over the years by the United Nations (and in cases heard before the International Court of Justice) to modify its control or remove it altogether. Meanwhile South Africa expanded its administration over the territory, even extending its apartheid laws to Namibia in 1966. In 1971 the International Court ruled that South Africa's presence in Namibia was illegal. When South Africa refused to withdraw, the African nationalist movement, the South West African People's Organization (SWAPO), led by Sam Nujoma, stepped up its guerrilla campaign to oust it. Major Western powers, particularly the United States, Canada, Great Britain, and West Germany, put great pressure on South Africa to resolve the issue. South Africa, however, stayed on in Namibia at great expense to its economy, its military forces, and its international position. It finally granted Namibia independence in exchange for a Cuban troop removal from neighboring Angola. Nujoma became the country's first president when Namibia attained independence in 1990. South Africa continued to administer Namibia's principal seaport of Walvis Bay until February 1994. These regional changes forced South Africa to increase its defense spending and border security. And as Angola, Mozambique, Zimbabwe, and other countries in southern Africa obtained independence, the world focused its attention and anti-racist sentiments on South Africa.

Steve Biko and the Black Consciousness Movement

The social, political, and economic revolutions taking place around the world in the 1960s did not go unnoticed by South Africa's Black student activists. The most prominent of these was Steve Biko, a student at Natal University's "non-White" medical school who led a breakaway of Black students from the White-dominated National Union of South African Students (NUSAS) in 1968 and helped form the South African Students' Organization (SASO) in the following year. Biko opposed not only White racism but also the White liberal paternalism that he believed characterized such multiracial organizations as NUSAS. By segregating Black students in Black universities, Verwoerd had unintentionally created a hotbed for Black resistance, from which emerged a new movement called Black Consciousness. Biko became its leader and chief proponent.

Black Consciousness drew on earlier South African traditions and from the world of the 1960s. For example, there was a strong sense of being African as found in Anton Lembede's Africanism and in African Christian churches. There were also the "winds of change" that brought independence and freedom to Africans across the continent starting in the late 1950s. The American civil rights and Black power movements also offered inspiration and ideas. In addition, the movement derived important theoretical distinctions from liberation writers such as Franz Fanon.

The Black Consciousness movement was open to "Blacks" (defined as all those who faced White racial discrimination) and included Coloureds, Indians, and Africans. The name itself challenged apartheid terminology, which still employed the negatives "non-Whites" or "non-Europeans." Black Consciousness philosophy emphasized Black self-esteem, self-assertion, and psychological emancipation from generations of being made to feel inferior to Whites and to view oppression, misery, and poverty as inevitable. The philosophy focused on race rather than class as the central issue in the liberation struggle. Its plans for actual political and economic change, however, were vague and consisted mainly of Black self-help, legal aid, and community programs. Its philosophy, devised by young Black intellectuals, found its most receptive audiences at Black universities, among educated African elites, and in schools. It did not reach far into the working class or peasant communities. Groups such as African trade unions rejected its emphasis on race. Nonetheless by the early 1970s the growth in primary and secondary education had produced an increase in the number of literate Blacks who could appreciate these ideas, and many responded to the strong emotional appeal of the Black Consciousness message.

Biko helped organize the Black People's Convention (BPC) in 1972. The BPC became a political umbrella organization for groups advocating Black Consciousness principles. It worked with the ANC, PAC, and Black trade unions to promote Black Consciousness. For a few years the Black Consciousness movement enjoyed considerable success. The government initially accepted it because of its apparent separate development tendencies, such as Blacks forming a separate Black student organization. These views soon changed though, as the government became more suspicious of the Black Consciousness movement and its activities. The government banned Biko and others following the 1973 Durban strikes. Police broke up SASO and BPC rallies in support of the new Frelimo government in Mozambique in September 1974. Nine SASO and BPC leaders were convicted in the following year under the Terrorism Act and sent to Robben Island. The men's provocative defiance before the court, however, and the assertive nature of the Black Consciousness movement in general, were passed on to the rebellious younger generations that confronted the apartheid system in 1976.

Workers' strikes, Angolan and Mozambican independence, Black Consciousness, South African military losses in Angola, and the pent-up rage and frustration that seethed throughout African townships by the mid-1970s created a powder keg that awaited a fuse. That fuse came in 1975 when the minister of Bantu education instructed all Bantu secondary schools that arithmetic and social studies must be taught in Afrikaans. This was an impossible demand because few teachers or students spoke Afrikaans. Parents, teachers, and students protested in support of English instruction, because English was an international language and the language of business and jobs. Afrikaans was the language of the oppressor, apartheid, the police. The Anglican bishop of Johannesburg, Desmond Tutu, warned Prime Minister Vorster in May 1976 that violence and bloodshed were likely to occur if he did not reverse the policy, but Vorster ignored him.

In Soweto township near Johannesburg on 16 June 1976, 15,000 secondary school children, partially organized by associations of school students, marched to Orlando West Junior Secondary School. The march began peacefully with signs and banners ridiculing Afrikaans and calling on Vorster to learn Zulu. Caught unawares, a small, hastily organized police contingent arrived to disperse the schoolchildren. When tear gas failed they opened fire, killing at least two children. The picture of an anguished fellow student carrying the body of the first of these martyrs, thirteen-year-old schoolboy Hector Petersen, was flashed across the world. Dozens of others were wounded as the children literally ran for their lives.

The police attack on the schoolchildren touched off waves of angry and violent rioting that spread from Soweto across the Transvaal and then to the Cape. Indian and Coloured teenagers joined the protests. Police offices, administration buildings, and state-run beer halls came under attack. The students shut down or destroyed businesses in Black townships. They stoned passing vehicles and halted buses. They called for general strikes, and groups of students forced workers to stay at home in the townships. Masses of angry, rock-throwing schoolchildren confronted rows of well-armed police. Although ANC, PAC, and Black Consciousness examples and ideas formed a backdrop to this explosion, liberation movements neither planned nor controlled them. They were spontaneous and led by local student leaders. The schools were closed and then reopened a month later after the instruction to teach in Afrikaans was rescinded. When the children returned they found police waiting to arrest student leaders, so they boycotted again, choosing "liberation before education." By year's end the government issued an official (although likely underestimated) casualty figure of 575 dead and 2,389 wounded. Many victims were teenagers, some only young children, as were the hundreds more arrested. While in prison the young people were sometimes kept in cells with hardened criminals and not allowed to meet with parents or lawyers. Neither parents nor lawyers were usually even informed of the child's arrest. Many died while allegedly trying to "escape," by allegedly committing "suicide," or simply while in police custody of allegedly "unknown causes." (These were the official explanations.) The Afrikaner novelist André Brink describes the agony and brutality of this dark period in *A Dry White Season*.

These were the largest and most widespread outbreaks of racial violence South Africa had ever experienced. The government reacted in its traditionally heavy-handed, violent manner. It placed much of the blame for the disturbances on the Black Consciousness movement. Steve Biko had been banned since 1974 and his activities restricted. On 18 August 1977 police arrested Biko under the Terrorism Act and kept him manacled and naked in a cell for twenty days. During interrogation he was beaten, suffering severe brain damage. He died on 12 September. The police said he fell against a wall or died during a hunger strike. Government-appointed medical doctors testified that Biko died of natural causes. The magistrate at the inquest failed to find anyone responsible for Biko's death. But Biko was no ordinary detainee, and this time the government had gone too far. Everyone knew who was responsible. There was a worldwide outcry over Biko's death. Yet the government only clamped down tighter. In October, Minister of Justice J.T. Kruger, who said that Biko's death "leaves me cold," banned the Dutch Reformed minister Beyers Naudé's Christian Institute, the South African Council of Churches, SASO, the BPC, and fifteen other Black Consciousness organizations and closed down two African newspapers, the Soweto *World* and the *Weekend World*.

REFORM: THE TOTAL STRATEGY, 1978–1989

Afrikaner leaders not just in government but in universities, churches, newspapers, and businesses were badly shaken by events in 1976–1977. Except for the extreme *verkramptes*, they generally agreed that these events marked a turning point and that there could be no returning to Verwoerd's strict segregationism. Compromises would have to be made in order for White dominance in South Africa to survive. But the riots in Soweto and the death of Steve Biko served only as immediate catalysts for change. It was South Africa's deteriorating defensive, economic, and social conditions that forced its White leaders to seek a new controlling strategy. Apartheid did not collapse overnight. National party leaders did away with many onerous and visible petty apartheid regulations, but they only tinkered with grand apartheid over the next twelve years without really ending it. They told the world that South Africa had changed, even that apartheid was dead; but White, particularly Afrikaner, political control over a White South Africa remained their goal.

The Soweto riots drove thousands of schoolchildren into guerrilla camps abroad, where they received sophisticated military training and advanced weapons. Events in Angola, Mozambique, Zimbabwe, and Namibia left South Africa with thousands of miles of difficult, unfriendly borders to defend. South African defense forces were stretched to the limit. Guerrilla activity within the country had already increased significantly by 1978. In 1980 ANC guerrillas set off bomb blasts at SASOL's two, critically important, oil-from-coal installations in the Orange Free State and the Transvaal. The government responded with a massive military build-up of both men and materiel. From 1977 all young White men had to perform two years of compulsory, fulltime military service, with periodic service in the military reserve until they were sixty years old. But a falling White birth rate coupled with significant White emigration, particularly of English-speakers, left the defense forces still far short of the numbers required. The government was forced to abandon its cherished principle of racial segregation in the military and of limiting Blacks to noncombatant roles. Africans, Indians, and Coloureds were now actively recruited, trained, and allowed to carry arms. It was a tough sell. The military needed to convince a significant portion of the Black community to join a war against organizations fighting for Black liberation from White oppression.

To counter the guerrilla activity, Defense Minister P.W. Botha and army commander General Magnus Malan also studied counterinsurgency techniques used over the previous twenty years, and they settled on one adopted from the French experience in Vietnam, the "total strategy." Botha argued that South Africa faced a "total onslaught" organized by Moscow that sought to overthrow the White government and replace it with a communist puppet state of the Soviet Union. The government's total strategy would win the "trust and faith" of the Black population, much as French and American leaders had talked of winning Vietnamese "hearts and souls." The total strategy required a carrot and stick approach, combining continued harsh repression of apartheid's opponents at home and abroad with significant social and economic reform. Military leaders such as Magnus Malan assumed a more active and important role in all aspects of government planning and policy, as military spending took a larger share of the national budget, border security intensified, and more troops marched to wars in Namibia and Angola.

The world reacted to the Soweto riots and Biko's death more loudly and more actively than it did after the 1960 Sharpeville massacre. The United Nations passed a mandatory arms embargo on South Africa in 1977. U.S. president Jimmy Carter informed Vorster that America would accept nothing less than majority rule and universal suffrage—one person, one vote—in South Africa. The economy went into recession as international investments dropped and capital flowed out of the country. Standards of living fell—especially for Whites, who had the most to lose. Businesses failed and the housing market collapsed. White conscription, White emigration, and the falling White birth rate also meant that fewer Whites were available for jobs in business and industry. Their places were filled by Black workers, putting more pressure on the apartheid system. In 1977 for the first time South Africa experienced a net loss of White citizens, more than 3,000 mostly highly skilled and educated professionals, through emigration. As the White population decreased, the

Black population increased at a much more rapid rate than expected. The White proportion of South Africa's total population dropped from a high of 21 percent to 16 percent.

Afrikanerdom changed as well. In 1948 support for D.F. Malan came from farmers, lower-class urban dwellers, and blue-collar workers. By the late 1970s Afrikaners made up 90 percent of the civil service and had control of 18 percent of the mines, compared with 1 percent in 1948. They also more than doubled the number of positions they held in private businesses and the professions. Fully 88 percent of them now lived in urban areas, and 70 percent of those held white-collar jobs. SANLAM, the Afrikaner insurance group, was one of the most powerful corporations in South Africa, and the Volkskas was one of the largest banks. These were *verligtes*, Afrikaners who could accept some change in return for stability, security, and a prosperous economy—with the caveat, of course, that White rule be maintained.

In 1977 Vorster appointed two commissions to look into the contradictions between apartheid and economic needs. The Riekert Report proposed a critical break from the apartheid concept of Africans being regarded as temporary visitors from the *bantustans*. The report concluded that skilled, employed Africans had to be accepted as permanent residents in urban areas and suitable housing made available to them. This would guarantee the business community a stable, permanent work force and also advance the "total strategy" objective of winning over some members of the Black community. It would create a Black middle class that owed its privileged positions to the system. Blacks working within this system would be economic equals to Whites and share in the nation's wealth. They would still have no political rights, however, and could immediately lose everything if they challenged the system in any way. The Riekert Report also recommended that pass and influx control laws continue to be actively enforced to keep "surplus" Africans in the *bantustans*.

The Wiehahn Commission, which had one Black member, studied industrial relations, particularly Black trade unions. Throughout the 1970s Black trade unions and Black workers made significant strides in both bargaining power and wages. White earnings rose by 79 percent between 1970 and 1978, whereas Black wages went up by 390 percent. International pressure on multinational businesses operating in South Africa to abandon racism in the workplace caused some of these companies to pay Black and White workers the same salary. Nevertheless there remained an enormous gap between the average take-home pay for Blacks and Whites. The Wiehahn Report recommended that job reservations be abolished; that Africans, Indians, and Coloureds be allowed to form trade unions; and that restrictions on multiracial unions be relaxed. These unions would become part of the country's industrial relations system, which meant conciliation and arbitration procedures as well as the right to strike. It also meant, however, official union registration and therefore wider government control over union activities.

Parliament enacted some of the recommendations of both the Riekert and Wiehahn reports in 1979. By the mid-1980s two large and increasingly powerful African trade unions had developed: the Congress of South African Trade Unions (COSATU), and the Council of Unions of South Africa–Azanian Confederation of Trade Unions (CUSA-AZACTU). The latter union had adopted the Black Consciousness philosophy. Altogether African trade unions had over one million dues-paying members and constituted an important, militant force in South African politics.

The government accepted other modifications to the apartheid system in the late 1970s as well. Many mines and industries made an effort to stabilize their African work force by hiring Africans to long-term contracts and allowing them to bring their families with them. As permanent residents, urbanized Africans were permitted in 1976 to obtain thirty-year (later extended to ninety-year) leases on their homes in African townships in White South Africa. In 1983 the government instituted a plan to help Africans buy their homes outright. Botha's total strategy also encouraged the relaxing of numerous petty apartheid laws. Many hotels and restaurants were opened to all races, as were movie theaters, venues for cultural events, and other public places. Sports teams and sporting events became more integrated. A critical component of the total strategy was the development of better-educated, more highly skilled workers of all races. In the late 1970s and early 1980s the government substantially increased the amount of money it spent on African, Coloured, and Indian schools at all levels. It also permitted these students to attend White universities if their own ethnic university did not offer certain courses of study. By the mid-1980s, 20 to 30 percent of students enrolled at Rhodes University, the University of Cape Town, and the University of the Witwatersrand came from these groups.

There was a fundamental contradiction, however, between allowing some Africans permanent residency in a White South Africa and arguing that all Africans had *bantustan* citizenship. This contradiction would shortly bring down the entire apartheid structure, but not yet. As the government made provisions for highly skilled Africans to remain in the country, it moved forward with the forced removal of "surplus" Africans to *bantustans*. It also continued to grant "independence" to some of these *bantustans*. The Transkei became "independent" in 1976. Bophuthatswana was next (1977), then Venda (1979), the Ciskei (1981), and KwaNdebele (1984). This charade of "decolonization" that Verwoerd so proudly trumpeted fooled no one: Foreign governments refused to recognize the "independent" *bantustans*.

By the early 1980s the *bantustans* were ludicrous embarrassments. Their governments, almost entirely funded by White South African taxes, were inept, corrupt, and authoritarian to the extreme. Some homelands created dens of inequity, such as Sun City in Bophuthatswana, where South African Whites could enjoy all the forbidden fruits denied them by their own puritanical rulers: pornographic movies, interracial sex, gambling. All the while, homeland populations sank deeper into abject poverty. Yet the South African government continued to deport thousands more "surplus" people year after year to these dumping grounds, destroying the environment through overcrowding, over-farming, and overgrazing.

Government modifications of apartheid caused more divisions within the Afrikaner community. On the left were many businesspeople, intellectuals, and clergy who viewed apartheid as immoral and inefficient and wanted the entire system scrapped. The right-wing *verkramptes* wanted to preserve Verwoerdian racial segregation to the letter. Vorster and the *verligtes* represented the "moderate" majority view in the Afrikaner community, and they held power.

Part of the total strategy was a propaganda scheme to convince the outside world that real change was occurring within South Africa. Throughout the 1970s Vorster used secret government funds, mainly from the Defense Department, to finance several propaganda operations not only within South Africa but also in the United States, Britain, and Europe. These included (1) purchasing newspapers and other publications, and (2) seeking to buy the support of politicians and prominent personalities abroad. When Vorster resigned the prime ministership due to ill health in 1978, his minister of defense, P.W. Botha, succeeded him as prime minister. Vorster assumed the honorary position of state president. He was forced to resign in disgrace just a few months later, however, when news of the misuse of these funds, known as the Information scandal, or "Muldergate" (named after Minister of Information Connie Mulder), came to light.

Unlike previous prime ministers who supported apartheid, P.W. Botha came to the post with no experience except in politics. He left university in 1936 to work for Malan's Purified National Party in 1936 and moved up through the party ranks before being elected to Parliament in 1948. Botha first joined the cabinet in 1961 as minister of Coloured affairs and of community development and housing. He served as minister of defense from 1966 to 1978. After taking office as prime minister, Botha selected General Malan to succeed him as defense minister. Botha could now implement the total strategy policy he and Malan had developed in the 1970s. He initially hinted publicly that he might substantially change the apartheid system. The Wiehahn and Riekert commissions' recommendations, for example, had his full support. He even questioned the need for the Mixed Marriages and Immorality Acts, one of the bedrock principles of apartheid. Botha seemed prepared to head off on a bold new path and speed the pace of change. At the National Press Club in Washington, D.C., in 1979, Botha's minister of co-operation and development (previously Bantu affairs), Piet Koornhof, told a somewhat startled audience that apartheid was dying. To make sweeping changes, however, Botha needed Afrikaner support.

The forced resignations of Vorster and Connie Mulder had considerably strengthened Botha's hand. Mulder was the National Party leader in the Transvaal and the favorite to become the next prime minister. After his resignation he formed his own Conservative Party. The *verkrampte* deputy minister of Bantu education, Andries Treurnicht, took Mulder's place in the Transvaal. Treurnicht—"Dr. No" as he came to be known—opposed any apartheid reforms. He led the hard-line right wing within the National Party. Hoping to obtain a mandate for change, Botha called an election for April 1981 and the National Party won a massive majority once again, but Hertzog's Herstigte Nasionale Party won nearly one-third of the Afrikaner vote. When Botha moved to adopt major governmental reforms following the election, Treurnicht called for a vote of no confidence but lost. Forced out of the National Party, Treurnicht and some of his followers, all still members of Parliament, formed the Conservative Party of South Africa, which soon absorbed Mulder's faction. At the same time a number of disillusioned low-level bureaucrats, subordinate police and soldiers, farmers, and blue-collar workers joined paramilitary right-wing extremist groups, such as the Wit Kommando (White Commando) and Wit Wolwe (White Wolves). These groups carried out numerous acts of sabotage against the government and random acts of murder and violence against Blacks in the 1980s and 1990s. By far the most important of the paramilitary bands was the Afrikaner Weerstandsbeweging (Afrikaner Resistance Movement, or AWB), led by Eugene Terre'Blanche, which adopted Nazi-style symbolism, salutes, and uniforms.

Thus, although Botha won the 1981 election and the no-confidence vote, thousands of Afrikaners voted for conservative parties that pledged to maintain apartheid. Botha pulled back from his aggressive campaign for change but did press forward with the major governmental reforms that Treurnicht and others adamantly opposed. Vorster had initiated these reforms in 1976. For years apartheid planners had been uneasy about the ambiguous position of Coloureds and Indians under apartheid. In the post-Soweto era the support of these two population groups was deemed indispensable and an integral part of the total strategy. Even though separate development created "homelands" for Africans where they could live and possess political rights, Coloureds and Indians in fact had neither a homeland nor political rights. Vorster appointed a National Party committee, chaired by Botha, that proposed the creation of three separate parliaments: one White, one Coloured, one Indian. Indians and Coloureds would thereby have some voice in national government while racial segregation and White supremacy were preserved. This plan was presented during the 1977 general election, which the National Party won by a huge majority vote, but hardliners managed to delay its implementation temporarily. The Schlebusch Commission was established instead to study other options for constitutional change. Its recommendations resulted in the establishment of a multiracial President's Council that replaced the White upper house of Parliament, the Senate. Although it possessed only advisory powers, the Council could make further constitutional proposals. The Commission also proposed a separate President's Council for urban Africans, but the plan was dropped when no representative Africans would join it.

In 1983 Botha announced there would be a new constitution that provided for three separate parliaments under a single executive presidency, as his committee had proposed five years earlier. The scheme was put to a vote in a Whites-only referendum. White hardliners on the right voiced harsh opposition to the plan. White progressives on the left condemned the exclusion of Africans. Nevertheless the referendum passed by a two-thirds majority. In its final form the new constitution provided for a new office of state president, who would be indirectly elected by an Electoral College that had a majority White make-up. The state president assumed new, wide-ranging powers. There would be three separate legislative chambers—a House of Assembly for Whites (178 members), a House of Representatives for Coloureds (85 members), and a House of Delegates for Indians (45 members)—with members of each house elected by voters from separate ethnic voting rolls. Each House would handle legislation for its "own affairs," such as education, health, and community administrations. Areas not covered under "own affairs" or matters affecting the nation at large, such as foreign affairs, taxation, industry, and defense, were "general" affairs to be acted on by a multiracial cabinet drawn from all three Houses. The state president retained complete control over all "Black [i.e., African] affairs" and decided what were "general" and "own" affairs. Because the White House of Assembly had more members than the other two Houses combined, Whites continued to hold absolute power. To further guarantee White control, any disagreements among the three Houses were sent on to the President's Council, where ultimately the state president made the final resolution. The National Party could now argue that Coloureds and Indians shared political power in South Africa. But the new constitution still distributed this power on the basis of race, it left Whites with absolute control over the political process, and most important, it excluded Africans, 75 percent of the country's population. The government did make provision for Africans residing in African townships to elect local authorities. The remainder could, according to apartheid theory, vote as they wanted in their *bantustans*.

Elections for the Coloured House of Representatives took place in August 1984 and for the Indian House of Delegates in September. Many Indians and Coloureds saw through this White ploy and refused to participate. Although some petty apartheid laws had been relaxed, Indians and Coloureds were still the objects of harsh racial discrimination and second-class citizenship. Young Coloureds and Indians also were dissatisfied because under the new constitution they were eligible for military conscription. A newly formed multiracial federation of over 575 organizations, including trade unions, called the United Democratic Front (UDF), organized a boycott of the polls. Most Indians and Coloureds refused to register; of those that did, only between 20 and 30 percent actually voted. In Cape Town the new constitution received the support of only 6 percent of qualified Coloured voters. Despite this less than impressive showing, Botha labeled the elections a start along the right road. The three new parliaments, with P.W. Botha as state president, held their first legislative meetings in September 1984.

Black Insurrection, 1984–1986

Botha had reformed apartheid enough for Blacks to want more, but not enough to satisfy any of them. Most Indians and Coloureds recognized that the new constitution only gave them the appearance of power, whereas Whites still held real control in South Africa. For Africans, the new constitution was a slap in the face. Rioting occurred in both Indian and Coloured communities before the parliamentary elections took place. Violence also erupted in the African townships, but this time on an unprecedented scale.

During the first violent confrontations between the apartheid government and the masses in 1960–1964, the government held a psychological advantage. Most Blacks, after centuries of oppression and treatment as inferiors, acted deferentially toward Whites. The generation of Black leaders in the early 1960s—Mandela, Sisulu, Tambo, Sobukwe, and others—overcame this timidity and led mass protests from above, but then the White man's superior weaponry and organization defeated them.

Steve Biko's Black Consciousness movement freed thousands of Blacks, especially the young, from these chains of diffidence and low self-esteem. The children of Soweto were bold, defiant, strident. Now the revolt came from below, much of it spontaneous and unplanned, as the masses simply refused to bow before White dominance again. Although they too were overpowered by the police and military, this time the government could not merely lock away a few leaders and end the resistance. While the ANC, PAC, and other liberation movements were banned and operating in exile abroad, Black South Africans created a culture of protest following Soweto that enveloped the country. Blacks were now openly defiant. Funerals, for example, became a popular occasion to demonstrate against the apartheid system, with large crowds openly waving banned ANC flags, singing banned ANC songs, and listening to emotionally charged speeches. Blacks danced the *toyi-toyi* and defiantly shouted *amandla ngawetu!* ("power is ours!").

It was this mass culture of protest that the multiracial United Democratic Front came to represent. The UDF coordinated the anti-apartheid actions of hundreds of church groups, community organizations, trade unions, sporting bodies, women's groups, and youth leagues. It was formed in August 1983 to organize a boycott of the new tricameral constitution, but it continued to promote other boycotts, protests, and work stoppages throughout the 1980s. Its most important function, however, was to serve as a national anti-apartheid political voice at a time when the government had silenced all the official groups.

Radical churchmen played a leading role in the UDF, filling in for the secular anti-apartheid leaders who were in exile, jail, or banned. These churchmen included Alan Boesak, Frank Chikane, and Beyers Naudé. The UDF's most well known spokesmen was the Anglican archbishop Desmond Tutu, who won the Nobel Peace Prize in 1984. These men and others used their pulpits and moral authority to condemn apartheid. Other UDF activists included Patrick Lekota and Popo Molefe, who were arrested with twenty others for treason in 1985. Both Lekota and Molefe became provincial premiers after the majority government came to power in 1994.

The UDF always remained an ephemeral organization, however, lacking formal leaders or property. Because the UDF had no real base, it was difficult for the government to halt its activities; to do so would involve arresting all the leaders of its more than five hundred affiliated organizations. Ideologically the UDF members were "Charterists," that is, they supported the multiracial, democratic principles of the Freedom Charter. Close ties existed between the UDF and the ANC, although many UDF members renounced the ANC's support for an armed struggle. UDF spokespersons made it clear, though, that the UDF did not intend to replace or oppose the ANC. UDF successes in leading anti-apartheid resistance in the mid- and late 1980s revived the ANC, caused its membership to increase, and helped the ANC replace Black Consciousness as the leading liberation movement.

Botha became state president, therefore, at the very moment when anti-apartheid opposition was more united, more defiant, and more militant than ever. The UDF not only led boycotts of the Indian and Coloured Houses of Parliament but also led successful boycotts against council elections in African townships. In many townships there were no candidates; where there were, only 2 to 3 percent of registered voters actually voted. The newly elected township councilors, as in the homelands, were mostly middle class and sought the power, prestige, and benefits of the office. They did not appreciate the bitterness and hostility their fellow Blacks felt toward the system.

The final struggle, leading to the end of apartheid, began on 3 September 1984, the day the new constitution took effect. The struggle broke out in Sharpeville, the site of an earlier turning point in South African history. This time Africans turned on Africans, killing Sharpeville's newly elected deputy-mayor. Other Africans, twenty-six altogether in September, were either burned to death or strangled. A similar number died in Sebokeng township near Vereeniging. For many Blacks, spontaneous violence now became the only response cathartic enough to release their pent-up anger and frustration. The so-called Black on Black violence that began in Sharpeville and Sebokeng spread to other townships. Black churches, school buildings, shops, and homes were destroyed, and buses and private vehicles in Black areas were destroyed or badly damaged. Black councilors, police officers, and other collaborators with the apartheid regime were either killed, injured, or forced to resign.

Much of this violence was carried out by young Blacks who took control of many Black townships and instituted their own forms of vigilante justice. Everyone, man or woman, who collaborated with the government or was suspected of being an informer became a target of their rage. When these Black youths, calling themselves the comrades, caught a suspected collaborator they sometimes punished him with "necklacing": They placed a rubber tire around his neck filled with gasoline and set it aflame. The lucky ones were only whipped. The comrades said their goal was to make the townships ungovernable by the government, by either frightening away or killing all those who collaborated with the apartheid regime. The impetus for Black on Black violence had various origins. Some of it was committed by rival gangs of Black youths who were simply fighting over territory. A significant number of the worst atrocities, it was revealed years later, were perpetrated by government agents as part of an elaborate "dirty-tricks" scheme that was responsible for hundreds of deaths.

By late 1985, informal Black groups ruled in many townships where police and government officials were afraid to enter. The comrades, most under twenty-five years of age, held control in some townships, although their powers and methods varied from place to place, as did their willingness to allow due process and justice. Many comrades worked with local UDF affiliates and, through them, the ANC. Together they organized boycotts of bus companies and of rents paid to African councils. They also encouraged strikes and worker and student stayaways. Other political activists remained loyal to the banned Black Consciousness movement. Some of these founded a new Africanist-Black Consciousness movement called the Azanian People's Organization (AZAPO), which derived its name for South Africa, Azania, from an ancient Arabic name for east Africa. AZAPO limited its membership to Africans, Indians, and Coloureds; called for a revolution to overthrow the White state and the capitalist system; and always represented a minority viewpoint.

The UDF's main rival for influence among Africans was Chief Mangosuthu Buthelezi, a controversial Zulu politician and descendant of Cetshwayo. Buthelezi was actively involved in the ANC through the 1970s but lost credibility when he became prime minister of the KwaZulu *bantustan* in 1975. The ANC and other anti-apartheid groups considered him a collaborator with the apartheid regime, but Buthelezi argued that he could fight apartheid from within the system. In the 1970s and 1980s he became a favorite of conservative politicians abroad and of the South African government and business community because he appeared less radical and militant than the ANC. He supported multiracialism, opposed sanctions, and encouraged foreign investment. He claimed that sanctions only hurt Africans. He rejected the armed struggle and publicly broke with the ANC over this issue in 1979. He consistently refused to negotiate any political arrangement with the White government, however, until Mandela was freed from prison and allowed to participate. He also steadfastly rejected KwaZulu independence. In 1975 he revived Inkatha, a Zulu cultural organization first formed in the early 1920s. Although Buthelezi promoted Inkatha as a national liberation movement, it was clearly an ethnic movement based on Zulu tradition and membership. From the mid-1980s, UDF and Inkatha supporters had violent confrontations in parts of Natal and KwaZulu.

APARTHEID'S DYING DAYS, 1985-1990

As opposition to apartheid grew, the government reacted in an indecisive and contradictory fashion, reflecting the various factions within the National Party leadership and within Afrikanerdom generally. Andries Treurnicht's Conservative Party, representing the Afrikaner right wing, consistently outpolled the National Party in by-elections and became the main opposition party. Its members included White civil servants who administered apartheid, White laborers frightened by Black competition, and racist ideologues. Many of Botha's advisers, as well as Afrikaner businesspeople, clergy, and other community leaders, advised radical change away from apartheid. In September 1985 a group of white businessmen flew to Zambia to discuss South Africa's future with Oliver Tambo and other ANC leaders. Throughout the 1980s, however, military and intelligence advisers, particularly General Magnus Malan, gained more power and influence within Botha's government and with Botha himself.

Botha continued his "total strategy" policy to stop the communists' "total onslaught." A key component of this policy involved preventing guerrilla incursions against the Republic from across its borders. South Africa used its military and economic clout to control its neighbors, all of whom were dependent in one way or another on the economic giant. In return for economic aid and jobs for migrant workers, South Africa's neighbors, the so-called frontline states, were required to withhold support and sanctuary for anti-apartheid refugees and movements. South Africa also practiced a destabilization policy against its neighbors. South African commandos regularly infiltrated neighboring countries, where they carried out acts of sabotage, terrorism, and assassination. South African armed forces, including the air force, attacked and destroyed ANC camps in these countries. Altogether these destabilization tactics caused one million deaths, left three million homeless, and inflicted $35 billion in damage to neighboring economies from 1980 to 1989.

South Africa also continued to occupy Namibia and became involved in civil wars in Mozambique and Angola. Samora Machel's Marxist government in Mozambique hoped that by signing the Nkomati Accord in March 1984 South Africa would halt its destabilizing attacks and stop providing arms and financial assistance to RENAMO (the Mozambique National Resistance Movement), an anti-government guerrilla movement in that country. In return, Machel agreed not to assist the ANC. Machel carried out his part of the bargain but South Africa did not, continuing its efforts to destabilize Machel's government. South Africa tried to win friends in America and England by supporting the anticommunist UNITA rebels in Angola, who also had U.S. support. In 1987–1988 South African forces fought Angolan, Cuban, and SWAPO troops to a standstill at the battle of Cuito Cuanavale in southern Angola, but the political and military costs were heavy. The battle eventually caused South Africa to withdraw from Angola and then from Namibia, leading to that country's independence in 1990. Although South Africa's destabilization policy had serious repercussions internationally, resulting in increased calls for sanctions, it did severely cripple the ANC's ability to make military incursions into the Republic. The Black insurrection in the townships was many times more effective in forcing change than were the ANC's limited guerrilla activities.

Botha's reform measures won him some sympathy abroad, whereas the so-called Black on Black violence hurt the image of the Black liberation struggle. Fortunately for Botha, he took office in 1979 just as Britain and the United States installed conservative governments that remained in power throughout the 1980s. British prime minister Margaret Thatcher steadfastly refused to impose sanctions, even though many members of Parliament and all the other members of the Commonwealth were demanding them. Ronald Reagan's administration in the United States practiced "constructive engagement," which called for reform—but not in a public way that would embarrass the apartheid regime, such as congressional sanctions or criticism in the United Nations. Reagan was ill informed about South Africa and generally supported the White government against what he viewed as the Black communist alternative.

But neither Thatcher nor Reagan could deny the township violence that appeared daily on television news around the world. Scenes showed heavily armed police and soldiers beating and firing on unarmed Blacks, many of them children. One of the worst incidents occurred in Uitenhage on 21 March 1985, the twenty-fifth anniversary of the Sharpeville shootings. Police there fired on a peaceful Black crowd marching to commemorate the event; nineteen people were killed and many more were wounded. Worldwide condemnation followed.

Despite the military attacks on his neighbors and his harsh repression of opposition at home, many outside observers still believed that Botha wanted reform and simply needed time to gather Afrikanerdom behind him. For this reason they placed hope on Botha's famous "Rubicon Address" before a National Party congress in Durban on 15 August 1985. Comments by Botha and by his foreign minister, "Pik" Botha, had fueled speculation that major changes to the apartheid system were coming and that South Africa was preparing to "cross the Rubicon" and head in a new direction. The speech was a colossal disappointment. Botha said he would not abandon apartheid and would not include South Africa's African population in the main political process. He also angrily rejected foreign "interference." As a result the international community reacted angrily to his speech. Economic sanctions were imposed, capital left the country, the value of the rand fell, the stock exchange had to shut down briefly, and foreign banks refused to roll over loans. These actions further weakened what was already a deteriorating economy suffering from high inflation, rising unemployment, and a decline in real growth per capita.

It was into this atmosphere of violence and disappointment that the British Commonwealth nations decided to send an Eminent Persons

Group (EPG), composed of seven senior British Commonwealth politicians, to South Africa to make policy recommendations regarding economic sanctions. EPG members were warmly greeted in March 1986 and met with both government and anti-apartheid leaders, including Mandela. The mood turned chilly, however, when EPG members asked the government to lift its ban on the ANC and other anti-apartheid organizations, release Mandela, and end apartheid. The mission was suddenly terminated on 19 May 1986 when South Africa carried out air raids against suspected ANC camps in Harare, Zimbabwe; Lusaka, Zambia; and Gabarone, Botswana—all Commonwealth members. The EPG's scathing report resulted in Commonwealth countries intensifying their sanctions. In September 1986 the U.S. Congress overrode President Reagan's veto and passed the Comprehensive Anti-Apartheid Act.

It was during the EPG visit that Botha and the National Party elite realized the world would never be satisfied until South Africa abandoned apartheid and moved to a democratic system of one person, one vote. Botha knew this would lead to a Black-ruled government, almost certainly led by the ANC. This he could not allow. Instead he would continue his efforts to win the "trust and faith" of the Black population. First, however, he needed to clamp down on the unrest and restore order to the townships. A state of emergency had been in place in several parts of the country from July 1985 to March 1986, but it was subsequently lifted because of international pressure. During this period 8,000 people were arrested and 22,000 charged with offenses. On 12 June 1986, Botha proclaimed a new, nationwide state of emergency for an indefinite period. Within a year another 26,000 people were detained, many of them children. Many anti-apartheid organizations were banned and their leaders arrested. Police were granted broad powers to detain, arrest, interrogate, and hold, with the accused having no access to a lawyer or due process in the courts. Torture became a routine part of interrogation, and assassinations of anti-apartheid activists were carried out both inside and outside the country by members of the security forces. After 1988 the Civil Co-operation Bureau, under the command of the Defense Force, coordinated these activities. To block news reports and the transmission of graphic images of police and military brutality in the townships, a nearly total ban was placed on all television, radio, and newspaper coverage of the unrest.

Within the townships a backlash had developed by 1986 against the excesses of the comrades, and many township residents took advantage of the state of emergency (with the government's encouragement) to reap their revenge. Groups of Black vigilantes formed, with names such as the *Witdoeke* or (the A-Team). They were generally older and politically more conservative than the comrades, and some had ties with homeland leaders, police, and councilors. Others were migrant workers living in single men's hostels. As elders they resented being told what to do by the young comrades; they wanted a return to the old order. They received support from the security forces, who were glad to have these men do their work of restoring order to the townships. The most notorious confrontation between the two sides occurred at the sprawling squatter settlement of Crossroads near Cape Town in 1986, when vigilantes with police help burned down the entire area occupied by comrades. Violent clashes—almost a civil war—between comrades/UDF and Inkatha supporters in Natal were also part of this backlash. Both sides were predominantly Zulu speaking; the battles were fought over issues between generations, rural and urban issues, different political views, and different understandings of Zulu traditions.

Yet none of the violence swirling around the townships ever seriously threatened White supremacy in South Africa. By 1987 the government had succeeded in bringing the townships under control and the passions of 1985 had subsided. Thousands of schoolchildren sat in jails awaiting trial, which often took months or more, and were routinely abused mentally and physically. Forty-three died in police custody by March 1987, and 263 were hospitalized. South African Defence Force units numbering 5,000 to 8,000 soldiers replaced the hated police in some townships. This lessened tensions but also caused more disillusionment among young White men, especially English-speakers, who joined the military to fight communism on the borders, not to protect apartheid in the townships. Little of this violence reached White areas; most Whites had little or no idea what was happening. The townships were often miles from White areas, and the news blackout prevented them from reading or hearing about the violence. The police and military guaranteed that Whites passed through the period almost as safely and securely as ever.

The government also passed a few reform measures during this period. Over thirty-four acts relating to pass laws were repealed. The Group Areas Act was slightly modified to allow some mixed-race areas. Two of the earliest and most hated pieces of apartheid legislation, the Mixed Marriages Act and Section 16 of the Immorality Act (which had outlawed sexual relations between all Blacks and Whites) were abolished, as was the Prohibition of Political Interference Act, which had segregated political parties.

The government's most critical problem was not township violence, but the economy. The government not only had to maintain White South Africans' high standard of living but also had to raise the living standards of those urbanized Blacks who were now permanent residents. To provide jobs, homes, and amenities for these Blacks, the economy had to grow; yet in 1987 South Africa had one of the world's worst growth rates. South Africa had always depended on outside capital investment for its growth and development, and no more so than in the mid-1980s. International financiers had always provided this capital with no questions asked, but worldwide protests and calls for sanctions finally influenced them. Large American and European banks refused to grant new loans or roll over old ones. Multinational corporations started withdrawing from South Africa. The U.S. Congress passed a comprehensive set of anti-apartheid measures in 1986. By 1987, organizations and nations around the world were pulling their investments out of South Africa and imposing severe sanctions. This all took an increasingly heavy toll on South Africa's economy, as did the high costs of managing apartheid, protecting South Africa's borders, and fighting wars in Namibia and Angola.

Botha, Malan, and their advisers were increasingly losing support from both right and left. In the May 1987 general elections for the White House of Assembly, the National Party received 52 percent of the votes, maintaining a still commanding majority with 133 seats. But the Conservative Party won 23 seats with 26 percent of the vote and replaced the Progressive Federal Party as the official parliamentary opposition. Whereas many average Afrikaner voters appeared to want a return to Verwoerdian apartheid, many White business, community, and religious leaders, English and Afrikaner alike, were looking to end apartheid altogether. They had accepted the fact that radical change was absolutely necessary, and they started to take the initiative themselves. Despite their attraction to Buthelezi, they recognized that a peaceful solution to South Africa's problems could not be reached without the participation of Mandela and the ANC. This explains the trip by a group of white South African business people to Lusaka, Zambia, in 1985, led by Gavin Relly of the Anglo American Corporation to meet with Oliver Tambo and other ANC leaders. The Broederbond, now chaired by the *verligte* Pieter de Lange, circulated a document in 1986 calling for Mandela's release, an end to group rights, and negotiations with the ANC. In 1987 the Progressive Federal Party leader Van Zyl Slabbert led a delegation of fifty Afrikaner intellectuals to Dakar, Senegal, for talks with ANC leaders.

By 1988 the situation had moved beyond Botha's control. He and his ministers spoke vaguely about future domestic reforms, but they could not think beyond racial categories, segregation, and White supremacy. In October 1988 segregated municipal elections were held, including those for new Black township councilors. Boesak, Tutu, Chikane, Naudé, and twenty-two other clergymen, representing sixteen denominations, defied the state of emergency regulations and called on all Christians to boycott the racist elections. Barely 25 percent of registered Black voters participated, and less than half the available seats were contested. Violence continued in the townships. Black trade unions were also active. There were 1,148 strikes in 1987, including one by the National Union of Mineworkers that lasted for three weeks and involved more than 250,000 miners. Cyril Ramaphosa led the strike. He would become general secretary of the ANC in 1991. At the same time, Indian and Coloured members of their respective houses of Parliament were becoming increasingly pessimistic about their ability to effect meaningful change. In October 1987 a military coup in the Transkei led by Bantu Holomisa ousted Matanzima. Holomisa openly supported the ANC. The SADF restored president Lucas Mangope to power in Bophuthatswana after a coup attempt in February 1988.

Circumstances both inside and outside the country now forced South Africa's White leaders to abandon apartheid and accept change. The resolution of the Namibian problem allowed international anti-apartheid movements to focus all their attention and resources on apartheid. Botha's total strategy of winning trust and faith was obviously not working, as the government's control over the Black population depended increasingly on sheer force. Demographically, Whites were becoming an ever smaller percentage of South Africa's total population, down to 15 percent in 1985 (from 19 percent in 1960; the number has dropped to 11 percent in 1999). The African population was not only growing, but despite government's attempts to tightly control migration to urban areas, Africans were leaving the homelands and settling in African townships in massive numbers. Africans were also becoming a powerful economic force, flexing their buying power, asserting their rights through strikes, and starting up businesses. As job reservations were relaxed, many Blacks were moving up through the business ranks, some into management positions. Although Black educational opportunities still remained segregated and inferior to that offered to Whites, millions of Blacks were attending school and a nearly equal number of Blacks as Whites were attending university. Finally, by 1988, the apartheid structure had become so unwieldly and inefficient that it threatened to topple of its own accord. Years of duplication of services for each racial group in areas of health, education, and welfare wasted millions of rands, as did the three parliamentary chambers and financial and security support to maintain the homelands. The massive state security system and military services also consumed more millions of rands that could have been used to provide a better life for all.

The ANC had to face a changed reality as well. A popular insurrection to overthrow the government was clearly not possible. For years the ANC had depended on the Soviet Union and its surrogates for training and equipment for an armed struggle. As Soviet communism itself moved closer to collapse, the USSR urged the ANC to abandon violent revolution and to negotiate with apartheid's leaders. The ANC leaders had little choice but to listen to this advice because no other country was able or willing to give them such aid. The hard-line South African Communist Party members in the ANC were also losing their credibility as the shortcomings of communism became increasingly evident. Most ANC members now favored negotiations and the establishment of a multiparty democracy and capitalist economy.

Botha suffered a mild stroke in January 1989 and temporarily resigned his duties. F.W. de Klerk, a lawyer and seventeen-year member of Parliament, temporarily took Botha's place. Botha abruptly resigned in August when it was evident he no longer had his Cabinet's support. De Klerk officially assumed office as state president following the House of Assembly elections in September. Although de Klerk's brother was a well-known liberal who had already met in informal negotiations with the ANC, de Klerk himself was a reputed conservative. Once in office, however, he revealed a pragmatic side, recognizing the need to make drastic changes and to negotiate with legitimate Black leaders. He began in October 1988 by releasing eight political prisoners, including Walter Sisulu. On 2 February 1990, the opening day of Parliament, de Klerk announced to an astonished world that he was unconditionally releasing Nelson Mandela and unbanning the UDF, ANC, PAC, SACP, and other liberation movements. The government, he said, planned to open negotiations with Mandela and other leaders with the intention of developing a new constitution based on universal suffrage. The Rubicon had finally been crossed.

CONSTRUCTING A NEW SOUTH AFRICA, 1990–1994

Holding hands with his wife, Winnie, Nelson Mandela emerged from twenty-seven years' imprisonment on 11 February 1990. It was an image and a moment equal to any of the other monumental events of the time—the fall of the Berlin Wall and the collapse of communism in Eastern Europe and the Soviet Union. In the space of a few feet Mandela went from being a prisoner to being a statesman of international stature. In several speeches following his release he identified himself as a loyal ANC member and thanked Umkhonto we Sizwe and the Communist Party for their sacrifices. Mandela also signaled his intention to continue the armed struggle and called for sanctions. Although many Whites both within and without the country, including de Klerk and Margaret Thatcher, were greatly dismayed, Mandela knew he had to maintain his base of support and also that he had to keep the pressure on until apartheid was ended and a multiracial, democratic government was in place.

Although he soon began a series of travels and meetings that took him around the world, often in an atmosphere most resembling a victory tour, he had little time for rest. He and the ANC were no longer on the outside looking in. They would soon be participating in constitutional negotiations as a legitimate political party and probably would be the next rulers of the country, yet in many ways they were a political party in name only. They had been banned for decades, which meant they had no internal organization within the country and no network of local branches. They also had few members with political and organizational experience, not to mention political leadership experience. Over the next two years the ANC created an organized national movement with a countrywide network of local branches. At a National Congress in Durban in July 1991, the ANC elected Mandela as president and the National Union of Mineworkers leader, Cyril Ramaphosa, as secretary-general.

Deep divisions were also present within the ANC in 1990 over questions of tactics and ideology: communism versus capitalism, private ownership versus nationalization, armed struggle versus negotiation. Those members who had never left the country and had suffered all of apartheid's hardships and violence deeply resented those exiles who had lived abroad and now returned home expecting to assume leadership positions. There were generations of radical young people who deserved credit for their massive rebellions that helped to bring down the government, but who now had to learn discipline and to obey the older ANC leaders. They also had to return to school, because many of them had sacrificed their educations for the revolution. The most difficult problem the ANC faced, however, was its opposition status. The White government still held political power. The ANC could not take the initiative on any matter—from building more homes, to asking for police protection at meetings, to holding elections—without first consulting with that government. The ANC could only force change by committing negative acts such as armed struggle, strikes, and demonstrations; continued calls for sanctions and boycotts; and leaving the negotiating table.

Mandela faced tragic personal problems after his release that also had wider implications for the ANC. Mandela's wife, Winnie, was tried and found guilty in February 1991 for complicity in the kidnapping and assault of a young activist, "Stompie" Mokoetsie, by members of her personal bodyguard, the "Mandela football team." Although she was—and still remains in 1999—popular among radicals, she had many enemies within the ANC. For numerous reasons Mandela announced in April 1991 that he and Winnie were separating. They divorced in 1996.

De Klerk and the National Party had serious problems as well. There had been hints of de Klerk's more enlightened tendencies as early as 1985 when he introduced the repeal of Mixed Marriages and Immorality acts. By 1990, however, he may have realized that apartheid had failed, that the economy was in deep trouble, and that Botha's initiatives of the 1980s, such as the tricameral parliament, enjoyed no support abroad. Nevertheless his actions in February 1990 took everyone by complete surprise. Black leaders such as Archbishop Tutu and Allan Boesak were elated, whereas far-right Whites such as Treurnicht and his Conservative Party, or ultra-rightists such as Eugene Terre'Blanche of the Afrikaner Weerstandsbeweging, were furious. Results from elections throughout the 1980s indicated that more and more of the National Party's core constituency, including many government bureaucrats and the police and military, were leaving the National Party and giving their support to the conservatives. Particularly troublesome were the members of the police and military intelligence units, such as the Civil Co-operation Bureau, who continued their covert operations against the ANC and other groups through arson, intimidation, and assassination. De Klerk announced in August 1990 that he had ordered these units disbanded, but their activities continued for at least two more years. These units received their orders from some of the highest officials in government, who still held to the dream that by disrupting the ANC, the National Party could ally itself with Inkatha and other ANC opponents and retain some degree of White power.

While both sides jostled for position, ANC and government representatives met to discuss conditions for starting formal constitutional negotiations, that is, "talks about talks." The ANC team included Walter
Sisulu, South African Communist Party general-secretary Joe Slovo, and
international affairs director Thabo Mbeki. On the government side were
long-time Foreign Minister "Pik" Botha, Minister of Constitutional Development Gerrit Viljoen, Minister of Justice Kobie Coetsee, and Minister
of Law and Order Adrian Vlok. The two sides met first on 2 May 1990
at the Groote Schuur manor house, the president's official residence in
Cape Town, and produced the "Groote Schuur Minute," which dealt
with the release of political prisoners and the general return of exiles. In
June de Klerk lifted the five-year-old state of emergency everywhere
except in Natal where violence continued between ANC and Inkatha
supporters. Parliament repealed the cornerstone of petty apartheid legislation, the 1953 Reservation of Separate Amenities Act, thereby opening
beaches, benches, restrooms, restaurants, hospitals, and hotels to everyone. Both leaders took trips abroad that June. To European leaders de
Klerk declared that the democratic process in South Africa was irreversible. In the United States Mandela was also positive about the future but
continued to ask that economic sanctions be maintained.

Before a second round of "talks about talks" could be held, the government uncovered a covert ANC military unit that was part of Operation Vula. Formed in 1988, Operation Vula connected exiles abroad with
internal activists and was intended as an insurance policy if negotiations
failed. Police arrested more than forty ANC members, including Mac
Maharaj, a member of the ANC's national executive and a SACP member. De Klerk tried to use these arrests to divide the ANC and SACP and
to force Joe Slovo off the negotiating team, but Mandela refused and
renewed his call for an investigation of armed government units operating against the ANC.

Because it was in the best interest of both parties to continue talks, the
two sides met again in Pretoria on 6 August, and Mandela announced
he was unilaterally and immediately ending the armed struggle, although Umkhonto we Sizwe would remain in existence. Even while the
Pretoria Minute proclaimed a historic truce between the government and
the ANC, many groups in South Africa at that moment were at war.

Shortly after de Klerk's unbanning of restricted groups in February,
violence erupted across the country. In Natal and KwaZulu, supporters
of the ANC, UDF, and COSATU (the large trade union federation) fought
with members of Buthelezi's Inkatha organization. By August 1990 the

clashes had spread from Natal to townships in the Transvaal and centered on single men's hostels accommodating Zulu migrant workers. These confrontations were particularly grisly, and more than 700 people died. The ANC believed the violence was fomented by a "third force" and called on the government to stop it. The homelands were also starting to crumble, as SADF troops were deployed in the Ciskei and Bophuthatswana following coup attempts, and South African police went to Gazankulu and Venda to restore peace.

Afrikaner far-right wing groups also became more numerous and more active in 1990 as reform gathered momentum. In June police arrested eleven far-right extremists involved in an alleged plot to assassinate prominent players in the reform process, including Mandela and de Klerk. Other right-wing activists began to disrupt National Party political rallies.

At the opening of Parliament on 1 February 1991, de Klerk again significantly advanced the reform process by announcing that all remaining apartheid laws, including the Group Areas Act and Population Registration Act, would be repealed. Only in matters relating to the franchise would race continue to have any legal significance, and these laws too would be revoked once agreement was reached on new constitutional arrangements. Once again de Klerk had caught the ANC by surprise. Of particular importance was the effect de Klerk's announcement had on the lifting of economic sanctions. Although the ANC continued to call for their retention, most countries including African countries, were soon knocking at South Africa's door to re-establish trade relations. The announcement also accelerated the dropping of cultural, sporting, and academic boycotts of South Africa, and the ANC generally supported these. South Africa would compete in the 1992 Olympic Games after an absence of thirty-two years.

Although the repeal of the apartheid legislation opened the way for the Black elite to move into previously reserved Whites-only neighborhoods and jobs, it did not make a great deal of difference to the millions of South Africans living in poverty. Unemployment stood at nearly 40 percent. Unchecked migration from the homelands led to shantytowns sprouting up around major urban areas containing 5 to 7 million desperately poor, malnourished squatters living in iron, wood, plastic, and cardboard hovels. Violence, crime, and drug use were rampant in these as well as in the traditional townships. Whites were not above the economic problems and political and social changes affecting the country in the early 1990s either. The "poor Whiteism" of the 1920s and 1930s returned, and it continues in 1999. The loss of high wages, job reservations and security, political dominance, and racial privilege have left many Whites on the street and lining up for relief. Far-right extremist groups played on White fears, which were now becoming very real for some, to attract new members.

Although there were good reasons for violence in the townships, the ANC continued to suspect government involvement in promoting it. Mandela and Buthelezi met in January and April to settle their differences, but violent clashes between Inkatha (now the Inkatha Freedom Party, or IFP) and ANC supporters only intensified. In July 1991 a newspaper reported that the IFP had received at least 250,000 rand from the South African Police to carry out anti-ANC activities. This "Inkathagate" scandal severely damaged Buthelezi's reputation and national and international respect for de Klerk's government. General Magnus Malan and Minister of Law and Order Adriaan Vlok were both subsequently demoted to minor cabinet posts. The ANC remained suspicious, however, that government security forces were still involved in violent attacks against the ANC and its allies. Later investigations proved them correct.

The government meanwhile was busy defending itself against its right-wing opponents. In August 1991 de Klerk took the fight right to the heart of ultra-right wing extremism. He went to address a National Party meeting in Ventersdorp, home of Eugene Terre'Blanche, the fiery leader of the militant Afrikaner Weerstandsbeweging (AWB). While de Klerk made his speech in a local hall; a violent street battle raged outside between police and 2,000 armed AWB members who had assembled to stop the rally. The event marked the first time since the National Party came to power that South African police had been used against a White, and mainly Afrikaner, demonstration.

De Klerk carried through on the promised repeals, and by June 1991 apartheid had been abolished except for the political legislation, which was, of course, the most critical legislation of all. For the remainder of the year the government and ANC played a chess match, each trying to be in the best possible position when constitutional talks began. Both sides published their preliminary constitutional proposals, the ANC in May and the government in September. To increase its membership and to change its image, the National Party opened its doors in October 1991 to people of all races and successfully gained large numbers of conservative Coloured and Asian voters who also feared African rule.

The government and eighteen other parties convened on 20 December 1991 for the Convention for a Democratic South Africa (CODESA). The

Conservative Party and the PAC refused to attend. The resulting Declaration of Intent contained a commitment from all parties to "an undivided South Africa with one nation sharing a common citizenship . . . free from apartheid or any other form of discrimination or domination." The parties also agreed that while the constitution was being drawn up an elected constituent assembly would serve as the National Parliament and that an Interim Government would exercise authority during this period. Five working groups were set up to work out arrangements for negotiations on the future of the homelands, the nature of the interim government, target dates for the establishment of a new democracy, principles for a new constitution, and general problems.

In a by-election early in 1992, far-right White fears and anger over the new constitution were expressed in an impressive Conservative Party (CP) victory in Potchefstroom. The CP now demanded that de Klerk call a general election. He took a gamble and did. A Whites-only referendum on support for de Klerk's reform initiative was called for 17 March 1992. Eighty percent of registered White voters turned out, and a stunning 68.7 percent of them voted for the pro-reform side. Only one constituency in the entire country recorded a "no" majority. De Klerk had crushed the right wing, received a mandate for continuing the reform process, and strengthened his party's position at the negotiating table.

De Klerk therefore came to the second session of CODESA talks in May 1992, taking a tough stand, and the talks subsequently collapsed. At issue were questions of power sharing, majority rule, and centralized power. The National Party also wanted a veto over any decisions taken by the Constituent Assembly. Refusing to accept the government's hard-line position, the ANC called on its members and those of the SACP and COSATU to participate in a campaign of rolling mass action (a series of sit-ins, marches, and work stoppages) to force government concessions.

The day after the mass action began, however, on 17 June, two hundred Inkatha men attacked a squatter camp near the Transvaal township of Boipatong and massacred forty-five people, including women and children. The men apparently arrived in marked police vehicles. When de Klerk visited the scene to express his sympathy, he was driven away by hostile crowds. The police, apparently acting without orders, then opened fire and killed at least thirty more. The killings reconfirmed the ANC's commitment to the mass action campaign and a set of new demands dealing with security before it would return to the negotiating table. The mass action campaign continued through July and culminated in a two-day general stayaway on 3 and 4 August that severely hurt the already ailing economy. A month later the ANC tried to extend its mass action to the homelands. On 7 September 1992 the ANC sponsored a march to Bisho, capital of the Ciskei, to gather support for the overthrow of the regime of Ciskei leader Brigadier Oupa Qozo. When the marchers broke through Ciskei police barriers, however, the police opened fire, killing 29 people and wounding over 200 more.

While the ANC stayed away from the formal talks, ANC secretary-general Cyril Ramaphosa, and Roelf Meyer, the minister of constitutional affairs, met for nineteen days in September 1992 to hammer out an agreement that CODESA appeared unable to produce. On 26 September Mandela and de Klerk signed a Record of Understanding, marking the most significant turning point during the transition period after 1990. The ANC agreed to resume the negotiations after the government agreed to release more political prisoners, fence migrant hostels, and prohibit the carrying and display of traditional weapons (as Zulu Inkatha members were wont to do, and then use in their violent demonstrations). For its part, the ANC made a historic concession by accepting "sunset clauses" (proposed by the communist Joe Slovo) that safeguarded White civil servant jobs and allowed for a coalition government. Any party receiving more than 20 percent of the national vote would have a deputy president in the coalition government. Cabinet seats would go to parties polling over 5 percent of the national vote. In the Record of Understanding the two sides agreed on the establishment of a consitutional assembly to construct a final constitution and a five-year transitional Government of National Unity.

Because the compromise was only between the ANC and the government, however, the small parties felt left out. Buthelezi in particular was angry because the clauses about migrant hostels and traditional weapons seemed aimed at the Inkatha Freedom Party. He organized a new alliance that contained some rather unlikely bedfellows. The Concerned South Africans Group (COSAG) consisted of nineteen organizations including Buthelezi's nearly all-Black IFP, several anti-ANC homelands governments, and the White ultra-right wing Conservative Party and Afrikaner Volksunie (Afrikaner People's Union.)

Despite Buthelezi's opposition, the government and ANC now appeared ready to move forward with the new constitution and government, even without the full support of all the other parties. Twenty-six parties met again at the World Trade Centre outside Johannesburg on 1 April 1993 to resume multiparty talks, which they called the Negotiating Council, to work out the final details. The talks had barely begun when the country was rocked by the assassination of Chris Hani, the South African Communist Party general-secretary and former chief of staff of Umkhonto we Sizwe. Since his return from exile, Hani had become one of the most respected and highly regarded ANC politicians. His funeral was massive, televised live by SABC, and set off rioting and demonstrations across the country. His assassination was all the more lamentable because he had become a passionate spokesperson for peace and political tolerance, urging young ANC militants to accept the negotiating process.

The talks had hardly resumed following Hani's death when, on 25 June 1993, two thousand members of white extremist groups, the Afrikaner Volksfront (Afrikaner People's Front, or AVF) and the AWB, broke through the gates of the World Trade Centre and then followed an armored car through the plate-glass front of the building. Hundreds of thousands of rands worth of damage was done, but no one was injured. Even this bizarre incident could not stop what Ramaphosa called the "democracy train," however. In early July the Negotiating Council fixed 27 April 1994 as the date for South Africa's first democratic election. New national and provincial governments would be elected to institute a nonracial, nonsexist, unified, and democratic South Africa based on the principle of one person, one vote. The Negotiating Council also developed a draft interim constitution and a Transitional Executive Council (TEC) to supervise the elections. Although representatives of the Conservative Party, the Inkatha Freedom Party, and the KwaZulu government walked out, the remaining parties approved the interim constitution in November 1993 and the Parliament approved it on 18 December. While Parliament was acting in Cape Town, Mandela and de Klerk were in Oslo, Norway, jointly receiving the Nobel Peace Prize.

Once the interim constitution took effect, the Transkei, Ciskei, Bophuthatswana, and Venda *bantustans* (seven million citizens in all) were to be reincorporated into South Africa. In March 1994, Lucas Mangope, the Bophuthatswana leader, declared that Bophuthatswana would not participate in the April elections because of this dissolution of his "country." Bophuthatswana public servants, who wanted to vote in the elections, demonstrated in protest with ANC support. They battled with police for four days until Mangope relented and agreed to allow participation in the elections. In the midst of the rioting, a group of White AWB extremists came to Mangope's assistance and attacked some anti-Mangope demonstrators. As television cameras rolled, three of the Whites were killed in cold blood by Bophuthatswana police. Mangope resigned on 12

March. The Ciskei ruler, Brigadier Gqozo, resigned without a fight on 22 March. Buthelezi was now isolated but would not abandon his opposition to the constitution. He refused to participate in the elections until an agreement was reached on the status of the Zulu kingship and Zulu territory, and until he received a guarantee that Inkatha would not be discriminated against. In March Inkatha supporters staged an armed march through downtown Johannesburg and then left their agreed-on route and headed to the Shell House, national headquarters of the ANC. In the subsequent confrontation, shots were fired and eight people died. Mandela and de Klerk met with Buthelezi on 19 April and agreed in general to his terms. Buthelezi would allow Inkatha participation with the understanding that internationally mediated talks with the government would take place after the elections, which were only one week away. The ballots had already been printed, but the electoral commission somehow managed to get Inkatha stickers added to the bottom of all of them.

The Independent Electoral Commission (IEC) made all the arrangements for the general election. Several weeks of violence carried out by ultra-right wing extremists preceded the election; the violent actions included a huge car bomb in central Johannesburg that left nine people dead two days before the voting, and another car bomb at Johannesburg's Jan Smuts Airport that left thirteen injured on election eve. Once voting began on 27 April, however, peace and good will seemed to prevail across the country. Nearly 20 million people cast their votes.

As expected, the ANC won the largest share of votes, 62.65 percent, which gave it 252 seats in the 400-seat National Assembly, plus the president and a deputy president. However, it did not win the two-thirds vote necessary to rewrite the constitution on its own. The National Party won 20.4 percent (82 seats), which allowed it to appoint a deputy president in the five-year transitional government. The NP also won the Western Cape province. Buthelezi's IFP won 10.5 percent (43 seats) and carried the majority in KwaZulu-Natal. No other parties won more than 5 percent of the vote, which would have allowed them to have ministers in the national unity government. The remainder of the seats went to the Freedom Front (9), the Democratic Party (7), the PAC (5), and the African Christian Democratic Party (2).

On 10 May 1994 Nelson Mandela was inaugurated president, and Thabo Mbeki and F.W. de Klerk deputy presidents. Under a new, brightly colored national flag, choirs sang the new South Africa's two national anthems, "Die Stem van Suid Afrika" (The Voice of South Africa) and the traditional Christian hymn and long-time anthem of the liberation movement, "Nkosi sikelel 'iAfrika" (God Bless Africa).

10

The Mandela Years, 1994–1999

Four years after leaving jail, Nelson Mandela became president of South Africa. He was not the first African to move from jail or exile to the corridors of power. Kwame Nkrumah had done so in Ghana in 1957, Jomo Kenyatta in Kenya in the 1960s, and Robert Mugabe in Zimbabwe in 1980. But South Africa was the most modern, industrialized nation in Africa, and Mandela and the African National Congress (ANC) had little experience in parliamentary government or state administration. Unlike the other three countries, South Africa was also a nation with a minority population of millions of well-educated, highly skilled Whites. Mandela needed their support to govern, at least for the foreseeable future. He would have to maintain their confidence while responding to the very real needs and high expectations of the Black majority.

No one in South Africa knew quite what to expect as Mandela took office. Years of propaganda about a communist "total onslaught," as well as scenes of rioting and looting in the weeks preceding the elections, had caused many Whites to stock up on food and other supplies in expectation of the worst possible conditions. In his first few weeks as president, however, Mandela's charm, apparent lack of bitterness, and kindly tolerance won them over. Soon Whites and Black alike were referring to him simply, and fondly, as "Madiba," his clan name. There was no communist revolution, no Black retaliation for centuries of oppression. In some ways South Africa assumed an air of normality and stability like nothing any South African, White or Black, had ever experienced. South Africa was a normal country, not the skunk of nations. In May it joined the Organization of African Unity and the Non-Aligned Movement. In June 1994 South Africa rejoined the Commonwealth of Nations after having been banned from membership for thirty-three years. On 16 June the United Nations lifted its embargo on arms sales to South Africa. On 24 June South Africa reclaimed its seat in the UN General Assembly, and in December it rejoined UNESCO after forty years.

THE INTERIM CONSTITUTION

With the elections an interim constitution took effect that would serve as the country's law until a permanent constitution could be written. Included within the interim constitution were a Bill of Rights and thirty-four entrenched principles. These would provide the framework for the final constitution. It was obvious that the authors of the thirty-four principles were recalling the abuses of South Africa's past. For example, the first principle provided for the "establishment of one sovereign state, a common South African citizenship and a democratic system of government committed to achieving equality between men and women and people of all races." Moreover there was a guarantee of fundamental rights, freedoms, and civil liberties; a prohibition against "racial, gender, and all other forms of discrimination"; and a commitment to "promote racial and gender equality and national unity." Although the legal system was to ensure equality of all, an affirmative action clause interpreted this equality as including "laws, programmes or activities that have as their object the amelioration of the conditions of the disadvantaged, including those disadvantaged on the grounds of race, colour or gender." The legislative, executive, and judiciary branches of government would have appropriate checks and balances. The judiciary would be independent and impartial and would enforce the Constitution. South Africa would have a representative, multiparty government with "regular elections, universal adult suffrage, and proportional representation." One provision addressed freedom of information, and another acknowledged and protected the diversity of language and culture. Citizens were free to form, join, and maintain linguistic, cultural, and religious associations; they were also free to form employer organizations and trade unions and to engage in collective bargaining. The public service sector was to be nonpartisan, career oriented, and "broadly representative of the South African community." Members of the police, military, and intelligence forces, and the security forces as a whole, were forbidden from "furthering or prejudicing party political interest." The remaining principles addressed relationships among the national, provincial, and local governments and the relative powers of each. South Africa now had nine provinces instead of four, and a federal system that gave increased power to local and regional authorities.

At the end of May the Constitutional Assembly (CA), comprised of the members of the House of Assembly and the Senate sitting together, chaired by Cyril Ramaphosa, began work on a final constitution. They were bound to follow, as much as possible, the constitutional principles contained in the interim constitution. The CA was given two years to complete its work, which it did in May 1996. An eleven-member Constitutional Court was also created to hear and settle constitutional issues, as well as to certify that the final constitution conformed to the thirty-four constitutional principles. The first Constitutional Court consisted of seven Whites and four Blacks—nine men, two women. Chairing the court was Arthur Chaskalson, one of Mandela's Rivonia trial lawyers. The first major constitutional question the Court ruled on was the death penalty. Mandela, who had once faced the death penalty himself, adamantly opposed it, believing that no civilized country should use it. In June 1995 the Constitutional Court found the death penalty unconstitutional, a ruling that was widely unpopular because the conservative Whites had always supported its use, which had mostly been against Blacks. Many Blacks now supported it as well, as the tortures, murders, and other apartheid era crimes were revealed.

Under the terms of the Government of National Unity, Mandela was obliged to include de Klerk and the National Party in his Cabinet, but he denied de Klerk's request for some of the important Cabinet posts, such as police or defense. In the end the National Party received four lesser posts. Mandela appointed Buthelezi as minister for home affairs. ANC Cabinet ministers included many well-known figures: for example, Mac Maharaj as transport minister and Dullah Omar, who had been a legal adviser to Mandela, as minister of justice. Mandela appointed the former Communist Party general-secretary and Umkhonto we Sizwe chief of staff, Joe Slovo, as housing minister. Slovo had played a key role in the constitutional negotiations, having proposed the "sunset clauses" and the coalition government. When he died of cancer in January 1995, he was widely mourned by the Black community and by many Whites as well. Cyril Ramaphosa, leader of the National Union of Mineworkers and chief negotiator for the ANC during the constitutional talks, turned down a position in the Cabinet, after he was not made deputy president. He continued to chair the Constitutional Assembly until that body completed its work.

ECONOMIC ISSUES

The second most pressing problem the government faced was the economy. Many ANC Cabinet ministers and Parliament members arrived in office with revolutionary dreams forged over years of opposition to the capitalist apartheid regime, but the harsh realities of tight budgets and international finance soon forced a more pragmatic approach. The euphoria of independence and Black majority rule were not new to Africa, of course. Mandela and the ANC were keenly aware of the fates of liberation movements across the continent that had seized power and then failed to create economically viable, democratic states. South Africa's new rulers were anxious to show that they were capable of administering this giant country, and Mandela knew that in order to do so he had to earn the confidence of the international financial community. The government initially hoped for a type of Marshall Plan (the financial aid-program the United States provided Europe after World War II) from the Western nations that would provide economic assistance to South Africa, but it soon became apparent that this was not going to happen.

In 1993 the ANC had developed an ambitious Reconstruction and Development Programme (RDP) that promised "a better life for all." There would be free education for everyone, water, electricity, and the construction of a million houses during the first five years of the Unity government. The RDP's goals were to alleviate poverty and reconstruct the economy. To accomplish these goals the government needed to promote economic growth in conjunction with economic reconstruction and social development. No good would come from economic growth if the benefits were not equitably distributed and the entire society did not benefit. Parliament approved the RDP in June 1994. During its first year several programs were initiated, including free health care for children and pregnant mothers, school meals, land reform, housing, roads, and clean water and electrification projects.

Yet it soon became evident that the RDP's extremely optimistic goals would not be reached and that unemployment would remain high for the foreseeable future. And although the RDP recorded impressive statistics, many people remained without basic services and other amenities. Part of the problem was the inability of provincial and local authorities to carry out the RDP programs. The years of Bantu education and missed schooling were now affecting the government, as there were not enough qualified Black middle managers to run provincial and local governments. Other legacies of apartheid's last years were rent boycotts, failure to pay for services, and bond-payment refusals. Blacks had formerly refused to pay these monies to the agents of apartheid and they continued to avoid payment under the new government. Yet local governments depended on these payments to operate and to provide amenities. In February 1995, Mandela launched the Masakane ("Let us build together") campaign to encourage people to pay their rents, pay for services, and end the bond boycotts. The campaign has had only limited success through 1999, and the people's refusal to make payments remains a critical problem. To encourage growth, in March 1997 the government introduced an initiative known as GEAR—the Growth, Employment, and Redistribution policy. It emphasizes competitiveness, job creation, more equitable income spreads, tariff reform, and partnerships between private and public sectors.

LOYALTY OF THE MILITARY

Another major concern to the government of National Unity was the loyalty of the military services. Mandela had appointed a former Umkhonto we Sizwe commander, Joe Modise, as minister of defense but retained de Klerk's head of the defense forces, General George Meiring, as chief of the reorganized South African National Defence Force. Many other Afrikaner generals still held important positions and access to important military and intelligence secrets and data. Thus, there was the potential for a possible military coup or revolt. The integration of Umkhonto soldiers into South African military units also proved difficult, as they had to serve side by side with Afrikaner soldiers and accept discipline from Afrikaner officers.

THE AFRIKANER POPULATION

The Afrikaner population at large remained an important, and in some ways dangerous, constituency. There was much talk of a Rainbow Nation, a phrase popularized by Archbishop Tutu that suggested the uniting of all racial groups in the new South Africa. Many Afrikaners were

either afraid of or rejected the idea of such a nation, however, and Mandela seemed to go out of his way to promote reconciliation. In the first
months of his presidency he paid a visit to Percy Yutar, the prosecutor
who had sent him to jail twenty-four years earlier. He held a tea party
for all the wives of the former White prime ministers and presidents,
hosted a dinner party for the former commander of Robben Island, and
met with Verwoerd's widow, Betsie Verwoerd, and former president Botha. Many ANC members opposed these good will gestures and refused
to trust their one-time oppressors, many of whom had blood on their
hands. But most of Mandela's former persecutors came away from their
meetings awed and overwhelmed by his magnanimity. Mandela remained convinced that given time the Afrikaners would accept the new
South Africa and make an important contribution to the Rainbow Nation. Mandela and Archbishop Tutu both often spoke of *ubuntu*, an African concept of human brotherhood, mutual responsibility, and
compassion. This was often linked to the proverb *Umuntu ngumuntu nga-
bantu*, which translates as "A person is a person because of other people."
Tutu interpreted the proverb as referring to gentleness, compassion, hos-
pitality, openness to others, and knowing that one's life is closely bound
to all other lives. These ideas, and Mandela's years in prison, helped him
transcend anger, bitterness, and vindictiveness and reach out to his
enemy.

By reaching out to the Afrikaner community, Mandela also displayed
a moral superiority to Afrikaner hatred while defusing White fears of
himself as the devil incarnate. Although the Afrikaner right wing had
been discredited and rejected in the 1994 election, Mandela still sought
to divide them further and bring the relatively moderate groups, such
as the Conservative Party and its leader, Constand Viljoen, over to his
side, and to isolate even more the extreme right-wing groups, such as
the Afrikaner Weerstandsbeweging.

A pivotal moment in the reconciliation process with Whites occurred
in June 1995 when the South African rugby team, called the Springboks,
defeated New Zealand in Johannesburg to win the World Cup. Rugby
was the Afrikaner sport, and to many Blacks it symbolized the macho,
physical arrogance of the White oppressor. Rugby remained the least
integrated of all sports, and the 1995 national team was all White but for
one Coloured player. Many Blacks called on Mandela to boycott the
games and also to change the Springbok mascot. Mandela refused to do
either and not only attended the game but wore a Springbok rugby jersey
and presented the winner's trophy to the Springbok captain. Standing

on the field in the middle of the vast stadium, Mandela received wild applause from thousands of Afrikaner rugby fans chanting "Nel-son, Nel-son!" Although the event won Mandela many White supporters, it did little to speed up the integration of sports. South Africa's national teams remain predominantly White in 1999, although good-faith efforts have been made in many sports to develop more young Black athletes and prepare them for world-class competition. Rugby continues to be the area in which the least progress has been made.

THE TRUTH AND RECONCILIATION COMMISSION

By far the most important and most controversial of all the initiatives undertaken by the new government was the passage in July 1995 of the National Unity and Reconciliation Act, which provided for the establishment of the Truth and Reconciliation Commission (TRC). The TRC's origins can be traced to the pre-1994 negotiation talks between ANC and National Party representatives. De Klerk had initially insisted on a general amnesty for all. The two sides eventually agreed that amnesty should be granted to individuals only after they came before a commission to give a full and truthful account of crimes committed during the apartheid era, from March 1960 (Sharpeville massacre) to May 1994 (Mandela's inauguration). They also had to prove their actions were politically motivated. Those who remained silent about crimes could be prosecuted. The Commission's stated purpose was not to punish but to help the country come to terms with its past. This was not enough for many victims' families and friends, who wanted punishment for crimes committed. Indeed, many South Africans remain deeply troubled by the sight of torturers, assassins, murderers, and other apartheid criminals being allowed to testify and then go free. Numerous conservatives, many of whom were themselves guilty of crimes, accused the TRC of dividing the nation by digging up past wrongs at a time when the nation needed instead to be brought together.

In November 1995 Mandela selected Archbishop Desmond M. Tutu to serve as head of the seventeen-member Commission, which was further divided into three committees: one addressing human rights violations; one dealing with amnesty; and one focusing on reparation and rehabilitation. The TRC began hearing testimony from victims of human rights abuses in April 1996. Over 20,000 victims testified before the Human Rights Violations Committee in public hearings across the country or made statements to its statement takers. Over 7,000 people made amnesty applications. Although amnesty hearings and prosecutions continue through the end of 1999, the TRC completed its primary task by submitting a report on 29 October 1998. It had gathered more information about political crimes and victims than any similar body in history had done.

THE NEW CONSTITUTION

In May 1996 the Constitutional Assembly sent its final constitution to the Constitutional Court for certification. The Court sent it back for revisions before approving it in November 1996. Mandela signed the new constitution on 10 December 1996. Shortly after the document received parliamentary approval in May, de Klerk announced he would not continue as deputy president through April 1999 as provided for in the interim constitution. He indicated that he planned to step down from his office as deputy president and that the National Party would withdraw from the Government of National Unity at the end of June 1996. He and many National Party members were upset that the new constitution made no provision for minority parties to continue to provide a deputy president or to have guaranteed minority party representation in the Cabinet until 2004 as they wanted. De Klerk also was frustrated at the relatively minor role (as he perceived it) that the National Party was allowed in the coalition. He publicly expressed his opinion that the new constitution, as passed by the Constitutional Assembly's ANC majority, had abandoned the principles of the interim constitution and moved the country closer to being a one-party state. He pledged to provide a vigorous opposition to the government, but the National Party carried the heavy burden of its apartheid past and found it difficult to generate either trust or good will among African voters. When Roelof Meyer, whom de Klerk appointed as general-secretary of the party in February 1997, suggested that the only realistic course of action was to dissolve the National Party and start anew, he was forced out. Meyer and Bantu Holomisa, whom the ANC had thrown out, subsequently started the United Democratic Movement Party in September 1997. De Klerk resigned from Parliament and from politics in the same month, leaving the National Party in much disarray.

Marthinus van Schalkwyk succeeded de Klerk as National Party leader, and in the 2 June 1999 elections the party ran as the New National Party (NNP). In a humbling fall from power the party of Malan, Verwoerd, Vorster, and Botha came in fourth place, receiving only thirty-eight seats in Parliament. By the late 1990s it has been reduced to an essentially regional party of the Western Cape, where it continues to receive Coloured support.

Members of the Inkatha Freedom Party (IFP) also withdrew from Parliament in April 1995 because the agreed-on mediated talks were not forthcoming. Because Inkatha had also won the majority in KwaZulu-Natal, it wanted more provincial autonomy than was allowed by the interim constitution. Inkatha members returned to Parliament after the May 1996 Constitution vote and remained the only other political party represented in the Government of National Unity after the National Party's withdrawal. Relations between the ANC and Inkatha Freedom Party improved after de Klerk's withdrawal, as did the relationship between Mandela and Buthelezi. Much to everyone's surprise, when Mandela and Thabo Mbeki (the deputy president) had to be out of the country at the same time, Mandela appointed Buthelezi acting president. Mandela repeated this gesture several times, much to Buthelezi's delight. Like the New National Party, however, Inkatha remains an essentially regional party and very much Buthelezi's creation.

On 14 May 1999, ANC and IFP supporters buried their differences and stood together in front of the Durban city hall to witness the signing of a peace pact intended to end years of rivalry between the two largest political groupings in South Africa. Thousands of ANC and IFP supporters had died in more than a decade of political violence in KwaZulu-Natal. The Truth and Reconciliation Commission would later hear evidence indicting the apartheid government's security forces, the so-called third force, for instigating and even carrying out many of these killings.

The Constitution took effect on the opening day of Parliament, 4 February 1997, although existing Parliament members and the executive branch remained in office until new elections were held in June 1999. Under the Constitution the president is selected for a five-year term (which began following the 1999 elections) by the majority party in Parliament. Minority parties can no longer appoint deputy presidents. The president can select one deputy president and all Cabinet members either from within the majority party or from other parties. The Constitution also makes provision for continued recognition of traditional chiefs and customary law.

The Parliament as instituted by the interim constitution consisted of a 400-member National Assembly and a 90-member Senate. Since the 1999 elections, the Senate has become the National Council of Provinces

(NCOP) consisting of 90 delegates, 10 from each of the 9 provinces. Of the 10, 6 are permanent and 4 are special delegates—thus there are 60 permanent and 40 special delegates for the NCOP as a whole. The 60 permanent members are appointed by parties in the provinces on the basis of their representation in the provincial legislatures. Following the election of June 1999, the ANC had 32 permanent and 28 special delegates in the NCOP; the National Party had 11 permanent and 6 special delegates; the Inkatha Freedom Party had 3 permanent and 2 special delegates; and the Freedom Party and the Democratic Party had 5 and 3 permanent members, respectively. Decisions made by the NCOP generally require the support of 5 of the 9 provinces, or 6 of the 9 in matters relating to the "entrenched" principles.

The National Assembly under the new Constitution is to have no fewer than 350 and no more than 400 members. Seats in the National Assembly are determined according to the percentage of votes each party receives in the national elections. Following the June 1999 elections, 400 members were elected to the National Assembly. Of these the ANC won the most (266), followed by the Democratic Party (38), Inkatha Freedom Party (34), New National Party (28), and United Democratic Movement (14). Other parties that gained seats were the African Christian Democratic Party (6), United Christian Democratic Party (3), Pan Africanist Congress (3), Freedom Party (3), Federal Alliance (2), Minority Front (1), Afrikaner Eenheids Beweging (Afrikaner Unity Movement) (1), and Azanian People's Organization (1).

South Africa's highest courts are the Constitutional Court, which rules on the constitutionality of all laws, and the Supreme Court of Appeals, which is the highest criminal court. The Constitutional Court consists of a president, a deputy president, and nine other judges. They are selected by the president of South Africa and serve for twelve-year, renewable terms but must retire at age seventy. The Supreme Court of Appeals consists of a chief justice, a deputy chief justice, and a number of judges as determined by Parliament. The Supreme Court of Appeals may decide appeals in any matter and is the highest court of appeal except in constitutional matters.

The 1996 Constitution recognizes nine provinces: Western Cape, Northern Cape, Eastern Cape, Free State, Gauteng, KwaZulu-Natal, Mpumalanga, Northern Province, and North-West Province. Each province has its own premier, legislature, cabinet, and limited financial powers. It may also have its own constitution as long as the document is not inconsistent with the national constitution. The provincial constitution

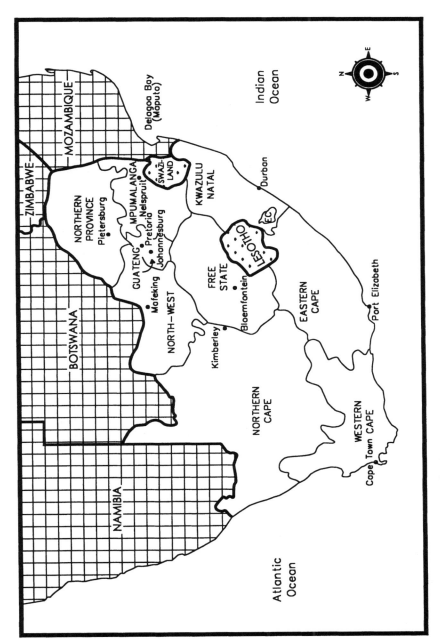

South African Provinces, mid-1990s

must be certified by the Constitutional Court before it takes effect. As of 1999, the Constitutional Court has only certified the Western Cape constitution. Representation in provincial legislatures is based on the percentage of the vote won by political parties in elections. The number of seats in each assembly is determined by the number of votes cast in each province. More densely populated provinces therefore have larger assemblies than do those with fewer inhabitants. Under this federal system, each province enjoys significant powers but ultimately is subject to the national Parliament and national Constitution.

In July 1997 Mandela turned seventy-nine years old and stepped aside as ANC president. By that time he had already handed over many of his presidential duties to his deputy president, Thabo Mbeki. In fact, Mbeki had been handling many of these duties since the new government was installed in 1994. Two of Mbeki's contenders for the position, Cyril Ramaphosa, who had chaired the Constitutional Assembly, and Tokyo Sexwale, premier of the Gauteng province, both dropped out of government in 1997 to go into private business. At the ANC annual party congress in December 1997, its fiftieth such meeting, the delegates elected Mbeki to succeed Mandela as ANC president and Jacob Zuma, ANC Party chairman, to succeed Mbeki as ANC deputy president. In July 1998 Mandela married Graca Machel, the widow of former Mozambican leader Samora Machel.

TESTIMONY ON CRIMES UNDER APARTHEID

While South Africa continued on the road to constitutional democracy, day after day of shocking testimony was given before the Truth and Reconciliation Committee. The TRC's five-volume, 3,500-page report, presented to President Mandela in October 1998, found many on all sides guilty of some crime during the apartheid era. The ANC initially refused to seek amnesty for any of its own members, arguing that they had been fighting a "just struggle." In the course of the hearings, details of ANC political crimes were exposed and the ANC eventually admitted to executing twenty-two members for such offenses as murder, rape, and mutiny. The TRC held the ANC accountable as well for killings committed during its military operations, for the killings of informers in its military camps in exile, and for killings and maimings as a result of its landmine campaign in the northern and eastern Transvaal from 1985 to 1987. The ANC was also blamed for the deaths of seventy-six Inkatha Freedom

Party members. The TRC charged the ANC with routinely using torture to extract information and confessions from detainees in its camps in exile from 1979 to 1989. In its report, the TRC recognized that the ANC and PAC were legitimate liberation movements, but it drew a distinction between a just war and just means.

The TRC included twenty-seven pages on the activities of Winnie Madikizela-Mandela and her Mandela United Football Club. This "club" of young men, which she organized and sponsored in the 1980s, became a private vigilante group. The TRC found that she personally committed gross human rights violations and participated in an assault on four youths. It found members of the Club guilty of killings, torture, assaults, and arson in the community.

It was the apartheid government's crimes, however, that received the most attention. No one was spared. There is not enough space in this book to summarize even a fraction of all the TRC's findings regarding governmental abuse of power. Both former state presidents P.W. Botha and John Vorster were found guilty of numerous violations of human rights and responsible for atrocities committed by their followers. The TRC accused Botha, for example, of personally ordering the 1988 bombing of Khotso House, headquarters of the South African Council of Churches. Botha was also held accountable for (1) the 1987 bombing of the African National Congress's London headquarters, and (2) a 1981 attempt to overthrow the Seychelles government. Most important, however, Botha had chaired the State Security Council, which systematically perpetrated every imaginable human rights violation and atrocity during the 1980s. Botha himself rejected a subpoena to give evidence before the TRC, said he had nothing to apologize for, and described the TRC as a circus. He was later charged in court for defying a summons. In June 1999 a Cape Town court dismissed the case against Botha on a technicality, but the TRC is considering an appeal. TRC findings about former president de Klerk were deleted shortly before the report was released because of various court appeals being made by de Klerk.

The details that came out of the TRC hearings were more horrible and damning than anyone could have imagined. Senior members of the apartheid government's security forces came forward to testify of systematic torture, rape, and murder; of death squads and assassinations; of cutting up and/or burning victims' bodies; of filling shallow graves. Gruesome and elaborate details were provided regarding famous cases such as the death of Steve Biko or the murders of other Black activists such as the "Cradock Four" and the "Pebco Three," both in 1985, in the Eastern Cape. The TRC also received solid evidence that government security forces had been responsible as a "third force" for instigating much of the so-called Black on Black violence that occurred during the 1980s and early 1990s. De Klerk continues to refuse to testify on the extent of his knowledge of, or approval of, these activities. Many other senior officials have accused de Klerk of being their ultimate boss. One such official was Eugene de Kock, known as "Prime Evil." He served as commandant at Vlakplaas, a farm outside Pretoria, that was used as a security police base during apartheid, a place where death squads were trained.

Hearings continue before the TRC's Amnesty Committee. In February 1999 five former members of the security branch were refused amnesty for the death of Steve Biko. In April 1999 amnesty was also denied to Chris Hani's two murderers. Hundreds of policemen who are found to have tortured, assaulted, or killed detainees may face prosecution if they are not granted amnesty.

TRANSITION UNDER THABO MBEKI

Nelson Mandela retired from public office in June 1999, and on 2 June for the second time all South Africans went to the polls to cast their votes in a national election—this time under the new Constitution. The ANC won 66.36 percent of the vote, coming within one seat of a two-thirds majority in the new Parliament. Altogether there are twelve opposition parties in the new Parliament as compared to only five in the Government of National Unity. Thabo Mbeki succeeded Mandela as the new president of South Africa, and Jacob Zuma became deputy president.

Mbeki was born in 1942 in the Transkei. His father was Govan Mbeki, a leading political activist in the eastern Cape. Thabo Mbeki joined the ANC Youth League in 1956 and became active in student politics. After moving to Johannesburg in 1959 he became a protégé of Walter Sisulu. In the early 1960s his father was arrested at Rivonia and sentenced to life imprisonment. Thabo left the country in 1962 under orders from the ANC and eventually went to Britain, where he completed a Master's degree in economics at Sussex University in 1966. He remained active in student politics in exile, playing a prominent role in ANC youth and student groups. In 1970 he went to the Soviet Union for military training and then went to Lusaka, Zambia, where he became assistant secretary of the ANC Revolutionary Council. He then held various ANC posts in Botswana, Swaziland, and Nigeria. Thereafter he returned to Lusaka, where he worked for Oliver Tambo. As head of the ANC Department of Information he directed anti-apartheid activities. Mbeki played a key role as an ANC negotiator with the government after he returned from exile in 1990. He was inaugurated South Africa's second democratically elected president on 16 June 1999.

Mbeki rules over both a developed and a developing nation. Most Whites still enjoy a standard of living and a way of life comparable to those in the most developed countries in the world. As in the apartheid days, most Indians and Coloured still enjoy a higher standard of living than do the majority of Africans. Although Africans make up about 77 percent of South Africa's population, they earn only 30 percent of the country's total income. By contrast, the 11 percent of the population who are White earn about 58 percent of the income. Asian and Coloured account for 4 and 8 percent, respectively, which relates more closely to their proportions in the total population. Putting a stop to rampant violence and crime; providing homes, basic amenities, education, health care, and jobs for everyone; and increasing economic growth without creating a larger gap between the haves and the have-nots are only some of the problems that Mbeki and South Africa face.

As the title of Nelson Mandela's 1994 autobiography suggests, it has been a long walk to freedom. South Africans, both Blacks and Whites, have gained their freedom. It remains to be seen what they will do with it. The next decade will tell whether South Africa will be able to overcome apartheid's terrible legacy and reach its potential as a leading nation, not only on the African continent but in the world. In many ways the Mandela years were an interlude, a transitional period of savoring the victory over apartheid. Now it is time to produce. Long-delayed expectations will have to be met, and promises kept.

Notable People in the History of South Africa

Abdurahman, Abdullah (1872–1940) Prominent Coloured political leader of the early twentieth century; president of African People's Organization.

Bambatha (ca. 1865–1906) Zulu village chief in Natal; led Zulu rebellion of 1906–1908, last armed revolt in South Africa by a traditional ruler.

Biko, Steve (1946–1977) Founder, leader, and martyr of Black Consciousness movement from late 1960s; founded South African Students' Association in 1969; died in police custody.

Boesak, Allan (1946–) President of the World Council of Reformed Churches; one of the founders of the United Democratic Front; career ended in scandal.

Botha, Louis (1862–1919) Afrikaner general in South African War; first prime minister of Union of South Africa, 1910–1919.

Botha, Pieter Willem (1916–) National Party prime minister of Republic of South Africa, (1978–1984); state president, 1984–1989; developed "total strategy" policy from late 1970s.

Buthelezi, Mangosuthu (1928–) Zulu political leader, who revived the traditional Zulu Inkatha movement that later became a political party, Inkatha Freedom Party; chief minister of KwaZulu homeland from 1972; became minister of home affairs after 1994 election, also served as minister of the interior; served as acting president when Mandela was out of the country.

Cetshwayo (ca. 1826–1884) Son of Zulu king Mpande; became Zulu king in 1872; led Zulu army in Anglo-Zulu War of 1879.

de Klerk, Frederik Willem (1936–) State president, 1989–1994; opened the way for end of apartheid; deputy president, 1994–1997; shared Nobel Peace Prize with Nelson Mandela, 1993; retired from government in 1997.

Dingane (1795–1840) Shaka's half-brother, who assassinated him and ruled Zulu kingdom, 1828–1840; defeated by *trekkers* at Blood River in 1838 and fell from power shortly thereafter.

Dube, John Langalibalele (1871–1946) Zulu educator, journalist, and politician; one of the founders of the ANC; served as ANC president, 1912–1917.

Fischer, Bram (1908–1975) Anti-apartheid Afrikaner lawyer and communist who defended Mandela and others in Rivonia Trial; sentenced to life in prison in 1966; died of cancer in 1975.

Hani, Martin Thembisile (Chris) (1942–1993) Anti-apartheid activist, ANC member, chief of staff of Umkhonto we Sizwe in 1987; general-secretary of South African Communist Party, 1991; assassinated in 1993.

Hertzog, James Barry Munnik (1866–1942) Afrikaner general in South African War; Union prime minister, 1924–1939; formed National Party.

Hintsa (ca. 1790–1835) Chief of the Gcaleka Xhosa and paramount chief of the Xhosa from 1804; captured during Frontier War of 1834–1835, held hostage, and murdered.

Huddleston, Trevor (1913–1998)   Anglican priest who served in the African suburb of Sophiatown and supported the African struggle to preserve Sophiatown; recalled by his superior to Great Britain in 1956; organized Harare Conference in 1987.

Jabavu, John Tengo (1859–1921)   African journalist, educator, and politician in the Cape colony and province; most prominent African spokesperson in the Cape in late nineteenth century; helped to found South African Native College, later Fort Hare University.

Kadalie, Clements (1896–1951)   Malawian-born labor leader; founded and led the Industrial and Commercial Workers' Union (ICU) during the 1920s.

Khama (Kgama) (ca. 1830–1923)   Ngwato Tswana king in Botswana; fervent convert to Christianity; led his people into British annexation; ruled from 1875 to 1923.

Kok, Adam III (1811–1875)   Griqua leader at Philippolis from 1837, then at Griqualand East in early 1860s; maintained Griqua independence under missionary influence until his death.

Kruger, Stephanus Johannes Paulus (Oom Paul) (1925–1904)   Afrikaner president of the South African Republic (Transvaal), 1883–1900; died in exile in 1904 after fleeing from Transvaal during the South African War.

Lembede, Anton (1914–1947)   One of the founders of African National Congress (ANC) Youth League and first president; developed a philosophy of African nationalism known as Africanism.

Luthuli (Lutuli), Albert (ca. 1898–1967)   President of ANC, 1952–1967; winner of the Nobel Peace Prize in 1961.

Malan, Daniel François (1874–1959)   Purified National Party leader; first apartheid prime minister of South Africa, 1948–1954.

Mandela, Nelson Rolihlahla (1918–   )   Co-founder African National Congress Youth League, 1944; joined ANC National Executive in 1949; founder and organizer of Umkhonto we Sizwe, 1961; imprisoned, 1962–1990; president of ANC, 1991–   ; Nobel Peace Prize winner, 1993; president of South Africa, 1994–1999; retired from politics in 1999.

Mbeki, Thabo (1942–   )   Son of veteran ANC activist Govan Mbeki; member of ANC Youth League in 1956; studied economics at University of Sussex from 1962 and then worked in ANC London office; became ANC director of information and publicity in 1984 and head of ANC department of international affairs in 1989; made deputy president in the Government of National Unity in 1994 and succeeded Nelson Mandela as president of South Africa in June 1999.

Moshoeshoe (Moshesh) (ca. 1786–1870)   Founder and king of Lesotho, 1830s–1870; brilliant statesman and strategist.

Mpande (1798–1872)   Half-brother to Shaka and Dingane; Zulu king from 1840 to 1872; maintained Zulu independence until his death.

Mzilikazi (ca. 1795–1868)   Zulu lieutenant under Shaka; founder of the breakaway Ndebele kingdom; settled in Transvaal in the 1830s, then migrated to the area of southern Zimbabwe in the late 1830s to an area that became known as Matabeleland; ruled until his death.

Ngqika (Gaika) (ca. 1775–1829)   Xhosa ruler of the Rharhabe clan in the Ciskei region; collaborated with Lord Charles Somerset while trying to maintain land and cattle.

Nongqawuse (1841–1898)   Xhosa prophetess whose prophesies led to the Xhosa cattle killing of 1857.

Philip, John (1775–1851)   London Missionary Society missionary and superintendent in South Africa from 1819 to 1851; greatly disliked by settlers for his work on behalf of Khoikhoi and slaves.

Plaatje, Sol (1876–1932)   African journalist, interpreter, writer, politician, and nationalist; first secretary of the ANC, 1912–1917; member of 1914 delegation to London to protest 1913 Land Act.

Pretorius, Andries Wilhelmus Jacobus (1798–1853)   *Voortrekker* leader during Great Trek; defeated Zulu at Battle of Blood River; helped established Republic of Natalia, then an independent Transvaal Republic; gave name to Pretoria.

Ramaphosa, Matamela Cyril (1952–   ),   Secretary-general of National Union of Mineworkers, 1982–1991; founder of Congress of South African

Trade Unions (COSATU); organizer of mass democratic movement, 1988; ANC secretary-general, 1991; member of Parliament, 1994; now in private business.

Retief, Piet (1789–1838)   *Voortrekker* leader during Great Trek; killed by Dingane in 1838; Afrikaner martyr.

Rhodes, Cecil (1853–1902)   British imperialist, mining magnate, and politician; prime minister of Cape colony; founder of British South Africa Company and colonizer of Rhodesia.

Sandile (1820–1879)   Ngqika's son; chief of Rharhabe Xhosa in Ciskei from 1840 to his death; member of last generation of Xhosa to have independence; killed in war of 1878–1879.

Sarili (1809–1892)   Hintsa's son; paramount chief of the Xhosa from 1835 during last generation of Xhosa independence; fought the British in 1846, 1850–1852, 1878–1879; died in exile in Transkei.

Sekhukhune (ca. 1810–1882)   Paramount chief of the Pedi from 1861; taken prisoner during war with British in 1879.

Seme, Pixley Kalsaka (1881–1951)   African lawyer and founder of the South African Native National Congress, later the African National Congress; later became mentor to Anton Lembede.

Shaka (ca. 1787–1828)   Creator of the Zulu kingdom; ruled as king, ca. 1817–1828; subject of intense historical debate and writing.

Shepstone, Sir Theophilus (1817–1893)   Natal administrator of African affairs from the 1840s to the 1870s; annexed Transvaal for the British in 1877; presided over dissolution of Zulu kingdom after Anglo-Zulu War of 1879.

Sisulu, Walter Max Ulyate (1912–   )   ANC Youth League member; ANC National Executive, 1949; senior ANC leader; imprisoned 1964–1989.

Slovo, Joe (1926–1995)   South African communist leader; head of Umkhonto we Sizwe; key figure in constitutional negotiations, 1990–1994; minister of housing in the 1994 Mandela government until his death.

Smuts, Jan Christian (1870–1950)   Afrikaner general in South African War; first deputy prime minister in Union government, then prime minister 1919–1924, 1939–1948; war hero in World War I; helped found League of Nations and United Nations.

Sobukwe, Robert Mangaliso (1924–1978)   Member of African National Congress who broke away in 1959 to found Pan Africanist Congress of Azania; believed in Africanist goals; was arrested and imprisoned on Robben Island in 1960 and held for nine years; thereafter was banned to Kimberley, where he died.

Soga, Tiyo (1829–1871)   Xhosa writer, linguist, composer, and London Missionary Society missionary; ordained in Scotland, 1846–1848, first Xhosa Christian minister; married Scottish woman, Janet Burnside; translated gospels and other works into Xhosa.

Somerset, Lord Charles Henry (1767–1831)   Governor of the Cape colony, 1814–1826; British aristocrat who shaped eastern frontier policy against Xhosa and introduced several colonial institutions, including improved agricultural and livestock methods, South African Museum, and South African Library.

Strijdom, Johannes Gerhardus (1893–1959)   Prime minister, 1954–1958; responsible for removal of Coloureds from the Cape common voters' roll.

Suzman, Helen (1917–)   Liberal politician; opposition member of South African Parliament, for United Party, 1953–1959, and then broke away to Progressive Party, for whom she served as the only Progressive Party member of Parliament from 1961 to 1974; outspoken critic of apartheid and South African government's human rights abuses.

Tambo, Oliver Reginald (1917–1990)   ANC National Executive, 1949; ANC president, 1967–1990; represented the ANC overseas during the years it was banned.

Treurnicht, Andries (1921–1995)   Afrikaner minister and politician; member of National Party; broke away in 1982 to form Conservative Party; refused to participate in 1994 election.

Tutu, Desmond Mpilo (1931–)   Archbishop of Cape Town and head of the Anglican Church in southern Africa from 1985; received Nobel

Peace Prize, 1984; served as chair of Truth and Reconciliation Commission after his retirement from Anglican Church in 1995.

van Riebeeck, Jan (1619–1677)   First Dutch East India Company governor of Cape colony, 1652–1662.

Verwoerd, Hendrik Frensch (1901–1966)   Minister of native affairs in Malan government, 1948–1958; responsible for "Bantu education"; prime minister, 1958–1966; chief architect of apartheid; assassinated in Parliament in 1966.

Vorster, Balthazar Johannes (John) (1915–1983)   Imprisoned during World War II for pro-Nazi sympathies; prime minister of Republic of South Africa, 1966–1979; promoted an "outward looking" foreign policy; fell from office after Information scandal ("Muldergate") broke in 1978.

Xuma, Dr. Alfred Bitini (ca. 1898–1962)   President of ANC, 1940–1949; revived ANC but was ousted as president in 1949 when he opposed calls for more militant action by ANC Youth League members.

Glossary

Amabutho (Zulu). Zulu military regiments formed by age-grades.

Assegaai (Zulu). A long spear used for throwing or a short spear introduced by Zulu for stabbing; used by both Khoikhoi and Bantu-speakers.

Azania (Arabic). Ancient name for east African coast; used by Black Consciousness supporters and others as an alternative name for South Africa.

Baaskap (Afrikaans). "Domination," "mastery"; usually refers to White domination under apartheid.

Boer (Dutch). "Farmer" (n.) or "to farm" (v.), a term for Dutch settlers used in a derogatory manner by the British in the nineteenth century; *Afrikaner* is the accepted term today.

Commando (Dutch). Initially a mounted militia of citizens and regular troops, but mostly only citizens, defended White territory and attacked indigenous peoples.

Heemraden (Dutch). Subordinate district councilor serving under the *landdrost* in the Dutch Cape colony.

Kaffir, Caffer, Caffre (Arabic). White term for Bantu-speakers, especially

Xhosa, in the nineteenth century; derived from the Arabic word for "infidel." Considered a highly derogatory, racist term in recent usage.

Knecht (Dutch). Usually a White man who worked for others, as a servant or overseer.

Kraal (Dutch, Portuguese). A term with several meanings: an enclosure for farm animals; a chief's home (a royal *kraal*); an African village; a cluster of huts belonging to one family or clan.

Laager (Dutch). The defensive circling of pioneer wagons against attack; the term was later used metaphorically to describe the defensive attitudes of apartheid South Africa.

Landdrost (Dutch). District magistrate under the Dutch East Company system in the Cape colony.

Matjeshuise (Afrikaans). Reed mat houses used both by Khoikhoi and White frontier farmers.

Mayibuye iAfrica (Xhosa). "Come Back Africa," also simply *Mayibuye.* African National Congress motto and song; now the name of the official ANC journal.

Mfecane (Zulu) or Difaqane (Sotho). Variously translated, such as "time of troubles" or "crushing." The term refers to the series of destructive wars associated with the rise of the Zulu kingdom between the 1790s and the 1820s, but recently it has been the subject of much historical debate.

Nagmaal (Dutch). Multi-day meeting of frontier Afrikaner families to hold Holy Communion service and to socialize.

Satyagraha (Hindu). "Truth-force"; Mohandas Gandhi's technique of active, nonviolent resistance developed during his twenty-one years in South Africa.

Strandlopers (Dutch). "Beach walkers"; Khoisan people living along the Indian Ocean coast.

Toyi-toyi. The name of a Black protest dance of unknown origin, probably introduced by ANC exiles from military training in Africa or Eastern Europe. Chanting protesters form phalanxes while dancing forward and punching the air with their right fists in rhythm with the chant.

Trekboer (Dutch). Migrant livestock farmers who spread out from the

Cape peninsula across the Cape colony in the eighteenth and nineteenth centuries.

Ubuntu (Bantu languages). African concept of human brotherhood, mutual responsibility, and compassion.

Uitlanders (Dutch). "Foreigners" who flocked to the Transvaal gold fields in the late nineteenth century; their economic and political grievances were one element in the crises leading to the South African War of 1899–1902.

Veldkornet (Dutch). District field cornet answerable to the *landdrost*; oversaw local policing and militia.

Verkramptes (Afrikaans). The "narrow ones"; a term used in reference to ultra-conservative Afrikaners.

Verligtes (Afrikaans). The "enlightened ones"; a term used in reference to relatively pragmatic and reform-minded Afrikaners.

Volk (Dutch, Afrikaans). The "people"; a term often used in the twentieth century in association with Afrikaner nationalism.

Volksraad (Dutch). The elected legislative assembly in the former Afrikaner republics of the Transvaal, the Orange Free State, and Natalia during their years of independence.

Voortrekkers (Dutch). Afrikaner pioneers who left the Cape colony in the 1830s and 1840s on the Great Trek.

Witwatersrand (Dutch). "Ridge of the white waters"; an area of deep gold-bearing reefs, to the east and west of Johannesburg, constituting the largest known gold field in the world.

Veld (Dutch). Grazing or farming land; more generally, the landscape or countryside—flat, hilly, or non-urban land.

Zuurveld (Dutch). Literally, "sour field"; the large area west of the Great Fish River in the Eastern Cape fought over by Whites and Xhosa for nearly one hundred years for access to land and water.

Bibliographic Essay

Since South Africa has emerged from the censorship and White view of history mandated by the apartheid regime, Black South Africans have reclaimed and proudly championed their own histories. A library of new books have recently appeared, many of them by authors whose biographies, memoirs, confessions, and points of view would have been banned a mere decade earlier. The books cited in this brief essay fall into two categories. First, they are generally broad surveys. The reader should refer to the more extensive bibliographies in these volumes for works on specific topics. Second, most of the books cited here were written in the 1990s. Again, important works written before 1990 are included in their bibliographies. The interested reader should also look at the *Journal of African History*, the *South African Historical Journal*, and the *Journal of Southern African Studies*. In addition, there are a multitude of sites on the World Wide Web, including several belonging to South African newspapers. Finally, a number of commercial films about South Africa are readily available at most video stores. These include *Cry, the Beloved Country*; *Bapho*; *Cry Freedom*; *A Dry White Season*; *The Power of One*; *Sarafina*; and *Mandela and de Klerk*.

The most comprehensive general history available today is T.R.H. Davenport, *South Africa: A Modern History*, 4th ed. (Toronto: University of Toronto Press, 1991). The fifth edition is expected to be published in 2000. Other good general histories include J.D. Omer Cooper, *History of Southern Africa* 2nd ed. (Portsmouth: Heinemann, 1994); Leonard M. Thompson, *A History of South Africa*, 2nd ed. (New Haven: Yale University Press, 1996); and Robert Ross, *A Concise History of South Africa* (Cambridge: Cambridge University Press, 1999). The *Reader's Digest Illustrated History of South Africa*, ed. Christopher Saunders, is very well done and has excellent illustrations, photos, and maps. For a more in-depth study of the present century, see William Beinart, *Twentieth Century South Africa* (New York: Oxford University Press, 1994).

The standard, and excellent, work on early Cape colonial history is Richard Elphick and Hermann Gillomee, eds., *The Shaping of South African Society, 1652–1840* (Middletown, CT: Wesleyan University Press, 1988). Richard Elphick and T.R.H. Davenport have edited a thorough study of Christianity as it helped shape South Africa's history: *Christianity in South Africa: A Political, Social and Cultural History* (Berkeley: University of California Press, 1997).

Two outstanding comparative studies of South African and U.S. history, written by one of America's finest historians, are George M. Fredrickson, *Black Liberation: A Comparative Study of Black Ideologies in the United States and South Africa* (New York: Oxford University Press, 1995), and *White Supremacy: A Comparative Study in American and South African History* (New York: Oxford University Press, 1981). Another good comparative analysis is Howard Lamar and Leonard Thompson, eds., *The Frontier in History: North America and South Africa Compared* (New Haven: Yale University Press, 1981).

As the centennial of the South African War approaches, a wealth of new material is appearing; good places to begin a study are Thomas Pakenham, *The Boer War* (New York: Random House, 1979); Bill Nasson, *Abraham Esau's War: A Black South African in the Cape, 1899–1902* (Cambridge: Cambridge University Press, 1991); and Iain Smith, *The Origins of the South African War, 1899–1902* (New York: Longman, 1996). The wealth and world of the diamond mines are described in Stefan Kanfer, *The Last Empire: De Beers, Diamonds, and the World* (New York: Farrar, Straus & Giroux, 1993). A more recent look at the gold mines and migrant labor is T. Dunbar Moodie with Vivienne Ndatshe, *Going for Gold: Men, Mines and Migrancy* (Johannesburg: Witwatersrand University Press, 1994). A good biography of Cecil Rhodes is Robert I. Rotberg, *The*

Founder—Cecil Rhodes and the Pursuit of Power (New York: Oxford University Press, 1988).

For a history of apartheid, one can begin with Brian Lapping, *Apartheid: A History* (New York: George Braziller, 1989); Saul Dubow, *Racial Segregation and the Origins of Apartheid in South Africa, 1919–1936* (London: Macmillan, 1989); and Dan O'Meara, *Forty Lost Years: The Apartheid State and the Politics of the National Party, 1948–1994* (Johannesburg: Ravan, 1995).

A partial listing of books about Black South Africans and their histories includes the following: Peter Delius, *The Land Belongs to Us: The Pedi Polity, the Boers and the British in the Nineteenth Century Transvaal* (Berkeley: University of California Press, 1984); Jeff Guy, *The Destruction of the Zulu Kingdom* (London: Longman, 1979); Shula Marks, *Reluctant Rebellion: The 1906–1908 Disturbances in Natal* (Oxford: Clarendon Press, 1970); J.D. Omer Cooper, *The Zulu Aftermath: A Nineteenth Century Revolution in Bantu Africa* (Evanston: Northwestern University Press, 1966); J.B. Peires, *The Dead Will Arise: Nongqawuse and the Great Xhosa Cattle-Killing Movement of 1856–1857* (Bloomington: Indiana University Press, 1989); and *The House of Phalo: A History of the Xhosa People in the Days of Their Independence* (Berkeley: University of California Press, 1982); Kevin Shillington, *The Colonisation of the Southern Tswana, 1870–1900* (Johannesburg: Ravan Press, 1985); Les Switzer, *Power and Resistance in an African Society: The Ciskei Xhosa and the Making of South Africa* (Madison: University of Wisconsin Press, 1993); and Leonard M. Thompson, *Survival in Two Worlds: Moshoeshoe of Lesotho, 1786–1870* (Oxford: Clarendon Press, 1975).

Several books are available about Nelson Mandela, but the best and most definitive is the recent biography by Anthony Sampson, *Nelson Mandela: The Authorised Biography* (New York: Harper Collins, 1999). One should also read Nelson Mandela, *Long Walk to Freedom: The Autobiography of Nelson Mandela* (Boston: Little, Brown, 1994). Books about South Africa's new president, Thabo Mbeki, are just appearing. Start with Thabo Mbeki, *Africa: The Time Has Come* (Cape Town: Tafelberg Publishers, 1998); and Adrian Hadland and Jovial Rantao, *The Life and Times of Thabo Mbeki* (Rivonia: Zebra Press, 1999).

The *Truth and Reconciliation Commission of South Africa Report* is available, but the five volumes are too costly to purchase. They should be available at most major libraries. The interested reader can also access all five volumes at the following World Wide Web site: ⟨http://www. polity.org.za/govdocs/commissions/1998/trc/index.htm⟩.

A powerful and moving description of the Truth and Reconciliation Commission's proceedings by a South African poet and reporter is Antjie Krog, *Country of My Skull* (Johannesburg: Random House, 1998).

Index